THE
WISDEN
BOOK OF CRICKET LAWS

THE
WISDEN
BOOK OF CRICKET LAWS

DON OSLEAR

WITH

DON MOSEY

STANLEY PAUL
London

This book is dedicated to my daughter Sara, who during her formative years – the early years of my close and intense study of cricket law – may have missed out on some of the love and attention which was rightfully hers.

Stanley Paul & Co Ltd
An imprint of Random House UK Ltd
20 Vauxhall Bridge Road London SW1V 4NE

Random House Australia (Pty) Ltd
20 Alfred Street, Milsons Point, Sydney, NSW 2061

Random House New Zealand (Pty) Ltd
18 Poland Road, PO Box 40-86, Glenfield, Auckland

Random House South Africa (Pty) Ltd
PO Box 337, Bergvlei 2012, South Africa

First published 1993
Reprinted 1993
Copyright © Don Oslear and Don Mosey

Set in Linotron Plantin Light and Plantin by Essex Composing Ltd, Rayleigh, Essex
Printed and bound in Great Britain by Mackays of Chatham

A catalogue record for this book is available upon request from the British Library

ISBN 0 09 177344 X (cased)
ISBN 0 09 177345 8 (paper)

Contents

Acknowledgements

My thanks are due to a number of people in my efforts to write this book: firstly to Don Mosey, who extended to me the invitation to do so, for his help and advice at all times, together with his perusal of my copy; to Colonel John Stephenson for his permission to print the Laws of Cricket and to Mr A. C. Smith for his permission to refer to certain incidents within the professional game; to a number of my ACU friends for their wise counsel over the years, in particular David Whiley, Robbie Robins, Peter Stevens and the late Lewis Trethewey; to a number of authors for allowing me to refer to certain points in their various publications, and to my many colleagues both amateur and professional.

For permission to reproduce copyright photographs the authors and publishers would like to thank Patrick Eagar, *Daily Mirror* and Express Newspapers.

Foreword

It is perhaps ironic that so many controversies in the game of cricket result from an incomplete knowledge of the Laws of the game and in my experience the players were often the worst offenders.

As a very high-profile game it excites a lot of media attention, naturally, and it is an extremely popular television sport. Detailed close-up pictures are thus brought right into the home while the man who pays to go into the ground to absorb the unique atmosphere of a cricket match has to be content with the 75-100 yards or more view with the naked eye, or with binoculars – not the most convenient method of long-term watching.

Cricket, so long synonymous with fair play and good sportsmanship that it has become part of the language, has had to endure its share of controversy since public attention has more recently been focused closely upon it.

A wider and more general knowledge of the Laws helps one understand the reasons for disputes, but far more importantly it enhances the watcher's appreciation of some of the finer points of the game and, indeed, of the alertness, concentration and expertise of umpires without whom, let's face it, the game could not exist.

Don Oslear cares personally about cricket. He is the most committed and dedicated umpire in the game. He also cares very much for the welfare of the players but he can be fiercely angry when they do not respect the accepted courtesies. No one is better qualified to be the spokesman on the Laws of cricket.

Don Mosey spent 25 years playing cricket in the tough atmosphere of the northern leagues before turning to writing, then broadcasting, about the game. He studied the first-class game, you might say, under the tutelage of two magnificent all-round cricketers, Brian Close and Ray Illingworth, both of them outstanding captains. Throughout his more-than-50-years involvement in the game, he has campaigned against "knocking" and gratuitous criticism of umpires, as he has consistently opposed the abuse of referees in his other love, rugby union.

SIR COLIN COWDREY

LAW

1

THE PLAYERS

I. THE NUMBER OF PLAYERS AND CAPTAIN

A match is played between two sides each of 11 players, one of whom shall be captain. In the event of the captain not being available at any time, a deputy shall act for him.

2. NOMINATION OF PLAYERS

Before the toss for innings, the captain shall nominate his players who may not thereafter be changed without the consent of the opposing captain.

NOTE

(a) More or Less than Eleven Players a Side

A match may be played by agreement between sides of more or less than 11 players but not more than 11 players may field.

T he first Law of the game should never cause complications if a match is played in the spirit of the Laws as envisaged by those who first staged the game of cricket in the sixteenth century in the Weald of Kent and Sussex. In those days it was merely a pastime indulged in by villagers on any piece of land available where they could obtain permission to play.

Everyone would take part, not merely 11 men a side; all would bat and all would bowl and I like to think it was a pursuit for the involvement and enjoyment of all the villagers. In time, challenges were issued by one village to another and there must have been some form of ad hoc Laws agreed by the opposing parties. It was not until 1744 that a form of Laws was first published. Nevertheless, it is startling to realise that not until the 1947 Code of Laws was it officially stated that a side should consist of 11 players, unless otherwise agreed.

Law 1 allows for more than 11 players (or fewer than that number) on either or each side *by agreement* but stipulates that no more than 11 can be in the field at one time. A match in which more than 11 players a side participate will not be regarded as first-class but now, in first-class regulations, a player may be withdrawn from a match, generally if he is required for England duty;

another player will take his place without sacrificing the match's first-class status. We also have to bear in mind that only a small percentage of cricket is played at first-class level, while the Laws of the game are formulated for all – from schoolboys to Test players.

In club cricket, many oddities occur in putting together a side. Players can be late in turning up because of work commitments or mechanical breakdowns. They may even be unaware of their selection. How many of us have received last-minute pleas to turn out because so-and-so has not arrived? How many young and enthusiastic boys have experienced their first taste of competitive cricket because a visiting side has turned up with one or two players short? And how many home players have done a stint in the field as a substitute until a latecomer has appeared? This, of course, is how the game always has been and always should be played and not only at grass-roots level. As I say, Law 1 should cause no problems so long as the spirit is observed.

In my first season as a senior umpire I was involved in an unusual case of changing a nominated side after the match had started. It was in a county championship match, on 30 August 1975 at Tunbridge Wells, and it involved two of the most experienced captains in the game – Ray Illingworth of Leicestershire, and Mike Denness of Kent. Leicestershire had won the toss and elected to bat and they had reached a score in the mid-forties for the loss of one wicket when – believe it or not – we left the field for bad light at midday. During the stoppage, Brian Davison, who was padded up ready to bat at No. 4, was informed of a family bereavement and left for Leicester immediately. He was, of course, one of the nominated players.

My colleague, Bob Barnard and I were approached by the two captains and asked if it was in order to include David Gower (the Leicestershire 12th man) in the side in place of Brian Davison. Permission was granted and our decision was based on two premises: (1) Brian had taken no part in the game and therefore there was no transgression of Law which might otherwise have robbed the game of its first-class status – more than 11 players a side competing; (2) not only had the substitution the *consent* of opposing captain but he actively *desired* it to take place. The incident took place in 1975 when the 1947 Code of Law applied. The change was in every sense agreed by all parties to be in the true spirit of the game, and when the TCCB read the captains' and umpires' reports, they agreed, too.

In the 1980 Code of Laws (which I still refer to as the "new" Code) it mentions in "Definitions" that a change in a nominated side should only be allowed up to the start of play in a competitive match. I am bound to say, however, that if faced with those circumstances of the Kent v. Leicestershire match I would take similar action. I do not regard the term "should" as mandatory, like "shall", "must" or "will".

It is probably unusual for umpires actually to be made aware of the names of a nominated side before the toss takes place and in cricket as a whole it may well be that umpires are remiss in not paying more attention to this point. In a limited-overs contest like the Benson & Hedges Cup or the NatWest Trophy, umpires must certainly be aware of who is the nominated 12th man, because if the original match is not concluded and another one has to be started the side can only be picked from the original 12 names – no others.

Two incidents have occurred in recent seasons which touch on the composition of a side. The first, which I believe reflects absolutely no credit at all on the home club, was in a Yorkshire League match. This is a league which provides high-quality one-day cricket, often involving first-class players of the past, present and future. Most of the visiting side, travelling 90 miles, were caught in a traffic jam – it was no fault of theirs: an accident had occurred to cause the hold up – and they had only three players on the ground at the scheduled time of start. Nevertheless, the home captain insisted that the toss took place and, when he won it, he put the "away side" in to bat. Two wickets fell and therefore the innings was at an end. With what feelings can be imagined, the visiting three then sportingly took the field to enable the home side to score the handful of runs needed to win. One has to say that the action of the home side brought no credit to them, or to the club or the competition in which they play. They have to live with the memory of what happened. But if I may, perhaps, jog the elbow of the umpires involved, "A match may be played *by agreement* between sides of more *or less* than eleven players."

The other incident involved a deputy making the toss. While the Law makes no mention of a deputy for the captain being a member of the nominated side (and perhaps the Law should make reference to this subject), I think it is fair to say we *assume* the deputy will come from the ranks of the nominated players. One has, of course, encountered cases of dignitaries or celebrities tossing the coin but it has been no more than a cosmetic gesture, usually on festive occasions. But in this case it was the captain of one club who was not, in fact, involved as a player in the match.

Now personally I am not bothered who tosses the coin – so long as he does not make ostentatious efforts to captain the side during play when he is not a member of the nominated team. In short, these were two incidents of a kind the game can well do without.

LAW
2

SUBSTITUTES AND RUNNERS; BATSMAN OR FIELDSMAN LEAVING THE FIELD; BATSMAN RETIRING; BATSMAN COMMENCING INNINGS

1. SUBSTITUTES

In normal circumstances a substitute shall be allowed to field only for a player who satisfies the umpires that he has become injured or become ill during the match. However, in very exceptional circumstances, the umpires may use their discretion to allow a substitute for a player who has to leave the field for other wholly acceptable reasons, subject to consent being given by the opposing captain. If a player wishes to change his shirt, boots, etc., he may leave the field to do so (no changing on the field) but no substitute will be allowed.

2. OBJECTION TO SUBSTITUTES

The opposing captain shall have no right of objection to any player acting as substitute in the field, nor as to where he shall field; however no substitute shall act as wicket-keeper.

3. SUBSTITUTE NOT TO BAT OR BOWL

A substitute shall not be allowed to bat or bowl.

4. A PLAYER FOR WHOM A SUBSTITUTE HAS ACTED

A player may bat, bowl or field even though a substitute has acted for him.

5. RUNNER

A runner shall be allowed for a player who, during the match, is incapacitated by illness or injury. The player acting as runner shall be a member of the batting side and shall, if possible, have already batted in that innings.

6. RUNNER'S EQUIPMENT

The player acting as runner for an injured batsman shall wear the same external protective equipment as the injured batsman.

4

7. TRANSGRESSION OF THE LAWS BY AN INJURED BATSMAN OR RUNNER

An injured batsman may be *out* should his runner break any one of Laws 33 (Handled the Ball), 37 (Obstructing the Field) or 38 (Run Out). As striker he remains himself subject to the Laws. Furthermore, should he be out of his ground for any purpose and the wicket at the wicket-keeper's end be put down he shall be *out* under Law 38 (Run Out) or Law 39 (Stumped) irrespective of the position of the other batsman or the runner and no runs shall be scored.

When not the striker, the injured batsman is out of the game and shall stand where he does not interfere with the play. Should he bring himself into the game in any way, then he shall suffer the penalties that any transgression of the Laws demands.

8. FIELDSMAN LEAVING THE FIELD

No fieldsman shall leave the field or return during a session of play without the consent of the umpire at the bowler's end. The umpire's consent is also necessary if a substitute is required for a fieldsman when his side returns to the field after an interval. If a member of the fielding side leaves the field or fails to return after an interval and is absent from the field for longer than 15 minutes, he shall not be permitted to bowl after his return until he has been on the field for at least that length of playing time for which he was absent. This restriction shall not apply at the start of a new day's play.

9. BATSMAN LEAVING THE FIELD OR RETIRING

A batsman may leave the field or retire at any time owing to illness, injury or other unavoidable cause, having previously notified the umpire at the bowler's end. He may resume his innings at the fall of a wicket which for the purposes of this Law shall include the retirement of another batsman. If he leaves the field or retires for any other reason he may resume his innings only with the consent of the opposing captain. When a batsman has left the field or retired and is unable to return owing to illness, injury or other unavoidable cause, his innings is to be recorded as "retired, not out". Otherwise it is to be recorded as "retired, out".

10. COMMENCEMENT OF A BATSMAN'S INNINGS

A batsman shall be considered to have commenced his innings once he has stepped on to the field of play.

NOTE

(a) Substitutes and Runners

For the purpose of these Laws, allowable illnesses or injuries are those which occur at any time after the nomination by the captains of their teams.

T his Law is so long and involved that it can be something of a minefield for all but those who have made a close and intense study of the Laws of Cricket. I propose to deal with it in two sections, as it applies (1) to a substitute for the fielding side and (2) to a substitute for the batting side.

(As a precaution, I should add that Law 2 now differs drastically in the regulations governing the playing of different TCCB competitions. Indeed, I sometimes wonder during the course of a season if Law 2 will ever again apply in the context for which it was originally written. And that is what we are concerned with here: the Laws in their purest sense.)

Substitutes for the fielding side

If a member of the fielding side has to leave the field because of illness or injury, that side can by right have a substitute. The injury can be as serious as a broken leg or as minor as a small blister on the toe; illness can range from an attack of malaria to a slight stomach pain. The substitute can be anyone recruited from anywhere. It can be an outstanding fieldsman like Derek Randall or Mark Ramprakash, enjoying a day off from playing, or a young boy sitting in the crowd with no specialist ability as a runner, thrower or catcher. The batting captain has no say in the matter at all except that he *can* refuse to allow the substitute to keep wicket but he is not allowed to specify any other position in which the substitute may or may not be occupied. A substitute cannot, of course, bat, bowl, run for an injured batsman or captain a side. All he can do is field.

In an experiment to Law 2.1 in 1985 an umpire can allow a substitute for "exceptional reasons" with the consent of the opposing captain. For instance, I am sure it would be correct for the umpire to allow, and the opposing captain to agree to, the use of a substitute if a member of the fielding side was informed that a member of his family was ill. It is possible to think of a host of situations of this kind where a player may wish to leave the field and I hope I shall never "stand" in a match in which the captain refuses such a request.

Now we come to the length of absence from the field and the player and his involvement on his return. If he has been absent for no more than 15 minutes he can take a full part immediately after coming back. He can take the ball and bowl straight away. If he has been off for more than 15 minutes he will not be allowed to bowl until he has been on the field for as long as he was absent. Now I have seen it written in books on Cricket Law that absent players should not be allowed to return until the end of the over which is currently being bowled. There is no way I can subscribe to this view and I certainly would not apply such a restriction in certain circumstances. Let us say, for instance, that an absent player has been off the field for 14 minutes and is now anxious to return and beat the deadline. If he is standing on the boundary edge, clearly wanting to get back into the game, but a bowler is delivering, say, the second ball of an over, it might be another three or four minutes before he has completed that over. The "absentee", therefore, will have exceeded 15 minutes by the time the over is completed and thus be prevented from bowling for 17 or 18 minutes. This seems to me to be manifestly unfair to the fielding side. What, therefore, would I do? I would stop play as soon as I see the "absentee" is ready to return, irrespective of the state of an over, and ask the fielding captain if he requires his missing player back on the field. If so, he will be allowed to return and everyone is happy.

I accept, and agree with, the interpretation which I have also seen written "that the 15-minutes-plus absence also applies to fielders who fail to return after an interval'. I also agree that "the restriction will not apply to a player who is late for the start of the match", because the player in this case has never *left* the field (in that he has never been *on* the field). What I am unable to agree with is the last line of Law 2, paragraph 8 which states, "This restriction shall not apply at the start of a new day's play." As it stands, this section has led to certain ambiguities and, as I saw it, was open to abuse. No one can tell me that in a three-day match a player can lie in bed until a late hour upon day two or three, arrive at the ground at 12.30 pm, and bowl straightaway; that is not correct. The player has failed to return after an interval to the field of play, the interval in this case being from close of play on one day to the start of play on the next. I therefore took it up at a meeting of the MCC Laws Committee of which I am a member. As a result, the Association of Cricket Umpires was given MCC approval to publish the following: "The last sentence of Law 2.8 ('This restriction shall not apply at the start of a new day's play') is to be interpreted as follows: 'If a Fieldsman fails to come on the field at the start of a new day's play (other than at the start of a match) this shall be counted as failing to return after an interval, except that any time for which he was absent from the field at the end of the previous day's play shall be discounted.' Hence, if a Fieldsman comes on to the field at the start of play on any day there will be no restriction on his bowling. If, however, for example, he does not come on to the field until 20 minutes after the start of play on the second day (or on a subsequent day) then he will not be allowed to bowl in that innings until he has been on the field for 20 minutes, irrespective of whether or not he was absent from the field at the end of the previous day."

This has cleared up the point to some extent. As the Law stood, a bowler could have been absent prior to the close on one day for, say, 20 minutes for good and sufficient reasons of injury or illness, then decided to have 20 extra minutes in bed on the following day, turned up late, taken the field and been able to go straight on and bowl. A small point, perhaps; an unlikely one, too, it may seem. But it is as well to have these matters made absolutely clear. In fact I would have preferred to see this change in Law 2.8, stating, "Any time a fielder was absent from the field of play at the end of a day would be waived as long as that fieldsman took the field of play at start of play the following day." But you can't win 'em all. I think the situation is now clearer.

7

Umpires must work together when a player leaves the field. The umpire who is formally told that a fieldsman is leaving must draw the attention of his colleagues to the matter. Both must note the time of departure and, when the player returns, both umpires must check and agree on the length of his absence. This is not always as straightforward as it seems. A returning player can sometimes escape the notice of one umpire and it is important that his colleague should keep him in the picture. It is very much to the fielding captain's advantage to ensure the umpires are absolutely clear when a player leaves the field and when he returns. As it happens, the onus is on the captain to make sure such comings and goings are brought to the attention of the umpires.

While I have no desire to cross swords with the cricketing Press, I saw one report in a newspaper which was, as far as I could judge, incorrect in almost every point. The writer had confused what was, in fact, an application of Law 1 (a change in the nominated side) with Law 2 (use of a substitute). The point I want to make is this: I would be glad, and I am sure it goes for my colleagues, to clear up any point of Law or Regulation if reporters wanted to knock on the door of the umpires' room and inquire. We can all help each other.

Under the pre-1980 Code of Law a term was used in Law 2 (Substitutes), "during the match" and no one was entirely sure what the exact definition of this was. Fortunately, in the 1980 code under "Definitions" the matter was cleared up. "During the match" meant "from the moment the coin was spun in the air at the toss to the ultimate conclusion of play on the last day of the match". Furthermore, the type or duration of the match was irrelevant. It could be 20-overs-a-side, played on an evening, or the way they play grade cricket in New Zealand: a two-day game played on successive Saturdays, with six rest days in between. An injury or illness which required the use of a substitute could take place at any time during those eight days (Saturday to Saturday), whether the injury/illness had occurred on the ground or somewhere else, at work or play, during day or night. A substitute could be fielded in compliance with the Law. The mind boggles at what may have caused the imposition.

The following is an addendum to Law 2 "Substitutes" and in particular to Law 2.8. Again it is a decision which was arrived at by the members of the MCC Laws Committee at the meeting held on 12 October 1992.

There have been many questions in regard to a member of the fielding side leaving the field of play more than once in the same innings. The question asked was in regard to the time which he had to be back on the field before he could bowl, and I set down a couple of examples.

(1) A fielder is off the field twice, both times for more than 15 minutes. On the first occasion he is off for a period of 17 minutes before his return and under the Law he would have to be back on the field for 17 minutes before he can bowl. After he has been on the field for 10, he again leaves the field. This

second absence is for a period of 20 minutes before his return and the question is: how long before he can bowl? In this case, he will have to serve the 7 minutes to complete the first time of his absence, plus the 20 minutes for the second one, a total of 27 minutes.

(2) Again the first absence from the field was for a period of 17 minutes, again leaving after being back on the field for 10 minutes. This time the second spell of absence was only for a period of 12 minutes. In this case when he returned he would only have to serve a 7-minute period before he could bowl, as the second absence would not count because it was for less than 15 minutes' duration. It is only when the periods are for more than 15 minutes that penalty time must be served.

(3) This is a further example which I feel could be open to abuse but the Committee decided that the clarification should apply. A fielder leaves the field and returns after 12 minutes. He then stayed on for one over and again left the field, returning after a further 12 minutes: how long would he have to wait to bowl? Answer: he can bowl immediately as neither absence was in excess of 15 minutes; not sure that I am happy about that.

It is clear to see that as long as the second absence is not in excess of 15 minutes, then they will not be added together. Of course if it is, then they will be. This ruling brings things more into line with what has been adopted in first-class cricket for a few years, and whilst some think that in certain instances it is unfair, it certainly helps to eliminate abuse.

Substitutes for the batting side
If a batsman is injured whilst actually batting or fielding (or, in New Zealand, at any time during or between the two Saturdays) he may have a substitute to run for him, as of right. The fielding captain has no right of objection to any other member of the side undertaking the duty of runner. What the umpires must try to ensure is that, if possible, the runner has already batted. This is not always possible, as when one of the opening pair is injured or ill. In such a case, there is one thing which I, personally, would not allow: the runner to be the next player in the batting order after the dismissal of one of the opening pair. In this contention, the only thing to support me would be Law 42 (Unfair Play) and while nothing unfair might be intended by the use of No. 3 batsman as a runner for numbers 1 or 2, it is possible that an unfair advantage *might* be gained from it.

The other thing the umpire must watch out for is the apparel worn by the runner. In the 1980 Code of Laws, Law 2.6, it is written that runners shall wear gloves and pads and then only if the injured batsman is wearing them. Since then, of course, we have seen helmets in profusion and I could count on the fingers of one hand those batsmen whom I have never seen wearing a helmet. In 1985 an experimental Law, replacing Law 2.6, was introduced: "The player acting as runner for an injured batsman shall wear the same external protective equipment as the injured batsman." I agree with this Law

9

except that I am at a loss to understand how the word "external" came into it. To me, this means that a runner has no need to wear a box, thigh pad, chest pad or arm guard (that is if the injured batsman for whom he is running was wearing an arm guard with his sleeves rolled down and buttoned at the wrist). Once he rolls up his sleeve the guard becomes *external*. If that were to happen I hope no umpire would instruct the runner to go and put on an arm guard. One or two might!

I believe simply that a runner should be dressed similarly, with similar protective equipment to the injured batsman, and that if there is a difference it should not be to the advantage of the runner. That belief is not strictly in accord with what is stated in the Law. For one thing, if the injured batsman is wearing a cap I would never insist on the runner wearing one (he may never have worn a cap in his life). In any case, I don't count a cap as "protective equipment". I would like to leave this part of Law 2.6 as it is, but delete the word "external".

The positioning of an umpire when a runner is being used is, to me, one of the most important points to be studied. The umpire at square-leg should immediately move over to point, and the square-leg position should be occupied by the runner and also be used by the injured batsman when he is not the striker. There are three reasons why I believe this is necessary. (1) The umpire can more clearly see the batting crease and its imaginary extension out to the runner. Thus he can observe the injured striker, and his runner, and their positions if he is asked to adjudicate on a stumped or run-out appeal. (2) The runner will be able to make his way from one end to the other over what is usually a more lightly populated area of the field – certainly less populated than the off side – and he will be less likely to be a hindrance to fielders. (3) The umpire in that (point) position will be a help to his colleague. An umpire at the bowler's end, especially one of lesser experience, has to remember that the only help he can get out in the middle is from his colleague. To get into position for a run-out decision it is wise always to run to the side of the pitch where his colleague is. In that position he will never be badly placed. For the umpire of greater experience, and when the injured batsman is taking strike, it is important for him to remember to run to the same side as his colleague, too, but when the non-injured batsman is taking strike treat it as a usual situation. You really do have to concentrate quite hard and remember which is the best side to get into a good position to give a decision.

There are a number of recorded instances of run-out incidents when a runner has been involved. I have adjudicated on three in England, all in championship matches, and in one such instance there were *two* runners because both batsmen had been injured. I have been involved in a situation when such a hilarious mix-up occurred with two runners that just about everyone was in tears of laughter and I thought my colleague would have a stroke. (See the story at end of this chapter.)

I advise that umpires follow three principles when judging a run-out decision with a runner being used. (1) If the *injured* striker has hit the ball and remained in his ground (i.e. behind the batting crease), he cannot be run out, so the umpires are left to judge the positions of the runner and the non-injured batsman. (2) After playing, or attempting to play the ball, should the injured striker be out of his ground and the wicket be broken *at the wicket-keeper's end*, he will always be *out* irrespective of where his runner or the non-striker may be. The runner and the non-injured batsman may have completed three runs and be standing safely in their ground, but if the injured striker is out of *his* ground and his wicket is put down, then he must be given out on appeal. It may be that the injured striker has (forgetting for a moment his injury) run down the pitch and made his ground at the other end – even here he is not immune from dismissal. If this happens, any runs which have been completed by the other two parties (runner and non-injured batsman), whether *they* have run one, two, three or more, will not be scored – none of them. (3) The injured batsman cannot be run out, no matter where he may be, by the fielding side breaking the wicket at the bowler's end. In such a situation his runner, and the non-injured player, will be considered to be the two batsmen (i.e. taking, for the moment, the injured batsman out of the reckoning). In Law 38 (Run Out) I will deal with more dismissals and situations where a runner is being used. For the moment, just let me emphasise the point I made in principle (2): if runner and non-injured batsman have "scored", say, three runs but the injured striker is judged to be *out*, none of the runs shall count. The non-injured batsman must return to the bowler's end and the new batsman will take strike (unless, of course, the run-out occurred off the last ball of the over).

When batting with a runner, an injured player, while he is the striker, will be subject to dismissal under all Laws, and when not the striker and standing in his passive position at square-leg, he can still be given *out* for infringements of Law 33 (Handled the Ball) or Law 37 (Obstructing the Field). The injured striker's runner, when standing away from the action at square-leg, is also subject to Laws 33 and 37 as well, of course, as Law 38 (Run Out). It is not difficult to imagine an injured striker's fury if he is well within his ground but finds himself given *run out* because his runner, relaxing his concentration for a minute, has strayed an inch or so in front of the line of the batting crease! It would indeed be an unusual dismissal, but good in Law.

Returning for a moment to my point that an umpire should move to the point position when a runner is in use (with the runner at square-leg), let us take the case of the arrival at the wicket of a left-hand batsman when he is taking strike. I believe the umpire should retain the same position even though he is now back at square-leg and the injured batsman is at point. There, the injured party can assume a place where he is of least impediment to the fielding side. He can be backward of point, or for that matter in front of point, because he is deemed to be "out of the game" except for Laws 33 and 37.

Why, I sometimes wonder, do we invariably have the injured batsman, when not the striker, positioned square with the wicket on the leg side? It is not essential. Why do we not place him behind the wicket-keeper, perhaps slightly to the leg side if the disposition of the fieldsmen permits? He would have a shorter distance to limp when it was his turn to take strike and he would rarely be in anyone's way! It's just a thought I have had for some years. I may try it out one day.

There is an interesting coincidence of how certain individuals knew that a "Run Out" situation was available to their side; certainly in two instances, when I have seen an injured striker using a runner. I recall that at Cambridge, in 1977, while rain caused us to spend a long time in the pavilion, I was asked to explain exactly what was involved in bringing about a dismissal when an injured striker is using a runner. The most effective way to do this, I find, is to demonstrate using three beer bottles. While I was doing this, Ray Illingworth happened to be watching and he called to several of his players, "Get yourselves over here and learn something." I must have spent the best part of an hour shuffling those beer bottles around and we had quite a crowd of spectators by the time I had finished.

Four years later I happened to be umpiring Sussex v. Warwickshire at Hove when Dilip Doshi, the Indian Test bowler (who played for Notts before joining Warwickshire), was injured and limping when he came in to bat in his usual position, No. 11, with Steve Perryman as his runner. Willie Hogg was the other batsman. Dilip played a ball backward of square on the leg side and set off with a hop, skip and a jump down the pitch. Steve Perryman completed the run with Dilip following not too far behind while Willie had made his ground comfortably at the wicket-keeper's end. Suddenly, from cover point, came a great shout, "Take the bails off," and Ian Gould, the wicket-keeper, did so, almost facetiously. The man who had shouted then turned to me and asked, "How's that?" and I replied and signalled *out*. I walked over to the wicket, picked up the bails and we all left the field.

The cover point who had been responsible for the shout was Paul Parker, one of those who, four years earlier, had been Secretary of Cambridge University Cricket Club and had watched my demonstration with the beer bottles. The Press advanced en masse as we reached the pavilion and I told them, "Doshi – run out and no runs to be scored. Happy?" They looked a bit doubtful but they left to write their stories.

It's always a great pleasure to realise that someone has benefited from a demonstration or a lecture. Another example of this occurred in 1981 and while I was able to see that a *player* had taken note of my advice on Law 2, I rather think that my umpiring colleague went away a bit wiser, too.

During the previous winter, 1980-81, I had undertaken an extensive umpiring-and-lecture tour of New Zealand where Brian Hardie, of Essex, was playing and coaching at the University of Auckland. He invited me to talk to the students, and one of the lectures was on injured strikers using a runner. Right – we now move on to the end of July, 1981, when Essex were playing Middlesex in the Southend Festival and my colleague was Khizar Hayat, the Pakistani Test umpire and a rather shy little man. In the Middlesex first innings, Paul Downton had Keith Tomlins as a runner because of injury and in an eighth-wicket stand with Mike Selvey, Paul had reached 46. With the bowling from my end, Paul hit a nice shot into the covers and, in his excitement (probably as he neared 50) he set for a run himself. It was the first time he had slipped up on this point since he came in to bat. Both he and Keith Tomlins duly arrived at my end and, by now standing square on to the wicket, I glanced down to the other end to see that Mike Selvey had run a good ten yards past *his* wicket. Ah, but there was Brian Hardie in the field, the man who had listened to my lecture in Auckland a few months earlier.

He shouted to Keith Fletcher, who had fielded the ball, to throw it to David East, the wicket-keeper, who, when the ball arrived, removed the bails and appealed. I looked towards my colleague, Khizar, who was motionless. I couldn't help wishing, "For goodness sake, do something." Khizar turned and looked at me as several Essex players were now appealing – especially Brian Hardie – and I nodded my head furiously to signify assent (to the appeal). He still made no decision so, as unobtrusively as possible I called, "That's *out*. Give him *out*." At last, he gave a batsman *out*, but then tried to insist that it was Selvey who had to go! By now, of course, I was completely involved in a situation which should not have been my responsibility. I walked back to the bowler's wicket, told Downton he was the man *out* and sent him and Tomlins on their way, asking them to send back Selvey.

While this was happening I had a chat with Khizar, and it was quite clear that he had never before been involved in an incident of this kind. But it happened back in 1981 and he is now Pakistan's best umpire. He was, in fact, that country's representative in the 1992 World Cup competition in Australia and New Zealand. Brian Hardie had obviously learned well, too, and later that week he told me that he and David East had been discussing that very situation only a short time earlier.

Twice I have been involved in matches where both batsmen have been injured and have been granted the concession of a runner. That, believe me, makes the situation very interesting indeed! One was at Dartford, Kent v. Middlesex, in 1983, which was, in fact, just two days before I officiated in my first World Cup match. Bob Woolmer had scored a fine century in the first innings despite breaking a toe during the second half of his innings, and he was required to come out to bat in the second innings, this time with a runner. I seem to remember he joined Chris Cowdrey, who also had a runner; but Chris was quickly caught at slip and the innings ended – rather to the relief of my colleague, Ken Palmer, and myself.

The other occasion was in New Zealand in January 1981, when both batsmen and their runners were there for a considerable time. I will try to shorten the story, but it is difficult.

In essence it has to be understood that club cricket matches in that country are two-day affairs, played on consecutive Saturdays, and on the first Saturday everything went well. During the week, on Wednesday I think, four of the players, two from each side, whilst making a journey by car to work, were involved in an accident. None was badly hurt but all were cut, bruised and stiff, therefore Law 2 (Substitutes) in regard to both batting and fielding sides was implemented on the second Saturday.

On that day, the side which was batting last required just over 200 runs to win and a reasonable time in which to get them but they had a disastrous start, losing four wickets for less than 20. One of those who had been injured was a good batsman and he came to the wicket batting at No. 6 with a runner; but with the ball being struck very hard to the boundary, there was no need for much running by either party, over the course of a hundred partnership before the next wicket fell. With 22 runs required, in came the other injured member of the batting side at No. 11, accompanied by a runner: imagine the scene. Injured striker batting well, injured striker's runner in the square-leg position, and alongside him was the injured non-striker; at the bowling end, the wicket at which I was standing, was the non-striker's runner. The bowler delivered the ball and bang, it was hit over the mid-on fielder down toward the boundary and his runner set off. But not the runner from my end: he stood, turned, looking upwards and admired the shot. Seeing his runner not moving, the injured non-striker decided that he had better run, so off he went. The injured striker seeing his batting partner running felt that he must get into the act and he also set off. By this time we had all three running toward the bowling end shouting to the stagnant runner, that he should be so-and-so running for the so-and-so far end, and as they arrived he set off accompanied by the other three – three on a second circuit and one on the first. In the ensuing confusion we had various parties running in various directions, at various times, shouting various things to each other; and then the fielding substitutes got into the act.

By this time I was down on one knee to observe any "run out", but I was shaking with laughter. My colleague was on both knees with tears running down his face; I am not sure that either of us could have seen to give a decision.

Fielding substitutes are usually young men, fleet of foot and strong of arm – and so it was in this case. Where do they usually field? Mid-off and mid-on, and again that was the case. As the ball sailed over the mid-on he turned and gave chase, overtaking the ball some three feet from the boundary line; if the fool had let it reach we would all have been in the clear. With the strong arm the ball was propelled the distance down to the wicket-keeper with a great throw, but not quite, for the wicket-keeper had to take a couple of steps towards it and away from the stumps. Catching the ball he glanced up to see four figures, all dressed in white, all clad in pads and gloves, all brandishing bats, running towards him in line abreast. Now, whether it was the chance of an immediate dismissal, or whether he took fright at the sight he saw, I never did find out; but he took half a step backwards towards the stumps, tripped, fell and flattened the lot. The action was still not yet finished, and there was no chance of my mate giving anyone "out" at his end, for by this time he was lying on his side with his legs twitching. I thought that he might have been having a stroke, but I could hear him laughing. The fielders were shouting to the wicket-keeper, "Get up, get up, throw it down the other end", and from amidst a welter of stumps and bails, he raised himself to his knees, drew back his arm and threw the ball towards a fielder positioned over the other wicket at my end. Unfortunately, too high, too hard and too far; for the last we saw of the ball, before everyone collapsed into tears, was it running under the sightscreen at one end of the ground. What I do not want is for anyone to write to me and ask, "How many runs were scored?" For in a situation as hilarious as that, who the hell cares?

LAW
3

THE UMPIRES

1. APPOINTMENT
Before the toss for innings, two umpires shall be appointed, one for each end, to control the game with absolute impartiality as required by the Laws.

2. CHANGE OF UMPIRES
No umpire shall be changed during a match without the consent of both captains.

3. SPECIAL CONDITIONS
Before the toss for innings, the umpires shall agree with both captains on any special conditions affecting the conduct of the match.

4. THE WICKETS
The umpires shall satisfy themselves before the start of the match that the wickets are properly pitched.

5. CLOCK OR WATCH
The umpires shall agree between themselves and inform both captains before the start of the match on the watch or clock to be followed during the match.

6. CONDUCT AND IMPLEMENTS
Before and during the match the umpires shall ensure that the conduct of the game and the implements used are strictly in accordance with the Laws.

7. FAIR AND UNFAIR PLAY
The umpires shall be the sole judges of fair and unfair play.

8. FITNESS OF GROUND, WEATHER AND LIGHT
(a) The umpires shall be the sole judges of the fitness of the ground, weather and light for play.
(i) However, before deciding to suspend play, or not to start play, or not to resume play after an interval or stoppage, the umpires shall establish whether both captains (the batsmen at the wicket may deputise for their

captains) wish to commence or to continue in the prevailing conditions; if so, their wishes shall be met.

(ii) In addition, if during play the umpires decide the light is unfit, only the batting side shall have the option of continuing play. After agreeing to continue to play in unfit light conditions, the captain of the batting side (or a batsman at the wicket) may appeal against the light to the umpires who shall uphold the appeal only if, in their opinion, the light has deteriorated since the agreement to continue was made.

(b) After any suspension of play, the umpires, unaccompanied by any of the players or officials, shall, on their own initiative, carry out an inspection immediately the conditions improve and shall continue to inspect at intervals. Immediately the umpires decide that play is possible they shall call upon the players to resume the game.

9. EXCEPTIONAL CIRCUMSTANCES

In exceptional circumstances, other than those of weather, ground or light, the umpires may decide to suspend or abandon play. Before making such a decision the umpires shall establish, if conditions allow, whether both captains (the batsmen at the wicket may deputise for their captain) wish to continue in the prevailing conditions; if so, their wishes shall be met.

10. POSITION OF UMPIRES

The umpires shall stand where they can best see any act upon which their decision may be required.

Subject to this over-riding consideration, the umpire at the bowler's end shall stand where he does not interfere with either the bowler's run-up or the striker's view.

The umpire at the striker's end may elect to stand on the off instead of the leg side of the pitch, provided he informs the captain of the fielding side and the striker of his intention to do so.

11. UMPIRES CHANGING ENDS

The umpires shall change ends after each side has had one innings.

12. DISPUTES

All disputes shall be determined by the umpires and if they disagree the actual state of things shall continue.

13. SIGNALS

The following code of signals shall be used by umpires, who will wait until a signal has been answered by the scorer before allowing the game to proceed:

Boundary – by waving the arm from side to side

Boundary 6 – by raising both arms above the head

Bye – by raising an open hand above the head

Dead ball – by crossing and recrossing the wrists below the waist

Leg-bye – by touching a raised knee with the hand

No-ball – by extending one arm horizontally

Out – by raising the index finger above the head. If not out, the umpire shall call "not out"

Short run – by bending the arm upwards and by touching the nearest shoulder with the tips of the fingers

Wide – by extending both arms horizontally.

14. CORRECTNESS OF SCORES

The umpires shall be responsible for satisfying themselves on the correctness of the scores throughout and at the conclusion of the match. See Law 21.6 (Correctness of Result).

NOTES

(a) Attendance of Umpires

The umpires should be present on the ground and report to the ground executive or the equivalent at least thirty minutes before the start of a day's play.

(b) Consultation between Umpires and Scorers

Consultation between umpires and scorers over doubtful points is essential.

(c) Fitness of Ground

The umpires shall consider the ground as unfit for play when it is so wet or slippery as to deprive the bowlers of a reasonable foot-hold, the fieldsmen, other than the deep fielders, of the power of free movement, or the batsmen of the ability to play their strokes or to run between the wickets. Play should not be suspended merely because the grass and the ball are wet and slippery.

(d) Fitness of Weather and Light

The umpires shall suspend play only when they consider that the conditions are so bad that it is unreasonable or dangerous to continue.

U mpires the world over have been (and to my mind always will be) individuals of the highest integrity. If not, they are quickly unmasked; but for my part I have yet to find one who fell short of the high standards required.

In England, umpires are known to be the best in the world and so they should be. Not only at first-class level but also in the better class of club cricket I know of umpires who officiate on around 75 days in an English summer which means that by sheer weight of experience they will stand out above many others in different parts of the world.

During my tour of New Zealand in our winter of 1980-81 I received from

Brian Langley, at the TCCB, my list of appointments for the 1981 summer at home. I showed it to Fred Goodall, New Zealand's most experienced umpire at that time, and after he had looked at it he said to me, "Don, this shows you will 'stand' on 87 days next summer. That amounts to more first-class cricket than I have umpired in the whole of my career." Fred had been a Test umpire for many years and was certainly the best in New Zealand. Today, some years after he has retired, he is the national umpires' training officer based in Wellington.

I have mentioned the name of Brian Langley, who retired from the position of Assistant Secretary to the TCCB in 1988. All of the first class umpires would refer to him as the "magic man"; he made us all feel that we were the most important people in the game of cricket. Should he require an umpire at one minute's notice to take on an extra match all he had to do was to ring any of us, he would never have a refusal; for whilst it was in his power to direct us to take the match, he always started the conversation with the words "Can you help me?" When he left the offices of the TCCB some of the magic which we felt he possessed left with him.

As many people know, I regard as part of my duties not just trying to improve knowledge of the Laws but to pass on something of the art and technique to umpires worldwide. To this end, I have travelled to Sri Lanka, Zimbabwe, Israel, West Indies, New Zealand and, more recently, to Malaysia and Singapore and have been asked to return in February 1993. All tours except one have been at considerable personal expense but I do not look on this as a burden. On the contrary, I feel it is a great honour to be invited. In all the countries I have visited I have found great eagerness and willingness to learn about all aspects of umpiring. All I ask in return is that those who attend my seminars are willing to work hard.

I flatter myself that after talking to a group of officials, without ever seeing any of them in a white coat or anywhere near a cricket pitch, I can tell who will, or will not, umpire well. Returning for a moment to that 1980-81 tour of New Zealand, of the many umpires with whom I "stood" or discussed the Laws of Cricket, one stood out from the rest. When I returned to England I said that Brian Aldridge would become New Zealand's next Test-panel umpire and in 1985 that prediction proved correct. He went on to umpire the 1992 World Cup Final in Australia.

It wasn't too difficult to get that one right. During that New Zealand trip I "stood" on 25 days, officiating for 2,496 overs, and I gave 86 lectures. More importantly, I "stood" with 17 of that country's umpires and formed a fair idea of their individual ability.

I have made four visits to Zimbabwe. (Who was it who said, "Once Africa gets into your blood it never leaves you"?) That country and its people have left a great impression on me and I greatly value some of the friendships I have made. My first visit was in 1985 when I first "stood" with a good friend named Don Arnott. I umpired with him when I went out with an English

Counties side and I honestly believe that if Don had devoted himself to umpiring he would have made a fine official. Another umpire with whom I worked in Zimbabwe was Clive Currin (mentioned elsewhere in this book – Law 11) and if he and Don Arnott were still officiating, how fortunate Zimbabwe would be in its umpiring standards! In Zimbabwe I have umpired on 54 days (taking 4,435 overs) and delivered over 150 lectures.

My trip to West Indies was short, and while I did not "stand" with their David Archer when he spent half a season in England, I did have the pleasure of umpiring with him during that tour of mine.

To spend three weeks in Sri Lanka in March, 1991, was an interesting experience, and some of my lectures lasted longer than any others I have delivered. But they were very well attended by people keen to learn. Not everyone who has played in Sri Lanka will agree with me but I feel the country has real potential for a strong and efficient panel of umpires. In particular, "Sammy" Samarasinghe had a good game when I "stood" with him, as did the two others. Twelve days' umpiring took in 887 overs and I gave 12 lectures.

Other tours in which I have undertaken both umpiring and lecturing have been to Israel where Geoffrey Davis and members of Harrow Cricket Club have been almost solely responsible for keeping the game alive. Little cricket is played but they are so keen, and work so hard to stage a match, that it is good to see. Nevertheless, there is very little umpiring structure and they have little knowledge of the Laws. After "standing" in a match at Beersheva I gave a 90-minute lecture in a school in the middle of the Negev desert where, it seemed, everyone in the community turned out – men, women, children and animals as well! An interpreter translated my words into Hebrew. I bet none of my fellow training officers can beat that!

So much for umpiring abroad; let's get back to umpiring in this country. Through the Association of Cricket Umpires there is a tremendous training programme at all levels for those who wish to take advantage. When I joined the first-class panel in 1975 there was only Lloyd Budd (a former Hampshire player) who had had any involvement with the ACU. I do not for one moment claim the Association is perfect in every way but it does have a great deal to offer umpires – current or aspiring.

Perhaps at this stage I might quote the words of Frank Lee, an excellent umpire of former years, who wrote in his book, *The Umpire's Decision*:

> "To any man who is about to embark on this job of umpiring I cannot give better advice than this: Study and learn The Laws and continually review them, for only by knowing each and every one is it possible to apply the correct decisions, particularly when an unusual point arises."

I would like to endorse every word of that, particularly the last six. How true.

It is correct to say that umpires who make the fewest mistakes will turn out to be the best. An umpire who is not fully conversant with the Laws and who makes a mistake in that area of his umpiring will have committed an unforgivable act. No umpire consciously makes a *bad* decision but some do make *incorrect* decisions, usually due to not noticing a point of fact or lacking the total concentration which is required of all umpires. Should an umpire realise that he has made an error, the best advice I can offer is: Forget all about it, immediately. Treat it as though it never happened. If you don't, and you worry about it, nothing is more certain than that it will affect the rest of your game.

One final point about the ACU. Two of its officers, Sheila Hill and David Whiley, are members of the MCC's Laws Committee and they bring a tremendous amount of sensible thought to our discussions. The game owes them a great deal.

There have been some magnificent umpires over the years, from "Honest Will" Caldecourt, who officiated in 1850, to the first-class panel of today; from Frank Chester and Syd Buller through the line of Arthur Fagg, Ron Aspinall (with whom I "stood" at Derby in my first game of 1975), Eddie Phillipson, Lloyd Budd, Bill Alley, John Langridge and Sam Cook. I owe them a great deal. They were all not only excellent professional cricketers but became splendid umpires and if it had not been for their encouragement and wise counsel in my early years I would not now be in the happy position I have occupied for nearly two decades.

There are 26 umpires on the first-class list and to my mind at least 16 of them could umpire a Test in any part of the world. I am not saying those 16 are the *best in the world*, nor would I claim that the eight nominated Test Match umpires are the eight I would select. Incidentally, eight is too many in my view; six is the ideal number. One other thought: players, officials and administrators in the game of cricket have voiced a certain view at great length – umpires must be strong and be prepared to stand up and be counted. I am sure that this is usually the case but some of those who are now ex-Test umpires, to my mind, are very strong umpires. Strange.

During the 1992 season I was the stand-by umpire for the Fourth Test at Headingley and I was there as support for two of the best, Ken Palmer and Mervyn Kitchen. That was not one of the easiest matches to umpire and, of course, they did not get through it without the odd mistake occurring. But in proportion to the number of appeals they heard requiring a decision I know that both of them turned in a fabulous performance. Also, the way they conducted themselves despite provocation, severe at times, from a number of the players, spoke volumes for their professionalism.

There are 14 notes to Law 3, some of which I do not intend to deal with at length. Note (1) states that the umpire *shall be* appointed and it is the mandatory word which is used. In club cricket we are lucky if one individual, let alone two, can be found to give up the necessary time. It is not a period of two hours or less which is required, as in football. For the efficient umpire a day's duty takes up almost ten hours, not counting his travelling time.

Note (2) states that no umpire can be changed during a match without the consent of both captains. In the early days of the game it was customary to change umpires after every innings but later the umpire's position was felt to be of such importance that he was not to be changed during a match. Judging by the autumn/winter series of 1992 in Zimbabwe and South Africa, when a number of umpires were used during a match, it seems that the thinking has changed; and the game, in my view, is the poorer for that.

On a lighter note, however, I can claim one-fifth of a world record after being one of five umpires who officiated in a first-class match in England. The game was Essex v. Sussex at Ilford on 14 June 1988 and the appointed officials were H. D. ("Dickie") Bird and Chris Balderstone. During the game Bird became ill, and to complete that particular session of play his place was taken by George Clark, the dressing-room attendant who is also a local league umpire. After that, John Jameson – the Sussex coach but a former first-class umpire – took over for the remainder of the day. Meanwhile, the TCCB had contacted me at Edgbaston where I was umpiring a second-team match, instructing me to go to Ilford for the final day of Essex v. Sussex. My researches, while admittedly not fully comprehensive, reveal a number of first-class matches which have had three different umpires for one reason or another. I myself have taken part in four such matches but I have not found a game which has had *four*, let alone *five*.

Note (3), in the main, will relate to unusual boundary-markings and their allowance. This is covered under Law 19.

Note (5) has a certain importance, as was shown one day at Trent Bridge in the first match of the 1986 season between Notts and Hampshire. The clock which is generally observed (the one opposite the pavilion, at the Radcliffe Road end) suddenly started going backwards! Umpires – do not forget your watches! Note (7) will be dealt with more fully under Law 42. Note (8) is the tricky one. In first-class cricket the umpires are the sole judges of light, state of the ground and rain but in Law in the case of rain when both captains wish to play, "their wishes shall be met". In other words, if a monsoon is sweeping over the ground and the captains want to play through it, we carry on. I have often joked that "if the captains wish to play I will stay out in the middle until the bails *float* off". But no one can expect players *or umpires* to perform at their best in farcical conditions.

Law 3.8 (ii) refers solely to light – or perhaps I should say "to dark". To those who abuse umpires when bad light stops play I would say this: You are laying the blame at the wrong door. It is never the umpires who call a halt to play because of a deterioration in the light; it is the batsmen at the crease. If the umpires, acting together, take the view that the light is poor they will inform the batsmen and leave the matter in their hands. It is they who decide whether or not to terminate play at the time. If the batsmen's views, for any reason, differ from the umpires', we can then leave the field only if two criteria are met. Firstly, a batsman may appeal to an umpire for play to cease because of a deterioration in the quality of the light. He may do this once during any session of play (I will explain "session" in a moment). Secondly, if, *in the umpires' opinion* (in TCCB competition it is certain, as we use a light meter), the light has deteriorated since the batsmen's decision to stay on the field was taken. A "session" in this particular case is not start-to-lunch, lunch-to-tea, or tea-to-close. We may have been on and off the field four times between lunch and tea, for instance, so we are looking at four different "sessions" in that period as far as Law 3.8 (ii) is concerned.

An appeal can then only be issued if the batsmen have decided to stay on the field after being informed of the umpires' view of the light.

Note (11) states that umpires shall change ends, after each side has completed one innings, which provides an interesting situation in a first-class match. Suppose Side A takes first innings but Side B forfeits its first innings and Side A decides to forfeit its second innings. At which end will the umpires take up their positions when Side B starts its second innings? Answer: the positions they would then occupy if two actual innings had been completed. Forfeited innings, in this instance, count as completed innings.

On Note (12), umpires should always try to come to an agreed decision and if they are unable to do so they should make efforts to appear as if they are in agreement. In cases where they *do* disagree, then what is in operation at the time should now apply (i.e. Keep on with what is happening. If play is taking place, *keep on* playing. If everyone is off the field, *stay* off).

"Standing" with umpires who are new to first-class cricket, and umpiring in other parts of the world, I have had colleagues say, "You are the senior umpire." This is an expression I do not accept. I have no objection to a colleague "leaning" on me, and perhaps taking advantage of my experience, but there should be no mention of seniority. We all go out to the middle as equals.

I have made the point that umpires in this country are able to acquire a great deal of experience, and perhaps I may illustrate this by listing the matches in which I have officiated from my start in 1975 to the end of the 1992 season: Tests – 5; other first-class matches – 342; one-day internationals – 11; Benson & Hedges Cup – 71; Gillette Cup and NatWest Trophy – 36; Sunday League – 202. There have been just over 50 "other matches" made up of games at Scarborough and Harrogate Festivals, various one- and two-day fixtures involving touring teams and, more recently, a number of Second XI games which must now add up to around another 50. It is not difficult to see, therefore, why English umpires become the best.

I am also a keeper of records and during the 1987 season I broke quite a number. I umpired on 115 days, taking in 10,108.3 overs, and I was on duty on another 14 days when no play took place because of rain or because a match had finished early. There was one spell which some people find it difficult to credit, which began on 15 July and ended on 24 August – 45 consecutive days of umpiring. The total of umpiring days in that season, the number of overs "taken" and that figure of 45 consecutive umpiring days are all records. No wonder English umpires are the best.

LAW

4

THE SCORERS

1. RECORDING RUNS

All runs scored shall be recorded by the scorers appointed for the purpose. Where there are two scorers they shall frequently check to ensure that the scoresheets agree.

2. ACKNOWLEDGING SIGNALS

The scorers shall accept and immediately acknowledge all instructions and signals given to them by the umpires.

T his Law is about what I like to call the Ladies and Gentlemen of the game – individuals who are even more dedicated to cricket than the umpires! Where would we be without those who meticulously note every incident which takes place so that it is recorded for posterity? Cricket is very much about records, certainly about statistics, probably more than in any other sport. One can leaf through a scorer's book and see games in the mind's eye, even though one might have been on the other side of the world when they were played.

At club cricket level, some of the scorers' positions are little short of abysmal and as scorers are asked to sit for up to eight hours in cold, dirty and cramped conditions, it's not difficult to see why some clubs struggle to find someone to take on the duties. To my mind, a good and conscientious scorer is worth his weight in gold and should be treated with the utmost courtesy and respect, not only by the members of his own club but by all visitors. Scorers are not only dedicated to their own clubs during the summer but they spend many winter hours compiling the club's records.

It was Milton who wrote, "They also serve who only stand and wait." If he had paraphrased that only slightly, I feel it would have been an entirely appropriate reference to scorers – who *sit* and wait . . . wait for a clear signal from the umpires of things which are a matter of record. I am at pains to impress upon my colleagues that *clear* signals to the scorers are essential to enable them to do their job properly. If there is a mistake in a scorebook it is not necessarily the fault of the scorer. It can be the result of poor or incorrect signalling – see the story under Law 26 (Bye and Leg-Bye). It is also essential to ensure that scorers acknowledge our signals to them.

When Pakistan toured Zimbabwe in 1987 I was happy to win two fans for myself from the worldwide congregation of scorers. While I umpired most of the matches, I was not involved in one game in Bulawayo but I was told I could fly down with the players and watch if I wanted. Meanwhile, a Qantas Airlines flight arrived in Harare bearing the Qantas Flight Stewards Cricket Club, and with them, two lady scorers. Over the weekend they were due to play two one-day games against Country Districts at Harare South and I jumped at the chance to umpire. It was extremely hot so I wore a hat. After giving a signal and seeing it acknowledged by the lady scorers I touched the brim of my hat in response. After the second match there was a bit of a party and one of those lovely ladies presented me with what is now one of my proudest possessions. It was a book of photographs of Australia, signed by all 16 members of the plane's crew. In presenting it, one of the scorers, Sue Hawes, described how I touched the brim of my hat in acknowledgment of the scorer's return signal. "Only an Englishman could have done that," she said.

In "Definitions" under this Law it is emphasised that umpires are responsible for the correctness of the score throughout the match and I am bound to say I know of some grounds where we would never finish a match if this was strictly applied! Imagine what it is like when just one person has to keep the book correct and up-to-date and is then responsible for posting all the details of the score as well – total, number of wickets, each batsman's score, number of overs, last batsman's score, score at the fall of the last wicket, etc. To observe the strict letter of the Law we would be running over to the scorer at least once an over. If I know that a scorer is having difficulties, all I ask of him is that *the book* is correct. That is the official record of the match and it is of paramount importance that it is accurate. If he has the total, wickets and overs right at the end of each over, that is good enough for me. If, at the end of a match, I was officially asked to check the scorebook then, along with the scorer, I would do so but I certainly don't carry out a check as a matter of course.

When I was asked to look at the final draft of the 1980 Code of Laws and suggest any changes I thought appropriate, there were (as I have said elsewhere) two changes I suggested. I won one and lost the other. This is the one I lost. But I am still convinced that there is no way an umpire can be responsible for scores throughout a match and I hope no umpire is going to tell me how he can keep a detailed score while standing as an umpire. If he tries that he will not do either job to the best of his ability and he will certainly not do justice to either role.

In county cricket the scoring position is often well away from the scoreboard and one day at Hove a batsman became rather indignant because he felt that runs he had scored had been credited to his partner. I told him to carry on batting and to take no notice of the board. It was, I insisted, what was recorded in the book which mattered, "and they don't get it wrong". At the same time, it is fair to say that there will occasionally be a miscount, just as occasionally there is an extra ball in an over. These are not officially recorded although certain difficulties can arise, like when a wicket falls off an "extra" delivery!

Scorers have my highest regard and respect and it has been a privilege to count many of them as my friends over the years. When I started in 1975 we had men like Claude Lewis (Kent), Jack Hill (Surrey), Jack Mercer (Northants), Charlie Grove (Warwickshire), Matt Taylor (Lancashire), Bill Thornley (Notts) and Carling Beadmore (Derbyshire). Jack Mercer was a member of the Magic Circle and in off-duty moments I used to watch spellbound as he performed sleight-of-hand tricks with a pack of cards. Unfortunately, one or two of those I mention are no longer with us, but I think of them all with great affection, for they constitute my first fond memories of this wonderful band of scribes.

There are some great characters amongst the present generation like Harry Sharp (Middlesex), known as "The Admiral", and Geoff Blackbourn (Leicestershire) who has an unusual hobby. He collects pubs. Well, not exactly: he collects pub-names and has visited over 5,000 different ones. Before he can "log" a new name he has to have had a drink in it. Len Chandler (Sussex) and Byron Denning (Glamorgan) send cards to each other bearing the rudest and most insulting messages it is possible to think up. I hasten to add that they are great friends! Bill Davis (Lancashire) and Ted Lester (Yorkshire) are great walkers – an understandable pursuit after spending so much time cooped up in their working premises. Peter Austin (Warwickshire) and Clem Driver (Essex) have been asked to accompany England abroad as official scorers. Can you imagine an umpire shouting to any of that distinguished band a complaint that the score is wrong? It can, of course, work the other way. I remember standing with Bill Alley when the scorer once shouted something to him. Big Bill was not exactly a modest, shrinking violet and by way of response he acquainted the scorer with a few of the facts of life – from a distance of around 75 yards!

The instructions to both scorers and umpires in relation to Law 4 are both simple and specific. To the umpires, they shall extend to the scorers whatever signals and/or instructions are required. To the scorers, they shall quickly acknowledge all such signals or instructions, as well as recording the runs which are scored and other incidents of the game.

It may be thought that an umpire only uses signals to dispense information to the scorers: but remember, in the case of "short runs" the umpire will bend the arm so that he touches that shoulder with his finger-tips, the signal. Added to this, he will verbally instruct the scorers as to how many runs were short and therefore not to be credited, the instruction.

In unusual circumstances it may require an item of correspondence to be relayed by the umpires to the scorers. The incident of illegal fielding at Edgbaston under Law 41.1 is one such instance. Four had all been run and the scorers, whilst probably observing the act of illegal fielding, would not know of an award of the five penalty runs, as there is no signal for such a happening. As the game continued and whilst standing in my position at the striker's end, I took out my pad and wrote, "An award has been made for illegal fielding from the second ball of the last over. Please add five runs to the total and also credit them to the striker." At the end of the over I ran to the fence and asked a member of the groundstaff to convey the note to the scorers. There was no need to halt the flow of the match as no undue haste was required; the batsmen were at their correct wickets despite the award of five runs as the penalty. These five runs were added to the four which had already been run, making a total of nine, and this is one of the unusual cases of the batsmen being at the same end after the incident, as they are prior to the incident taking place – although an odd number of runs will be credited to the striker.

Many of the scorers have their own way of acknowledging an umpire's signal to them: some have a handkerchief, some a scorecard, some just wave a hand. Vic Isaacs waves various coloured table tennis bats. Vic, by the way, is the Hampshire scorer and compiles many of the one-day statistics for magazines. Not many signals are as unusual as the one used by the two scorers David Oldham and Tony Kingston, to my colleague Kevin Lyons, during the Somerset v. Northants match in 1990.

I am sure that Nigel Felton will not mind me saying that he is not renowned for hitting that many boundary 6s, but during this match he hit one just to the on side of the wicket and it carried a long way over the boundary boards. The scorers' box at Taunton is in quite an elevated position, and the ball was heading straight for it; but it seemed inconceivable that it would strike the large glass windows in front of David and Tony. In my position at the striker's end, and as I turned to my left, I was exactly in front of the box and saw the ball crash down on to the windowsill. At the same time there was a tremendous flurry of bodies and much noise as the two scorers disappeared from view, taking avoiding action from what they expected to be a shower of glass and a red spherical projectile. Kevin signalled the boundary allowance of 6, to be acknowledged by Tony, who by this time had gone to the floor on his knees, by raising his arms above his head; but all that we could see was a pair of hands appearing above the ledge. David went much better than this, for unable to get out of his seat he went backwards, still in it, and we had the sight of two legs frantically waving in the air as an acknowledgment to Kevin's signal. Needless to say, this incident did stop the show for some time, far in excess of the time taken by David and Tony to gather not only themselves together but also their chairs, books, pens and pencils.

Things can never be the same as they used to be but I must say that whenever the term "scorer" crops up I think of a drawing, dated 1842, of William Davis, of Brighton. He is sitting at a table in the open air, wearing a frock coat and a wide-brimmed straw hat, long-stemmed pipe in left hand, pencil in right, poised over the scorebook, with a glass of stout on the table beside a half-full bottle, an empty bottle lying on the grass under the table. If that was still the way the job is done I might now be a scorer rather than an umpire.

LAW
5

THE BALL

I. WEIGHT AND SIZE

The ball, when new, shall weigh not less than 5½ oz./155.9 g nor more than 5¾ oz./163 g; and shall measure not less than 8¹³⁄₁₆ in./22.4 cm nor more than 9 in./22.9 cm in circumference.

2. APPROVAL OF BALLS

All balls used in matches shall be approved by the umpires and captains before the start of the match.

3. NEW BALL

Subject to agreement to the contrary, having been made before the toss, either captain may demand a new ball at the start of each innings.

4. NEW BALL IN MATCHES OF THREE OR MORE DAYS' DURATION

In a match of three or more days' duration, the captain of the fielding side may demand a new ball after the prescribed number of overs has been bowled with the old one. The governing body for cricket in the country concerned shall decide the number of overs applicable in that country, which shall be not less than 75 six-ball overs (55 eight-ball overs).

5. BALL LOSS OR BECOMING UNFIT FOR PLAY

In the event of a ball during play being lost, or, in the opinion of the umpires, becoming unfit for play, the umpires shall allow it to be replaced by one that, in their opinion, has had a similar amount of wear. If the ball is to be replaced the umpires shall inform the batsmen.

NOTE

(a) Specifications
The specifications, as described in (1) above, shall apply to top-grade balls only. The following grades of tolerance will be acceptable for other grades of ball.
   (i)   Men's Grades 2-4

Weight: 5⁵⁄₁₆ oz./150 g to 5¹³⁄₁₆ oz./165 g
Size: 8¹¹⁄₁₆ in./22 cm to 9¹⁄₁₆ in./23 cm
(ii) Women's
Weight: 4¹⁵⁄₁₆ oz./140 g to 5⁵⁄₁₆ oz./150 g
Size: 8¼ in./21 cm to 8⅞ in./22.5 cm
(iii) Junior
Weight: 4⁵⁄₁₆ oz./133 g to 5¹⁄₁₆ oz./143 g
Size: 8¹⁄₁₆ in./20.5 cm to 8¹¹⁄₁₆ in./22 cm

T his is just one of the Laws which has stood the test of time and it says much for the wisdom, not only of the law-makers of an earlier era but of modern administrators as well. In general they have left alone regulations which have worked well for around 200 years.

As early as February 1744, the ball to be used had to weigh between 5½ and 5¾ oz., but we had to wait nearly 100 years (until 1838 to be precise) for the first Law laying down the circumference – between 9 and 9¼ in. (i.e. slightly larger than today). It leads me to think that bowlers of 150-odd years ago either had larger hands (which is manifestly not the case) or were simply pleased to have any sort of ball to play with! Some modern bowlers kick up a bit of a fuss if the ball feels large in their hands, larger that is than the regulation 8¹³⁄₁₆ to 9 in. I must admit, however, that a ball may increase in size after a number of overs, especially if it is being struck regularly by a Vivian Richards or an Ian Botham.

It was in May 1927 that the present measurement came into use. I call it a silly measurement, one which no one should ever forget because it is so strange . . . 8¹³⁄₁₆ minimum, 9 in. maximum. I sometimes wonder precisely who dreamed it up, and why. It was not until the 1980 Code of Law arrived that the words "when new" were included in the first line. Before that date bowlers perhaps had some justification in trying to persuade umpires to change the ball. Today they are less successful. It either has to be damaged in such a way that it might cause injury to the players or badly out of shape so that each time it is struck the change becomes more pronounced. I have seen the ball thrown to the umpire for inspection and immediately thrown back after a *cursory* inspection so frequently that one almost becomes dizzy.

Mostly this is the bowler trying to get a replacement, a partly used ball which sometimes will swing around like a boomerang. If this happens, the umpire feels a bit of a mug but it is one of the hazards of our occupation. Obviously, if a ball becomes lost or unable to be recovered, then another ball will be taken into use. I have at times wondered, when the bowlers are not able to make a ball swing, if the captain has not put on, for an over, a very occasional bowler. It could be with the hope that one of the batsmen will hit the ball into the far distance so that it will never be found again; this way he can extract from the umpire's pocket a spare. One of the instances of a ball being changed in a Test must have been at Edgbaston in 1975, when the umpires agreed it had gone out of shape after only ten deliveries. After all efforts to find a suitable replacement had failed, Alan Oakman, then the Warwickshire coach, went into the nets and had a new ball bowled to him ten times and this was then used to resume the game between England and Australia.

Umpires have always been able to keep a check on the shape of the ball by putting it through a gauge supplied for that specific purpose; but it was not possible to check the weight until 1984, when the TCCB issued instructions to every county that scales must be provided. It was then discovered that there was an astonishing disparity in the weights of some balls. Not many were under weight but plenty were above the 5¾ oz. mark. Sometimes we had to go through as many as two dozen balls to find six which were correct in weight and dimension. Manufacturers had to pay a good deal more attention to this aspect of their products after that.

At present they appear to have tightened up considerably on the weight problem but a more recent one has arisen in the dyeing process of the leather. In some reports I have submitted to the TCCB I have had to say that "after only a relatively small number of overs the ball resembled in colour something more like a snowball than a cricket ball". Manufacturers have also had trouble with the colour of the stitches after the two halves of the outer casing have been secured together with white twine. The stitches have turned pink, to the obvious dislike of the fielding side when its representative came to choose a ball after the toss.

This regulation for the fielding side to select a ball came into operation in 1985. Previously the umpire selected any ball from the box of new ones presented to them and handed it to the fielding side at start of play. It was not unknown to get comments throughout the innings on its size, shape and colour – not to mention its usefulness! Selection of the ball by the fielding side has made our task a little easier and I hope we may be forgiven a little smile if the score sometimes reaches 300 for one wicket with the bowlers gnashing their teeth in frustration.

In club, and some league, cricket the captains often agree to use just one ball throughout the match, generally for reasons of economy, but if no provision or agreement is made, then "either captain may demand a new ball at the start of each innings". Occasionally, in first-class matches when the side batting last requires only a few runs to win, I have been approached by the fielding captain with the suggestion that he will use any old ball, since a new one costs more than £30. It has then been necessary to explain that the captain of the batting side must also agree. Almost always agreement has been reached but on one notable occasion it was not.

The game was between Northants and Leicestershire, and a lot of time had been lost because of rain. Northants scored 202 for seven, thus gaining two bonus points and Leicestershire three. Leicestershire, on a badly rain-affected pitch (no covered wickets in 1976), then declared at 22 for two, which meant they scored no further bonus points but neither could Northants. Leicestershire had, however, put themselves in a follow-on position and, naturally, it was enforced. With about 20 minutes, plus the final 20 overs minimum to play and the pitch "turning square", Northants were in with a chance, and their captain said he would like to use the ball which they had had in Leicestershire's first innings. It was 18½ overs old. I went to the Leicestershire dressing-room with this ball in one hand and a brand new one, still in its wrapping, in the other, knocked and went in. I held out both hands and had time to utter just one word, "Captain . . ." before Ray Illingworth pointed to my right hand and said, "That one." It was the new ball. He had anticipated what his opposite number would do and he made exactly the right counter-move. Bishen Bedi and Peter Willey opened the Northants attack, even with a shiny new ball, and the score went: 1 run for one wicket; one run for two wickets; five runs for three wickets. It was left to Brian Davison and Illingworth himself to battle out the last 45 minutes against that new ball whilst I speculated on what might have happened with the older one. I also felt rather pleased that Law 5.3 had been observed to the letter.

This is by no means the only time that Ray Illingworth's name appears in this book (which is intended to feature umpires more than players), but I make no apology for that. Ray may have been a hard taskmaster but he knew his cricket Law, probably better than any cricketer I have known in my career. And the characteristic which, above all others, commended him to me was that he was utterly, scrupulously fair. As captain, player and tactician, neither Yorkshire nor Leicestershire have ever been able to replace him and I doubt if they ever will.

There is, of course, provision for a new ball to be used by the fielding side, at their request, after a certain number of overs have been bowled with the old one. The Regulations, and number of overs, have changed from time to time and from one country to another but at the time of writing it is 100 overs in first-class championship matches and 85 in Tests and tourist matches in England.

The only other reason for a change of ball is when it is lost or becomes unfit for play. Fortunately, in club cricket these are generally the only ones – and the ball becomes unfit for play only very rarely. The Law states that "it will be changed for one with a similar amount of wear". Now at first-class level these days there are a small number of bowlers who do interfere with the ball. They can be counted on the fingers of one hand. Application of lip-gloss to improve the shine is easy to detect. You can smell it and it is used very rarely. It is the opening up of the quarter-seam and the widening of the cross-seam which are more prevalent. There has been a regulation in first-class cricket for the last few years which allows umpires, if they observe interference with the seam, to change the ball for one "in much inferior condition". I have always said that if I ever had to apply this I would give to the fielding side a ball which had been gnawed by a dog for a couple of years but in the past twelve months I have changed my view slightly because that might be playing straight into the hands of the fielding side.

What happens is that one side is kept with as much shine as possible while the other is "scoured" – I can't personally vouch for the metal bottle-top treatment, though others can, but I can for damage inflicted by a large thumbnail. It is used to peel the duller side of the ball, like peeling an orange. If this fails, the cross-seam is opened up, and then just watch it go! I never thought this to be a problem, but in the past two years it certainly has become one. Umpires must be very wary and ensure that it ceases. They should also ensure that, if any such action is observed by them, the ball is changed. This is by no means the only type of interference with the ball, though the picking of the seam has been a problem for years.

When a ball is changed it is the duty of the umpire to inform the batsmen. Occasionally when it has been changed and batsmen have asked to see the replacement, they have been critical, but it is the umpire who chooses the replacement, not the batsmen or fielders. It is unfortunate that interpretation of this Law forces one to look at a certain unsavoury aspect of the game. There is so little about cricket which is unsavoury.

No one could possibly have anticipated (and most certainly not those who sat down to frame Law 5) the controversial events in the England v. Pakistan series of 1992. In my opinion, one thing which may have upset the tourists was that they initially wanted to use one brand of cricket ball and England wished to used another. Consequently, it was decided before the series started that as there were to be five Tests and five One-day Internationals, a coin was tossed ten times during a meeting with each manager having the "call" alternately, the winner of the toss to decide on the ball of his choice. Eight times out of ten the coin came down in England's favour so one might say the pot was boiling before the teams even took the field.

At MCC's Laws Committee meeting on 12 October 1992, a question was considered regarding the replacing of a ball with one of a similar degree of wear and use. Part of the question was, in my view, quite sensible; the other took about 30 minutes to answer. The "sensible" part of the question referred to the replacement of the ball which had been used in wet conditions and continually dried with a cloth provided by the umpires and asked: "Should the 'similar wear' include the ball being made wet then dried in a similar manner" (i.e. with a cloth provided by the umpire). What I would do in those circumstances is take the replacement ball from my pocket and roll it across the ground to my colleague for *his* inspection. He would then roll it back to me. If the bowler then wished to dry the ball on the cloth, that would be fair enough. But I would not allow needless time to be wasted by the deliberate wetting and drying of the ball.

With the second part of the question, one could have less patience: "Suppose the ball is hit out of the ground and into a river from where it is not retrieved. If it *had* been recovered it would have been wet. Should the replacement, therefore, be made wet?" This, to me, was absurd. The ball was not wet before it was hit into the river. Why should the replacement be wet after the hit? Certainly not – I would not allow it to be made wet.

6

THE BAT

I. WIDTH AND LENGTH

The bat overall shall be not more than 38 in./96.5 cm in length; the blade of the bat shall be made of wood and shall not exceed 4¼ in./10.8 cm at its widest part.

NOTE

The blade of the bat may be covered with material for protection, strengthening or repair. Such material shall not exceed ¹⁄₁₆ in./1.56 mm in thickness.

T he bat, to me, always has been and always will be the eternal symbol of the game of cricket.

Law 6, along with Law 17 (as will be seen later, under that Law), has had one addition made to it which, to my mind, is one of the most sensible ever made. The change to Law 6 was made in September 1771, and the one to Law 17 came as a result of an incident at Edgbaston in 1967 but both, in my view, have been equally valuable and sensible.

We will deal with Law 17 in context. For the moment, let's go back 222 years to when the width of a wicket was 6 in. A player named White took out on to the ground at Hambledon a bat of the same width. It took the officers of the club only a matter of days to call a meeting and stipulate that, henceforth, a bat should measure no more than 4¼ in. at its widest part, and that has remained in force until the present day. The measurement of the wicket, of course, has been increased by 50 per cent, to 9 in. The overall length of the bat – 38 in. – was laid down in May 1835, so here is another measurement which has stood the test of time. Even though the bat may be long- or short-handled, the overall length must not exceed 38 in.

Apart from the first bats, which had a curved blade, the shape has remained basically the same, though with many different designs. There has been the bat with the scooped out back and the one with the "shoulders" cut away. And there was one which I am glad to say I spotted, around 1978, which was, fortunately, very quickly declared illegal. It was being used in a match at Cleethorpes by a Minor Counties cricketer (a very good one) and had a number of holes bored through the blade, about pencil-thickness. And it was soon obvious that every time the bat made contact with the ball it ripped away the cover as if someone had used sandpaper on it. When the TCCB were contacted they informed the manufacturer that the bat was illegal and I like to think my report saved him a lot of money. I believe only two of these bats were made.

Then came the double-sided bat, which had a certain vogue around the end of the eighties; but it was not new. About ten years earlier I had seen Ray East, of Essex, use one, with the philosophy that "he never knew which side he played with anyway, so he might as well have a two-sided one". Ray was, of course, one of the great jesters of the game – Essex had more than their share at the time – and certainly Ray got a lot of good runs for his county.

To provide extra protection against hand injuries, a prototype was produced which had an extension of the blade, about half an inch thick, running in front of the handle and for the full length of the handle. Although it did not transgress the Laws regarding length or width, it was outlawed by the MCC on the grounds that "it significantly changed the recognised structure of the bat". Next came a bat with extremely rounded edges – reminiscent of a baseball bat, in fact – which died a quick death after several batsmen using it in trials received nasty blows in the most delicate part of the anatomy. In the very process of writing these notes I have held in my hands a new idea from Australia – a bat with a large bend in the handle, the idea being to bring the bottom hand behind the blade. Ah well! We shall see.

It was in Australia, of course, that we saw the aluminium bat wielded by Dennis Lillee (I have also had that in my hands), which was not held to be illegal because of shape or dimensions but simply because of the damage it could do to a ball. One would have thought that Lillee, of all people, would have been very much against it. But at least he caused a change to the working of the Laws with the addition of "the blade of the bat shall be made of wood".

I am not a believer that willow is replaceable by any other material. The sound of good willow meeting the leather of a cricket ball is so much part of the English summer, a lovely sound. My very good friend John Cook, who farms in Hampshire, has had the foresight to plant a number of willows over a period of several years. I hope I am still around when the first of those trees is made into cricket bats. John is a great lover of the game and it is a pleasure to be associated with someone who sustains the symbol of the game.

In recent years I have seen a number of bats being used which have led to damage to the ball. In the main it was one certain make, but not exclusively so. The bats were made with a sheathlike cover, the top of which came away from the bat just below the splice. When the batsman played forward, and low, the ball could be deeply sliced by the (loose) top of the cover. It was like a bacon-slicer shaving a piece from the surface of the ball – a piece which was often to be found between the blades of the bat and the loose bit of sheath. I took to looking closely at these coverings and also to carrying in my pocket a reel of bat-tape. If the sheath broke loose I would tape it. I was told, though I cannot vouch for the story, that the sheath was made from the covering used on helicopter blades. The problems were brought to the attention of bat manufacturers and they quickly took steps to deal with it.

Batsmen were fond of using "Elastoplast" for covering a bat-blade at one time and this was frowned upon, especially by bowlers who felt it took the shine off the ball. In fact it was quite possible to see why they complained when the red dye from the ball was quite clearly imprinted in the rougher surface of the "Elastoplast". Umpires were quickly told not to allow its use.

There have been instances of a bat exceeding the permitted width of 4¼ in.; but I believe these have occurred because a bat, after a lot of use, has "spread". For an umpire to spot this he must be pretty lucky or rather officious and I have personally never tried to measure a bat-blade. As for the thickness of material used to protect the blade of the bat – ¹⁄₁₆ in. each side – how are umpires supposed to check that, and how often? My view is that umpires should have to concern themselves with whether a bat is damaging the ball and all other considerations should be the province of the manufacturers.

We have all seen bats split and even break with splinters flying into different parts of the field. On one occasion a splinter hit the stumps but failed to remove a bail. If it had done so the square-leg umpire would have had to sustain an appeal for "hit wicket" (Law 35). But all in all, Law 6 seems to me to be one of the great Laws which have served the game well.

There has never been any mention of the length of the blade of the bat in Law 6 but MCC have now instructed John Jameson, the Assistant Secretary (Cricket), to look into this and submit a report. The thinking at the time this instruction was given was, I believe, that the blade of the bat would not be allowed to exceed 24 in. (I am reliably informed that the blade-length of most bats used is 22 in.) It will be interesting to see the outcome of this.

There will also be a ruling on all types of hand-guards fitted to the handle of a bat. Most of them have not, or would not have been, allowed in the past as their construction would obviously cause damage to the ball.

LAW

7

THE PITCH

I. AREA OF PITCH

The pitch is the area between the bowling creases – see Law 9 (The Bowling, Popping and Return Creases). It shall measure 5 ft/1.52 m in width on either side of a line joining the centre of the middle stumps of the wickets – see Law 8 (The Wickets).

2. SELECTION AND PREPARATION

Before the toss for innings, the executive of the ground shall be responsible for the selection and preparation of the pitch; thereafter the umpires shall control its use and maintenance.

3. CHANGING PITCH

The pitch shall not be changed during a match unless it becomes unfit for play, and then only with the consent of both captains.

4. NON-TURF PITCHES

In the event of a non-turf pitch being used, the following shall apply:

(a) *Length*: That of the playing surface to a minimum 58 ft/17.68 m.
(b) *Width*: That of the playing surface to a minimum of 6 ft/1.83 m.

See Law 10 (Rolling, Sweeping, Mowing, Watering the Pitch and Re-Marking of Creases), Note (a).

A part from the land upon which village, town and city war memorials stand, there is probably no more respected and loved piece of ground in any community than the cricket field. Law 7 describes it as "an area" but what other area of ground is mown at least twice a week for nearly six months a year, scarified, seeded and top-dressed in autumn and fertilised continuously throughout the year, not to mention frequent rolling? Where the pitch has the edge on the war memorials is that it was in place rather earlier than the memorials erected to our heroes.

The dimensions of the pitch – at least, its length of 22 yards, or one chain – is the one Law which has never changed. It is found in the 1755 Code of

Laws. But the width, 10 ft, appears for the first time, so far as I am aware, in the 1947 Code. Whilst the length of the bowling crease became greater over the years, I would suggest that the pitch width was always looked upon as having corresponding measurements.

Before 1823 there is a mention in Law of the bowling crease being 6 ft 7 in., and after 1825 it was increased to 6 ft 8 in. in length. In the 1902 Code it became 8 ft 8 in., the width it is today but as we have seen, the width of the *pitch* is now 10 ft.

In my time as a first-class umpire I have been a member of the MCC Pitches Committee under the chairmanship of Freddie Brown, a man dedicated to cricket – not just as a player and an England captain, but as an administrator as well. It was Mr Brown's idea, along with one or two others on the Committee, to hold a seminar for groundsmen each spring at Edgbaston. I personally learned much by going along to these seminars, in particular how to fill in bowlers' foot-holds. This came in useful when, in 1982, I had to undertake the filling in of the foot-holds on the second and third mornings of a match between Yorkshire and Gloucestershire at Bradford. It was the year before the ground lost its first-class status. Things were not going well at Park Avenue and suddenly the club found itself without a groundsman, which is why I pitched in.

None of this would have been possible without the expert guidance I had received from Trevor, assistant to Bernard Flack, that guru of the turf at Edgbaston. Apart from watching Trevor at the seminars, I had been allowed to observe, and even to help, while umpiring at the ground. The material of his foot-holds never came out and I am pleased to say that neither did mine at Bradford. And as we have mentioned Bernard Flack, I am reminded of arriving on the day before the Edgbaston Test between England and Australia in 1981 in what became known as "Botham's summer" (he took five wickets for one run at Edgbaston). Just about everybody went out to look at the pitch before it was covered for the night – players, Press, TV, and my colleague "Dickie" Bird and myself – and there was general agreement that it looked in the finest condition possible. Yet in the Test which followed, 40 wickets fell and no batsman managed to score 50 – the first time this had happened in 668 Tests since 1935, and that was on a rain-affected pitch in Barbados. At Edgbaston the pitch was certainly not badly affected by rain; it produced one of the most exciting matches ever, which England won by 29 runs, after Australia had needed only 142 with nine wickets in hand.

This prompts the thought that top groundsmen, I believe, are good enough to prepare whatever type of pitch they like. Yes, they are that good. Unfortunately, some are required by certain factions within their clubs to provide pitches which they (the groundsmen) would otherwise be reluctant to prepare. A case, I suppose, of "He who pays the piper calls the tune."

Rain-affected pitches are the umpire's nightmare. You can bet that one side will want to play and the other won't. And, of course, the one that wants to play will be the one that feels the conditions will give it an advantage. In deciding whether or not to play, the umpires will usually upset one side or the other. It's a no-win situation.

A pitch has to be cut and it can be rolled (Law 10). The Laws require it *all* to be rolled but it rarely is; they require *all* the pitch to be cut but it rarely is. The roller is only used between the two batting creases for reasons which are fairly obvious: if it passed over the white-painted creases it would then deposit white paint at intervals down the pitch. And it is not really necessary to roll between the batting and bowling creases; the ball is not usually going to land in that area.

One sees and hears many odd things during the rolling of the pitch. At Worcester one day, "Little Cyril" (who unfortunately is no longer at the ground in person but will always be there in spirit) was in charge of the rolling when the starting handle fell, unobserved, and was inadvertently rolled into the pitch. Fortunately, it was not in the middle and Worcestershire managed to get away with it. It is said that on the same ground a boy on the roller was not concentrating fully and rolled a set of stumps into the ground, but I can vouch for an incident at Portsmouth in 1979 when I was personally involved.

In those days I used to run round cricket grounds every morning, and on the second day of the match I had just finished this exercise, had a shower and was getting into my umpiring gear when the door burst open and one of the players breathlessly asked if I could come out to the pitch. His manner was so urgent that I thought something catastrophic had occurred but I could see nothing amiss as we walked out to the middle. There were, however, one or two people gazing earnestly at an area of the pitch. Closer inspection revealed that there had indeed been a catastrophe and those who know the Portsmouth roller – a monster of gigantic proportions and weight – will understand why. A ball had been hit by one of the players practising on the outfield and it just happened to coincide with the roller as it went along the pitch! It was now completely embedded, to a depth of some 3 inches in the ground. And there was about a quarter-of-an-hour to go before play was due to start. Very carefully, the ball was removed and I asked the groundsman to bring out some of the soil he used to repair bowlers' foot-holds. Then I scoured the bottom of the hole, rammed the soil down tight and added a sprinkling of grass cuttings to complete the camouflage. The match started on time.

As far as the cutting of the pitch is concerned, a groundsman, I feel, has got to be very careful. If the grass between bowling and batting creases is not cut it can cause the bowler to slip on the slightly longer blades. It is a fallacy that longer grass provides better protection of this area. I have been asked by a number of captains who are going to be in the field to ask the groundsman to cut the area. I can do this, of course, but only *after* the toss; before it, the selection and preparation are in the hands of the ground authorities. I must say it is lovely to walk out and see a pitch that has been cut to the exact width of 10 ft; but in local and club cricket umpires are not usually fortunate enough to have the pitch presented to them in this ideal state. This makes judgments under Law 41 (The Fieldsman) more difficult and we then have to rely on our eyesight to compensate for what we see as shortcomings under Law 10.

A pitch can be changed after the match has started but only if it becomes clearly unfit and then only with the consent of *both* captains. It is a very rare occurrence and I have seen it (almost) happen only once. I say "almost" because the captains did not agree and the match was abandoned.

LAW
8

THE WICKETS

1. WIDTH AND PITCHING
Two sets of wickets, each 9 in./22.86 cm wide, and consisting of three wooden stumps with two wooden bails on top, shall be pitched opposite and parallel to each other at a distance of 22 yards/20.12 m between the centre of the two middle stumps.

2. SIZE OF STUMPS
The stumps shall be of equal and sufficient size to prevent the ball from passing between them. Their tops shall be 28 in./71.1 cm above the ground and shall be dome-shaped except for the bail-grooves.

3. SIZE OF BAILS
The bails shall be each 4⅜ in./11.1 cm in length and when in position on the top of stumps shall not project more than ½ in./1.3 cm above them.

NOTES
(a) Dispensing with Bails
In a high wind the umpires may decide to dispense with the use of bails.
(b) Junior Cricket
For junior cricket, as defined by the local governing body, the following measurements for the wickets shall apply:
  Width – 8 in./20.32 cm
  Pitched – 21 yds./19.20 m
  Height – 27 in./68.58cm
  Bails – each 3⅞ in./9.84 cm in length and should not project more than
      ½ in./1.3 cm above the stumps.

A wicket is not only 9 in. in width but it also consists of three pieces of wood (the stumps) with two other pieces of wood (the bails) across the top. It is *not*, as some observers within the game would have us believe, an area of ground covered in grass and measuring 22 yds. by 10 ft. Just why the term "wicket" is used when people are talking about the pitch is beyond my comprehension, and I believe if the practice were discontinued it would not cause too much confusion amongst those who follow cricket via TV and

43

radio, even if the term "a sticky wicket" has become part of our language (outside cricket) as a figure of speech.

In early Law, the wicket started with a height of 22 inches with a width of 6 inches. In 1785 there is mention of a three-stump wicket, but this was possibly in use in parts of the country prior to this date. There is reference to bails in 1786, but it was not until 1803 that bails were mentioned in the official Laws. In 1798 the size of the wicket was increased to 24 inches in height, by 7 inches in width, and there is reference to one bail of 7 inches in length being used. 1821 saw the dimensions increased to 26 inches in height, still by 7 inches in width and in 1823 to 27 inches in height, by 8 inches in width. It was not until 1931 that a wicket could be of 28 inches in height, by 9 inches in width, but this was a maximum measurement. There was a minimum measurement, which could still be of 27 inches in height by 8 inches in width, but I do not think that the latter was really used. It was not until the 1947 Code of Laws was introduced that a specific stipulation was for a wicket of 28 inches in height, by 9 inches in width. In 1884 a thickness of bail was specified, so as no confusion of the maximum height of a wicket existed, and as we know, with bails in position, a wicket can measure under present Law 28½ inches high, as the bails can project above the stumps, to a maximum of half an inch. Each bail will be of 4⅜ inches in length.

It may surprise many – it certainly surprised me – to learn that it was not until 1931 that the width of the wicket was increased to 9 in.

In the 1947 Code it is stated that there should be a distance of 22 yards between each wicket; many followers of the game believe that is so but it is not, and never has been. It is the pitch (Law 10) which is 22 yards in length, whereas the distance between the wickets is 22 yards less the thickness of one stump. A fine point, perhaps, but Law 8.1 clearly establishes it.

Whilst the Law regarding the composition of the wicket and its measurements was different in the early days of the game, the term "wicket" has always been used. Today the height of a stump is 28 inches from ground level and the bails can add a maximum of an extra half-inch to make it 28½ inches high. The bails lie in grooves and the top of the stumps should be dome-shaped. However, I'm pretty sure most of us have seen stumps with very flat tops and almost no groove at all because of frequent hammering with the bat handle. I have also seen in some very hot countries (with very hard ground) in which it is still one of the duties of the umpire to site the wickets, a mallet provided to whack the stumps into the ground.

One story about bail-grooves. The only time I have officiated at Fartown, Huddersfield, was in May 1976 in the old John Player League (later the Refuge Assurance League), and when my colleague and I walked out to look at the pitch just before lunch, about 12.15 pm, everything seemed to be in order and at each end of the pitch lay three stumps. When we walked out at 1.55 pm to start the match, the stumps were now in position and as I checked them and placed the bails on top I found the bail-groove of the middle stump had been cut quite a way *down* the stump. The bails slipped down into this groove and jammed so tightly I don't think a hand grenade would have dislodged them. I had to rush to the pavilion, passing the incoming batsmen, to get another middle stump. As the set was brand-new, someone had slipped up somewhere in cutting the depth of the groove.

In the 1980 Code of Law it is now stipulated that both stumps and bails must be made of wood. I am sure this was instituted to dispense with the older type of stump which had a metal ferrule at the point. This could be dangerous on occasions. I have seen both Wayne Daniel and Alan Donald bowl balls which picked out stumps and sent them flying, head-high, in the direction of the wicket-keeper.

During the 1992 season, in a match at Headingley, Yorkshire v. Hampshire, 7-10 May, Malcolm Marshall bowled a ball which hit the striker's off stump and sent it cartwheeling a number of times before it embedded itself point-first into the ground a couple of yards in front of the wicket-keeper. It can now be seen why the metal ferrule on the point of the old stump was outlawed: if one of these had hit a wicket-keeper it could cause serious injury. It is on record that a wicket-keeper in India lost his life after being impaled by a stump in flight.

The Law does not stipulate how thick a stump may or may not be, nor does it specify a particular shape. One day we may see someone try out a set of square stumps. Law 8 does say that each stump must be of equal and sufficient size to prevent the ball from passing *between* them and so if someone wanted to be completely pedantic in his interpretation of this we might possibly see three stumps, each 3 inches wide, forming a wicket.

As early as 1786 there is a mention in the Laws of two bails being used for each wicket but, as we have seen, it was not until 1931 that the width of the wicket was increased to 9 inches and not until 1947 is there any reference to bails of 4⅜ inches being used.

I have twice seen a stump being snapped in two by the ball. Bails are constantly being broken and an umpire must ensure he has a replacement in his pocket. If I may offer a tip – never take out an odd bail; take a pair. And if one of those in use is broken, replace both bails with the spare set. There is nothing worse, in my view, than having two bails of different design, and possibly different colours, for the umpire to look at for half the day. It offends one's sense of what is right and proper.

Another tip is to ask the groundsman to pour water into the stump-holes during an interval. This ensures that not only will the stumps "sit" nicely in the ground but the bails do not keep falling off because of fractional movement of the stumps – other than when the ball hits the wicket, of course. But watch out for one point which I picked up from H. D. ("Dickie") Bird. As we arrived at our respective ends after an interval, Dickie pressed down hard on top of his set of stumps. Water spurted upwards, covering Dickie's face, coat and trousers with a dirty, muddy deposit! It was something I have been very careful about, ever since.

9

THE BOWLING, POPPING AND RETURN CREASES

1. THE BOWLING CREASE
The bowling crease shall be marked in line with the stumps at each end and shall be 8 ft 8 in./2.64 m in length, with the stumps in the centre.

2. THE POPPING CREASE
The popping crease, which is the back edge of the crease marking, shall be in front of and parallel with the bowling crease. It shall have the back edge of the crease marking 4 ft/1.22 m from the centre of the stumps and shall extend to a minimum of 6 ft/1.83 m on either side of the line of the wicket. The popping crease shall be considered to be unlimited in length.

3. THE RETURN CREASE
The return crease marking, of which the inside edge is the crease, shall be at each end of the bowling crease and at right angles to it. The return crease shall be marked to a minimum of 4 ft/1.22 m behind the wicket and shall be considered to be unlimited in length. A forward extension shall be marked to the popping crease.

F or the purposes of commenting on this Law (as others) I shall not use the term "popping crease" because today, in all grades of cricket, it is better known as the *batting* crease and referred to in that way.

In the early Code of Laws (1744) no limit to the length of the bowling crease is stipulated and the distance between the bowling and batting creases was 3 feet 10 inches, not, as it is now, 4 feet. By 1744 the Laws decreed that the bowling crease would extend for 3 feet in length on either side of the wicket; but remember that the wicket itself at that time was only 6 inches wide, not 9 inches as it is now. It seems that since those early days all the creases, and the wicket itself, have increased in dimensions.

As we have seen, there was a reference in 1744 to the length of the bowling crease having no limit; but by 1774 it had to be 3 feet in length on either side of the wicket, so it was 6 feet 6 inches in overall length, the extra 6 inches being to accommodate the wicket. In 1823 the length of this crease was increased to 6 feet 7 inches to accommodate the wider wicket, and in 1825 it was again increased, by 1 inch to 6 feet 8 inches, again because of a wider wicket introduced two years earlier. In 1902, we saw a substantial increase in the length of the bowling crease to 8 feet 8 inches. Again, eight inches were to accommodate the wicket but the crease now measured 4 feet each side of the wicket.

This distance was of considerable use to the bowler and by now a return crease had been added – marked at each end of the bowling crease and at right angles to it. The measurement of 8 feet 8 inches for the length of the bowling crease is still in operation, even though the wicket is now *nine* inches in width. It might be thought that if the law-makers had been consistent its length would have been increased to 8 feet 9 inches. All in all, I believe this steady increase in sizes and measurements points to the fact that cricket is now played by individuals who are fitter, quicker and of better physique than those of earlier days.

The Laws of the 1980 Code are, in the main, clear and specific as far as these markings are concerned but I do feel there is ambiguity in Law 9.1 regarding the positioning of the stumps. We see white line-markings at each end of the pitch and they may vary from as thick as two inches to as thin as half an inch. Now, if you take the last six words of Law 9.1 – "with the stumps in the centre" – you find the cause of the ambiguity, as a result of which the stumps are sometimes slightly forward of where they should be. "Centre" means the centre of the *length* of the bowling crease (all 8 feet 8 inches of it) but some groundsmen also take it as meaning the centre of thickness of the line-marking itself. If the white paint-mark is a mere half-inch, there is not much difference, but if it has been painted with a 2-inch width the difference is proportionately greater. In both batting and bowling creases it is the *back* of the white line which defines the crease – where the white paint meets the green grass. A glance at the wording of Law 9.2 shows us that the point of the stumps should be placed at the back edge of the white line marking the bowling crease. But in the main, at all levels of cricket, the pitch and the various markings are presented by the groundsman in a splendid manner, with white lines one inch in width, stumps correctly positioned and, with very rare exceptions, correct dimensions. In the very early days of the game, the creases were not marked by painting a white line upon the grass: they were cut into the turf to a depth of about one inch.

The length of the return crease, backwards from its junction with the bowling crease, is deemed to be unlimited in length; but it must be *marked* for a minimum of 4 ft, and it is this aspect of the Law which I have often found, especially when umpiring overseas, has not been followed. Quite frequently it has been marked for no more than 15-18 inches in length. It is the *inside* edge, the one nearer to the stumps, which marks the actual return crease.

The batting crease must have a minimum marking of 12 feet – 6 feet either side of an imaginary line drawn down the centre of the pitch. It is also deemed to be unlimited in length, and some groundsmen continue marking with a white dot (at intervals of about four feet) for as much as 12 yards further than the distance required by Law. This is a great help to an umpire in his judgment of a run-out decision.

On the evening before a big match I love to walk out on to a ground and look around. Just to gaze at the results of the hard work of preparation put in by groundstaff gives me enormous pleasure.

10

ROLLING, SWEEPING, MOWING, WATERING THE PITCH AND RE-MARKING OF CREASES

1. ROLLING

During the match the pitch may be rolled at the request of the captain of the batting side for a period of not more than 7 minutes before the start of each innings, other than the first innings of the match, and before the start of each day's play. In addition, if, after the toss and before the first innings of the match, the start is delayed, the captain of the batting side shall have the right to have the pitch rolled for not more than 7 minutes. However, if in the opinion of the umpires, the delay has had no significant effect upon the state of the pitch, they shall refuse any request for the rolling of the pitch.

The pitch shall not otherwise be rolled during the match.

The 7-minute rolling permitted before the start of a day's play shall take place not earlier than half an hour before the start of play, and the captain of the batting side may delay such rolling until 10 minutes before the start of play should he so desire.

If a captain declares an innings closed less than 15 minutes before the resumption of play, and the other captain is thereby prevented from exercising his option of 7 minutes' rolling, or if he is so prevented for any other reason, the time for rolling shall be taken out of the normal playing-time.

2. SWEEPING

Such sweeping of the pitch as is necessary during the match shall be done so that the 7-minutes allowed for rolling the pitch, provided for in (1) above, is not affected.

3. MOWING

(a) Responsibilities of Ground Authority and of Umpires
All mowings which are carried out before the toss for innings shall be the responsibility of the ground authority; thereafter they shall be carried out under the supervision of the umpires. See Law 7.2 (Selection and Preparation).

(b) Initial Mowing
The pitch shall be mown before play begins on the day the match is scheduled to start, or in the case of a delayed start on the day the match is expected to start. See 3(a) above (Responsibilities of Ground Authority and of Umpires).

c Subsequent Mowings in a Match of Two or More Days' Duration
In a match of two or more days' duration the pitch shall be mown daily before play begins. Should this mowing not take place because of weather conditions, rest days or other reasons, the pitch shall be mown on the first day on which the match is resumed.

d Mowing of the Outfield in a Match of Two or More Days' Duration
In order to ensure that conditions are as similar as possible for both sides, the outfield shall normally be mown before the commencement of play on each day of the match if ground and weather conditions allow. See Note (b) to this Law.

4. WATERING
The pitch shall not be watered during a match.

5 RE-MARKING CREASES
Whenever possible the creases shall be re-marked.

6. MAINTENANCE OF FOOT-HOLES
In wet weather the umpires shall ensure that holes made by the bowlers and batsmen are cleaned out and dried whenever necessary to facilitate play. In matches of two or more days' duration the umpires shall allow, if necessary, the returfing of foot-holes made by the bowler in his delivery-stride, or the use of quick-setting fillings for the same purpose, before the start of each day's play.

7. SECURING OF FOOT-HOLDS AND MAINTENANCE OF PITCH
During play, the umpires shall allow either batsman to beat the pitch with his bat and players to secure their foot-holds by the use of sawdust, providing that no damage to the pitch is so caused and Law 42 (Unfair Play) is not contravened.

NOTES
(a) Non-turf Pitches
The above Law 10 applies to turf pitches. The game is played on non-turf pitches in various countries at various levels. Whilst the conduct of the game on these surfaces should always be in accordance with the Laws of Cricket, it is recognised that it may sometimes be necessary for governing bodies to lay

down special playing conditions to suit the type of non-turf pitch used in their country.

In matches played against touring teams, any special playing conditions shall be agreed in advance by both parties.

(b) Mowing of the Outfield in a Match of Two or More Days' Duration

If, for reasons other than ground or weather conditions, daily and complete mowing is not possible, the ground authority shall notify the captains and umpires, before the toss for innings, of the procedure to be adopted for such mowing during the course of the match.

(c) Choice of Roller

If there is more than one roller available, the captain of the batting side shall have a choice.

I n the earliest Codes of Law, little attention is given to the matters dealt with in Law 10 until the 1809 and 1820 Codes. Pitches could be given no attention at all, except by mutual consent. We can deal with two parts of this Law in just a few words.

Watering is not carried out during a match, but in the early Codes there was a provision for watering, with the consent of the opposing captain. *Re-marking of creases* should be carried out by ground staff at each interval of play and it is a considerable help to umpires. I have seen this work carried out very expeditiously. After all, an interval of 10 minutes between innings is not a long time but the re-marking gets done and as we walk out to resume the match, everything is in order. There is more discussion of this point under Law 9.

Mowing is mandatory before play begins on each day of a match, the only exceptions being if there is no play because of the weather or if a rest day (as in Tests) should intervene. I have had a captain ask if we could start a day's play without the pitch being cut. I had to decline this request and refer him to Law 10. Mowing is then carried out before start of play on the day the match resumes. Pitch preparation is in the hands of the ground authority, and this includes mowing before the pitch is "presented" to the captains before the toss. After the first mowing, it is desirable that the mower-blades should remain at the same level for subsequent days of the match. Umpires must try to ensure that this is done but I have to confess that I am not into measuring the length of blades of grass from one day to the next!

One of the duties of umpires is to make sure that a pitch is mown before play starts on each day of a match. That is one reason why we are required to report to the ground at 9 am, two hours before play begins, or resumes. I have always thought this was a bit of an imposition on the head groundsman. I can't cut my own lawn properly, so there is no way I can tell him how to do his job, any more than I would expect him to tell me how to umpire. But the

Laws require me to be there at 9 am and there is no doubt justification for this.

I have had requests for a pitch *not* to be cut and, indeed, "if it would be all right for only one end to be cut". These requests didn't come from head groundsmen and, needless to say, I refused both of them. *All* the pitch has to be cut.

When pitches were not fully covered and left open to the elements there was often a delayed start and umpires had to be very careful about when they instructed ground staff to start cutting the grass on the pitch because if operations started too early, small pieces could be chipped off the surface. This was the time when we needed the expert advice of the head groundsman.

Discussing Law 7, I have mentioned the area between the batting and bowling creases which we often find has not been cut. If we receive a request before start of play for it to be mown we are entitled to instruct the groundsman to undertake it and comply with Law 10. Also, if we arrive at a ground for a first-class match and consider an undue amount of grass has been left on the pitch to be used for the match we are empowered to instruct the groundsman to shave off more grass than he has done, even though selection and preparation of a pitch (before the toss) is the responsibility of the ground authority.

In a match of two or more days the outfield, if possible, should be mown on each morning before play starts. If weather prevents this we have to try to ensure that such cutting as can take place favours each team equally.

One point which is *not* adhered to is that "any renovation by re-turfing must be confined to the foot-hold of the bowler in his delivery-stride". For one thing, turf is an unsuitable filling for a foot-hold; it will move about when a bowler's foot descends on it and it will wear quickly because it is soft. Experienced groundsmen now use a very strong loam which hardens quickly and will remain hard.

Furthermore, I have allowed bowlers' footmarks to be repaired *behind* the bowling crease and also up to a distance of 4 ft in front of the batting crease (i.e. not merely in the bowling-stride). Also, I have allowed sawdust to be used by bowlers in their foot-holds as they approach the wicket to deliver the ball and I allow any player, on either side, to secure foot-holds as long as it is not on the pitch more than 4 ft in front of the batting crease, and batsmen are allowed to replace divots and beat the pitch with their bat. As long as there is no unnecessary time-wasting, all these actions are allowed in full but it is interesting to note that when a declaration stage of an innings is being reached, the replacing of divots by the batsmen suddenly ceases.

The main thrust of Law 10 concerns the rolling of the pitch, which may take place at the request of the batting side in two instances. Firstly, before the start of each day's play *except the first day of the match*. The last seven words have been added to Law 10 as set out in the 1947 Code of Law. Before

1980, the captain of the side which, after the toss, was to bat first could, if he wished, have the pitch rolled, This, of course, would be in addition to all the preparation and rolling which had already taken place.

Secondly, the pitch can be rolled between innings at the request of the captain of the side to bat next. It should not be forgotten that this interval is only of 10 minutes' duration, which is why you will probably see a member of the groundstaff approach the fielding side (usually the captain though not necessarily – he may have passed on instructions as a matter of geographical convenience) to ask if he requires the pitch to be rolled and, if so, which weight of roller is to be used. Sometimes a captain, for tactical reasons, declines to have the pitch rolled.

While the maximum time of 7 minutes' rolling is normally applied, a captain might conceivably ask for just a couple of minutes to iron out slight blemishes to the pitch. So it is occasionally advisable for the groundsman, in addition to asking if rolling is required and what weight of roller, to add a supplementary question: "For the full 7 minutes?" Groundstaff are rarely taken by surprise. If it does happen, it is usually in the case of a sudden declaration of an innings or a side being unexpectedly asked to follow on. When 7 minutes out of an interval of 10 have to be earmarked for rolling, staff obviously do not want to be taken by surprise. They have to be ready to work as a team: one to roll, one to sweep, one with the marking frame and one with the water-bottle (for the stump-holes). When they emerge as the rest of us are leaving the field at the end of an innings they remind me of a sheriff's posse riding out of town.

Any rolling of the pitch before start of play on the second or any subsequent day must not start more than 30 minutes before the scheduled commencement of play. If it then rains before play actually begins but after the rolling has taken place, then no further rolling is allowed. The batting captain can elect to delay the rolling until 10 minutes before play starts. Ergo: on second and subsequent days' play, rolling can be requested by the batting captain to start any time between 30 and 10 minutes before play.

The last sentence of Law 10.1 is worded in a way which has always puzzled me. It is, as we have said, only a 10-minute interval between innings, and the pitch is rolled (if the captain wishes) to comply with this Law. As long as there is time for the rolling to be carried out, then I ignore the reference to "15 minutes before the resumption of play". Of course, if the rolling cannot be carried out, then any time which is longer than the interval will be taken out of playing time in the match.

Another fault in the wording, in my view, occurs in the second sentence of Law 10.1. I ask you, for a moment, to look back at Law 8 – in discussing it I refer to the unusual depth of a bail-groove. In that instance the batting captain would have been able, by right, to ask for the pitch to be rolled. The start of the innings, after the toss, has been delayed. Many times, as we have been about to get a game under way, there has been a delay because a batsman has wanted some spectators moving from near the sightscreen or behind the bowler's arm. Would we then have to agree to the batting captain's request for another 7 minutes' rolling of the pitch? There has been most certainly a delay, but the Law makes no mention of the length of a delay. It may not happen very often but, as I see it, the way is open for an extra rolling of 7 minutes if a captain wanted to insist on the strict letter of this Law being observed – and it would be absurd.

When I arrived in New Zealand in October, 1980, and read through their Regulations I saw an item which delighted me. It was an extension of Law 10.1, and I have at last succeeded in having it incorporated in the Laws of Cricket. It reads:

> "In the first paragraph, penultimate line, delete 'shall have the right' and insert 'may request'. Then add the following: 'However, if in the opinion of the umpires the delay has had no significant effect upon the state of the pitch, they shall refuse any request for the rolling of the pitch.'"

If a club happens to have several rollers of differing weights the batting captain can select which one he wants. In 1991, while umpiring in Sri Lanka, there were two words in the language that I thought I should learn: "Poddi" and "Locco". I'm not entirely sure the spelling is right but there is no difficulty about the pronunciation. They mean "small" and "large" in terms of the rollers.

I have had groundsmen ask if it is in order for them to roll only one end of the pitch, as requested by the batting captain. I informed them that it was not and referred them to the wording of the Law, which states, "that the *pitch* may be rolled", 22 yards in length by 10 feet in width. Again I have been asked if one end could be rolled with the heavy roller and the other end with the light roller. I again drew the attention to the wording of the Law, "that the captain of the batting side has a choice of roller", not the plural, "rollers" in Law 10. Any such rolling of the *pitch* is optional and the batting captain can decline to have it rolled.

In the 1980 season when rolling was not allowed after the toss, I was umpiring Yorkshire v. Glamorgan at Bradford. Sitting in front of the pavilion on the first morning talking to some friends – yes, umpires do have them! – I noticed the large roller was being trundled out on to the square. It was after 10.30 am and I thought, "This is a bit late to be rolling any other pitches which might be under preparation." But when the roller moved into position on the pitch to be used in the match which was shortly to begin I vaulted over the wall and ran out on to the square, boot-laces (which I had been in the process of tying) flapping around my ankles. I asked the groundsman what he was intending to do. He said that Geoff Boycott had told him to use the heavy roller because Yorkshire had won the toss and were going to bat. I told him, amongst other things, that this was not allowed and to remove the roller immediately. And I waited, at the end of the day's play, for some reaction.

When it came, Geoff said that when he had captained the side in the previous season he had always had the pitch rolled after the toss if he was batting. My reply was that while that was in order last season, it was no longer applicable in 1980. "Anyway," I added, "you are not captain now so I suggest you ask John Hampshire if there is anything else you want to know."

I don't suppose that went down too well. But I hate to think what might have happened if I hadn't spotted that the heavy roller was about to be used on the pitch for that match!

There is a time during a match when the choice of roller lies entirely in the hands of the umpires – if a pitch is to be artificially dried. Umpires are often reluctant to exercise this decision as they are usurping the right which usually lies with the batting captain. It is something which is very rare since 1981 with the full covering of wickets. When water has seeped on to the pitch, perhaps overnight, and blankets or an absorbent sponge are used in conjunction with a light roller to mop up, we might ask for a sponge-roller to be used, but it would depend on the volume of water to be moved. But the right does lie with us to give whatever instructions are necessary to the groundsman to facilitate the quickest possible start, or resumption, of play. After any such drying procedure, any rolling which the umpires feel shall take place lies entirely in their hands.

I remember that my colleague and I had to take such action on the morning of the last day of play at Cardiff. Now I was never fortunate enough to see Wilf Wooller play for Glamorgan but I was very well aware that he was something of a legend; that stories about him were, and still are, told whenever former cricketers gather together. Nor had I ever known him except in terms of passing the time of day. Nevertheless, he endeared himself to me on this occasion. Before play began, blankets had been used to soak up excessive moisture from the pitch. We had asked the groundsman to use a light roller to "tidy up" the surface of the pitch – we wanted to avoid bringing up any more moisture – and we had asked him to use the light roller for that reason, starting 15 minutes before play. Coincidentally, Mr Wooller had come to the umpires' room to ask for information for a newspaper article he was writing and he was sitting in a corner of the room, almost behind the door when it opened.

Enter Alan Jones, the Glamorgan captain, who did not notice Mr Wooller. Not unpleasantly, but certainly questioning our instructions to the groundsmen, he said, "I wanted the heavy roller. Why have you ordered the light one?" Before I had a chance to explain things WW intervened, firmly: "Go away, Alan," he said. "The umpires are quite correct in their instructions and you are not to question them."

The captain departed without a word. It was as if God had spoken. And He knew His cricket Law.

In 1972 at Newark in a Notts v. Glamorgan Second XI match, the pitch had been rolled between the innings of the last afternoon of the match, and as the roller was moved off the pitch it gave a splutter and stopped. It took fully another 10 minutes to tow it away and we felt it fair to add on 10 minutes after the close of playing time, simply because the time had not been a delay in rolling but after the rolling had taken place. In the report I acquainted the TCCB with what we had done, but they were not in agreement with our action, and I am not sure why. Their reason was that the rolling time should come out of playing time. I do not agree: the delay was after the pitch had been rolled.

LAW

11

COVERING THE PITCH

1. BEFORE THE START OF A MATCH

Before the start of a match complete covering of the pitch shall be allowed.

2. DURING A MATCH

The pitch shall not be completely covered during a match unless prior arrangements or regulations so provide.

3. COVERING BOWLERS' RUN-UP

Whenever possible, the bowlers' run-up shall be covered, but the covers so used shall not extend further than 4 ft/1.22 m in front of the popping crease.

NOTE

(a) Removal of Covers

The covers shall be removed as promptly as possible whenever the weather permits.

T his Law is almost extinct, for as far as I am aware full covering of pitches has been allowed in every league and every competition in which I have played or umpired. Most cricket clubs of any standing now have excellent standards of covering so that the pitch on which they are playing, at the very least, can be protected from the weather.

Under the 1947 Code of Law covers were allowed to be used at each end of the pitch but they could only extend for a distance of 3 feet 6 inches in front of the batting crease. This distance was increased by 6 inches (i.e. to 4 feet) under the 1980 Code. This distance could extend as far as necessary *to the rear* so that the bowler could always have dry and firm ground for his run-up. Some administrators feel this is not fair as it allows a fast bowler to operate off his full run and deliver the ball at maximum pace on to the rain-affected part of the pitch, therefore giving the fielding side a double advantage. In some quarters the view has been put forward that if pitches on which first-class matches are played are to be left open to the elements at all, then no covers whatsoever should be allowed. I feel this school of thought may have a point but it does create dangers for both bowlers and batsmen.

I started my professional umpiring career when the pitch could not be fully covered and my memory played a few tricks. It seemed that I umpired for only three years (1975-77) under the old regulations – until I looked back through my diaries and realised it was not until 1981 that pitches were fully covered in the event of rain. And the diaries showed that in those six years, before the introduction of full covering, I had only four one-day matches and four championship games in which no play at all took place because of rain. None of these was in 1975 or 1976, which were two hot and settled summers – not good for England, incidentally, since they led to home defeats by Australia and West Indies. In 1979 it was a different story when a county championship match in which I was appointed to "stand" at Lord's on 26-28 May was abandoned without a ball being bowled. Not only that – the following day at Sheffield my colleague and I called off any possibility of play at 11 am for the following day and we did this daily for the next three days. Six consecutive days without a ball bowled! It was that very wet spell which persuaded the TCCB to adopt full covering of the pitch in the event of rain and it duly came into operation in 1981. Covering for the wicket-ends, incidentally, was instigated as early as 1913.

In the early years of my first-class career I thus saw some of the great spin bowlers operating (at close quarters) in conditions which suited them – Ray Illingworth, Derek Underwood, Norman Gifford and Bishen Bedi, to name but four. I remember in particular a 1975 game at Northampton where Kent were bowling on a drying pitch on the morning of the last day. Derek Underwood was not having a great deal of success but at the lunch interval I saw the Kent scorer, Claude Lewis (no mean slow left-armer himself and a man who spent well over 50 years with Kent as player, coach and scorer), take him on one side and advise Derek to slow down his delivery a little and give the ball more air. After the break Underwood took five wickets for no run and from 136 for five Northants were 138 all out!

One other thing I believe rain-affected pitches reveal is not only the better bowlers and batsmen but the very best umpires. With the ball turning across the face of the bat and rearing off a full length, taking bits out of the top of the pitch, concentration has to be absolute and nerve unflinching in the face of constant and concerted appeals. Close fieldsmen are there in profusion in such conditions and appeals follow every sound of contact between two objects. More often than not the sound is not of contact between bat and ball.

To my mind, there were two reasons for incorporating full covering of the pitch in the event of rain into the playing regulations. The first was that it was desirable that all cricket should be played under similar conditions, so general covering was agreed upon. I think this makes sense; also, trying to ensure the paying spectator was not deprived of one ball if it could be avoided made as much sense. I am not so sure with regard to the covering of large areas of the middle of the ground. This ensures that that territory remains, in the main, dry. But what happens to the large volume of water which falls on the covers? It has to go somewhere and this means it is usually deposited just off the edges of the large, flat tarpaulins. And these are the areas which, despite all the efforts of the groundstaff, cause most of the delays in resuming play.

I ask the question: If we allowed rain to fall evenly over all areas of the field, would they dry more, or less, quickly than a smaller area with a greater concentration of water on it? I do feel that the areas where a bowler delivers the ball and where the striker takes his stance should be protected – let's say five yards in length and five in width. To add a personal note to this, I may say I like to keep my own feet dry, too!

The whole question – to cover, or not to cover – is debatable and it is also debatable, to my mind, whether covering ensures appreciably more play. On the whole I support the present regulations if only to spare us the spectacle of an accomplished batsman struggling to save his county side on a rain-affected pitch on Tuesday afternoon, then going out to bat on a firm, dry pitch in a Test two days later.

Another cause of delay in resuming play is the worn pitch-ends, used in previous games, which have been repaired and re-seeded. It goes against the grain for me to have to instruct a groundsman, whose job is difficult enough at any time, to remove these areas – top soil and seed as well. And it is always frustrating for spectators to see large areas of the field apparently quite fit for play yet no play taking place for long periods.

Some grounds now have extensive covers – Edgbaston, for instance, where the "Brumbrella" rolls out as a huge sheet covering a large area of the ground, even though it is not as extensive as when it was first installed. Then, it covered most of the playing area and when it was rolled back and the canvas was taken up by the roller, a tidal wave of water was deposited near the boundary lines at the Raybank side of the ground, causing a few problems from time to time. At Worcester, Old Trafford, Cardiff and Canterbury they have the inflatable type of "umbrella" under which practice games can be staged, which is in itself useful. I am sure that all these venues have been able to stage matches which otherwise might have had to be called off and while a lot of water is deposited around the edges the effect of this has been countered by the laying of drains to take the water away.

An incident in 1988 with regard to the large inflatable cover at Old Trafford nearly caused the dismissal of Graeme Hick. It was not really the cover but the sections of board which were on top of the aperture into which the cover is lowered when not in use. All grounds which installed such covers had some teething problems, and on this day one of these boards was not flush with the ground: the edge nearest to the pitch upon which the game was being played projected about two inches above the surface. Graeme was batting, and from a distance of about 15 yards a very hard-cut short which he played down past gulley hit the ground and edge of the board and bounced back straight to third slip. Graeme had set off for a run without thinking as the shot sped away, and he must have been nearly halfway down the pitch when the slip fielder, himself taken by surprise by the ball flying back toward him, did not take it cleanly. If he had done so he could easily have effected a dismissal under Law 38 (Run Out).

At this point I feel it is time to pay tribute to the hardest-worked of all those who help stage the game of cricket – the head groundsman and his staff. There are many other aspects of groundsmanship but to deal with only their work in covering a ground: (1) I wonder if everyone realises how physically dangerous it can be? I have seen a member of groundstaff holding on to a wildly flapping, flat sheet which has whipped him off his feet, quite literally. (2) I have also seen the wheeled covers at Lord's blown by gale-like winds down towards the Nursery End. Personally, I love to get out and give a hand when the covers are being removed. For one thing, it is not easy pulling tarpaulins about when they have a large volume of water on them; for another, the umpire can see very quickly which areas are going to need extensive drying, and where applications of sawdust will be required. It is necessary, too, to take into consideration the groundsman's views on the timing of the next inspection. He knows his ground, and prevailing conditions, better than anyone.

All staffs do everything possible to protect the ground and to get it ready for further play, and there are two matches which I shall always remember when I think of the efforts made to bring one-day matches to a conclusion in spite of the most terrible conditions. The first of these was a Benson & Hedges quarter-final at Old Trafford on 1-3 June 1983.

Play started late after rain and with Lancashire 186 for two wickets a most tremendous storm hit the ground. From the relative comfort of the pavilion we watched as the ground was flooded to such an extent that for some time no grass at all was visible and beer cans and assorted rubbish floated about on the lake. No play was possible on the second day and it really did look as though the result was going to hinge on that unsatisfactory method – the toss of a coin. So I decided to go to the ground at 7 am on the third day to see if I could help get ground-drying operations started. As I walked up to the pavilion at 6.45 am I found I had been beaten to it by at least half-a-dozen others. Not only were the groundsman and his staff hard at work but three motormops were being driven to and fro by Jack Bond, at that time the Lancashire cricket manager (now one of my colleagues on the first-class panel of umpires), by Peter Lever, one of the coaches, and by Ken Shuttleworth. I am glad to say we were able to complete a game of limited-overs cricket in a proper manner.

The second of these memories involves a NatWest Trophy semi-final at New Road, Worcester, on 13-15 August 1986. Almost a week of rain before the match had given the head groundsman tremendous difficulties in preserving a dry, firm pitch and just as we were about to start more rain came. When it stopped we almost despaired of getting the ground fit for play, and when we had tried everything else a helicopter was summoned. While it hovered overhead, providing a strong downdraught, we used hot-air blowers directed into "tunnels" made from the boundary-boards. They were novel ideas but they give some idea of how much thought and effort are put into attempts to stage the game by the groundstaff and, if I may say so, by the umpires as well.

I have one particularly sad recollection of implementing this Law at Kwe Kwe, in Zimbabwe, in January, 1988. The previous year I had umpired much international cricket and some club games in that country without much interference by rain. But in 1988 I was "standing" in a two-day match between Midlands and Matabeleland with Clive Currin, who was a good umpire then and would have been better now. I am sure he would have been Zimbabwe's representative amongst the World Cup umpires in 1992.

On the second afternoon of the game at Kwe Kwe very heavy rain hit the ground – when it rains there it really does rain – and tarpaulin covers were brought out. Supervising the covering, Clive and I restricted covering to 4 ft in front of the batting crease. We were then told that full covering was in order so we produced the regulations as laid down by the Zimbabwe Cricket Association. Not only did it *not* say full covering was allowed but it actually did say "that unless provided otherwise, MCC's Laws of Cricket would apply".

The upshot of it all was that I was not invited to umpire again, which caused me no particular problem – I am quite happy to go to Zimbabwe simply to visit friends – but Clive, too, was banished and that was Zimbabwe cricket's loss. He would have been a top umpire in all classes of cricket and would have helped the country, I am sure, to gain full membership of the International Cricket Conference.

LAW

12

INNINGS

1. NUMBER OF INNINGS
A match shall be of one or two innings of each side according to agreement reached before the start of play.

2. ALTERNATE INNINGS
In a two-innings match each side shall take their innings alternately except in the case provided for in Law 13 (The Follow-on).

3. THE TOSS
The captains shall toss for the choice of innings on the field of play not later than 15 minutes before the time scheduled for the match to start, or before the time agreed upon for play to start.

4. CHOICE OF INNINGS
The winner of the toss shall notify his decision to bat or to field to the opposing captain not later than 10 minutes before the time scheduled for the match to start or before the time agreed upon for play to start. The decision shall not thereafter be altered.

5. CONTINUATION AFTER ONE INNINGS OF EACH SIDE
Despite the terms of (1) above, in a one-innings match, when a result has been reached on the first innings, the captains may agree to the continuation of play if, in their opinion, there is a prospect of carrying the game to a further issue in the time left. See Law 21 (The Result).

NOTES
(a) Limited Innings – One-innings Match
In a one-innings match, each innings may, by agreement, be limited by a number of overs or by a period of time.
(b) Limited Innings – Two-innings Match

In a two-innings match, the first innings of each match may, by agreement, be limited to a number of overs or a period of time.

W hilst there have not been a great number of changes to this Law over the years it does embody one of the most important features of any game – the toss of the coin before the start.

I think that the picture by Robert James, 1845, "Tossing for Innings", symbolises the whole essence of the game. It shows four young boys who are about to embark on a game of cricket. One of them is spinning a very crude bat into the air. Probably most of us remember that when a coin wasn't available we had to call whether the bat would land with its face or the back upwards.

The early Laws made no mention of the number of innings which constituted a match but in the major games it was usual for two innings each side to be played – one reason why we see so few genuine ties resulting. Sides are required to take their innings alternately except when they have to follow on (Law 13). One of the more gentlemanly aspects of the game is that the term generally used is "invited to follow on", although if the captain of the fielding side offers such an invitation it cannot be declined. Going in to bat a second time is mandatory.

In recent years there have been some unusual and misunderstood occurrences associated with Law 13 (The Follow-on) and Law 14 (Declarations) as far as forfeiture of a second innings is concerned, yet under the first-class regulations, forfeit of a *first* innings is allowed. Personally, I try to distance myself from any discussion of such matters by the captains unless I am asked for advice. I don't want to know what is going on in these discussions. The game is for the players, and if they are attempting to reach a satisfactory conclusion for their respective sides, that is fine in my book so long as Law 12 is complied with. I do feel that Laws 12, 13 and 14 to some extent hinge upon each other and indeed Law 10.1 can be involved as well.

The toss is the age-old way of starting a game, and although there have been claims from time to time that it can provide an unfair advantage it is quite remarkable how thing have evened out over the years in which records have been kept. Law 12.3 states that "the captains *shall* toss" (the mandatory verb) but that is not strictly correct, because a deputy can toss for the captain and make the decision whether to bat or field if he wins the toss. A recent clarification adds, that "though desirable, a deputy need not be a member of that side". Law 12.3 requires the toss to take place on the field of play (presumably so that everyone can see everything is above board) but I do know there have been tosses which took place *not* on the field of play, not even on the ground and, in one case, not even on the same day!

Once I turned a blind eye to a toss which was carried out in the pavilion. It was at a club ground in Scunthorpe – Normanby Park Works, who play on the outskirts of the town and also on the fringe of the Lincolnshire Wolds, with a lovely view over the Trent Valley. The view wasn't particularly good on that occasion, however, with a cold wind blowing from the north-west and April showers hitting us at regular intervals. The captains had gone out to the middle to toss when a sudden, heavy shower hit the ground and they both raced back to the pavilion. And, realising they still hadn't tossed, up went the coin and I turned my back and walked away. I hadn't seen the non-compliance with the Laws!

That ground, by the way, is close to the Flixborough works which was devastated by an explosion in 1974 in which a number of people were killed. I imagine that Normanby Park Works play their cricket only half a mile away and fortunately no game was taking place when the explosion occurred, despite it being a Saturday.

But back to Law 12: the winner of the toss must convey his decision – whether to bat or field – to his opposite number no later than 10 minutes before the start of play. Some may say that conditions can't have changed much in such a short time but the actual toss may have taken place some time before the decision is conveyed. I have seen a toss take place at 9 am – quite legally, by the correct parties, in the correct manner, in the correct place and the decision passed on to the other captain *6 hours* before the scheduled start of play. Once a decision has been made and notified to the other captain it cannot be changed.

Apart from the professional game, cricket in the main is of one innings per side, although it is not so long ago that the first innings, in first-class matches, was limited to 100 overs per side maximum. I once saw Geoffrey Boycott, at Lord's, score 200 not out in those first 100 overs without giving a chance and, as far as I can remember, without having an appeal against him. Yet in the second innings he was out first ball. Cricket really *is* a great leveller. As for freak happenings, I remember all 22 players trying to come out to field at Worcester at the same time, all under the impression that their side had lost the toss!

LAW

13

THE FOLLOW-ON

1. LEAD ON FIRST INNINGS

In a two-innings match, the side which bats first and leads by 200 runs in a match of five days or more, or by 150 runs in a three-day or four-day match, by 100 runs in a two-day match or by 75 runs in a one-day match, shall have the option of requiring the other side to follow their innings.

2. DAY'S PLAY LOST

If no play takes place on the first day of a match of two or more days' duration, (1) above shall apply in accordance with the number of days' play remaining from the actual start of the match.

I n the early days, this Law produced many acrimonious situations. In 1835 it was compulsory for a side to follow on its first innings if it was 100 runs or more behind the opponents' score. In 1854, it was reduced to 80 runs or more which was, of course, far too low a figure. Yet there was no option; it had to be applied. Very often the side with the higher first-innings score may not have wanted a follow-on situation to be enforced. No doubt it happened then, as it does now (when it is *not* compulsory), that a side does not particularly want to bat last on a worn pitch, particularly when the opposition have spin bowlers of high ability.

In Australia, in the early 1890s, the follow-on was made optional but MCC could not agree to follow suit and merely raised the lead required from 80 to 120 runs. It was not until 1900 that the margin was increased to 150 runs or more but of much greater significance was that the follow-on was then made optional. I imagine that one of the great thrills of the game is for a side to win after being made to follow on, not only for the players but for their supporters as well. It is fairly rare in county cricket but even rarer at Test level. When England registered that dramatic win by 18 runs over Australia at Headingley in 1981, for instance, there had been only one previous instance of it happening in a Test Match – again, England over Australia way back in 1894-95.

The extent of lead required for a side to be able to "invite" the opposition to follow on is set out in Law 13.1 as it applies to games of various durations. It's a short Law and relatively free of complications, but it still must be thoroughly understood by captains and umpires. There was a famous incident in a three-day match at Worcester where a captain declared after his side had got to within exactly 150 runs of the opposition's total. It must have been a nasty shock when he was promptly asked to bat again! It may well be that he knew his Law but got his arithmetic wrong, but since I regard him as a good friend we won't pursue the matter further.

If no play takes place for a whole day from the start of a five-day match, the follow-on figure is reduced from 200 to 150 runs as it has now become a four-day game as far as Law 13 is concerned. In a two-day game in which no play takes place on the first day, the side batting second must be within 75 runs of their opponents' score to be safe from an "invitation" to follow on. It is only time lost before the start of a match which governs this situation. For example, if there is play for 30 minutes on the first day of a five-day Test Match and then rain intervenes until, say, after the tea interval on the fourth day, then the follow-on figure will still be 200 or more.

One of my most wonderful cricket memories of a match being saved after a side had followed on comes from Peterhouse College in Zimbabwe. It was an inter-schools match and one side was vastly superior to the other – not unnaturally since the boys of one school were two years older than the others. The game was played on two consecutive afternoons (two hours each day) on the first of which the "good" side had scored 186 for five declared and then dismissed eight of the opposition for seven runs. Before play resumed on the second day I got all the younger side together and we sat on the grass and talked about what had to be done. I pointed out that while there was no way they could win, they could certainly save the game by fighting as long and hard as possible. The last two wickets then added 13 more runs but, more importantly, they used up 50 minutes of the two hours' play available in getting them. They followed on, of course, but by now the fighting spirit was strong enough to give them a second-innings total of 32 for one at close of play.

The boys were proud of their efforts and I was proud of them. As I told their headmaster, I abandoned hopes of getting my reward in heaven; I have received it already, that afternoon, upon the back field at Peterhouse.

During a trip to Sri Lanka in 1991 I umpired Central Districts v. Colombo City in a four-day game in Kandy in which the home side finished 162 runs short of their opponents' total in the first innings. When I inquired whether they would require a roller on the pitch if they were asked to follow on the players looked at me as if I was someone from outer space. The match manager told me that the follow-on figure was 200 or more in a four-day game! Fortunately, I had studied the local regulations which included nothing of that kind so I had to insist (as I had in Zimbabwe when threatened with a breach of Law 11) that the match be played in accordance with the Laws of Cricket, 1980 Code.

14

DECLARATIONS

1. TIME OF DECLARATION

The captain of the batting side may declare an innings closed at any time during a match, irrespective of its duration.

2. FORFEITURE OF SECOND INNINGS

A captain may forfeit his second innings, provided his decision to do so is notified to the opposing captain and umpires in sufficient time to allow 7 minutes' rolling of the pitch. See Law 10 (Rolling, Sweeping, Mowing, Watering the Pitch and Re-Marking of Creases). The 10-minute interval between innings shall be applied.

A side is always going to bat on if the score is low; and the game has only seen really high scores over the past 100 years, so it is not entirely surprising to find the earliest reference to "Declarations" as comparatively recently as 1889. Before that, a side was not allowed to declare an innings closed at all, which led to certain wilful actions by batsmen (making sure they were dismissed) and fielding sides (in certain situations making no efforts to take wickets).

After 1889, sides were restricted in the timing of a declaration. At first, the batting side were only allowed to declare on the last day of a match. In 1900, an earlier declaration was allowed – after the start of the luncheon interval on the second day. And in 1910 a declaration could be made at any time on the second or third day. It was as recently as 1946 that we saw an experimental Law introduced allowing a captain to declare on the first day – but only after his side had scored 300 runs. And this did not apply in Test Matches.

It was in 1949, and at Lord's too, that George Mann, leading England against New Zealand, declared on the first day at 313 for nine, an action which was actually illegal. Fortunately, England gained no unfair advantage by the taking of wickets in the time remaining that day and the gentlemanly Walter Hadlee, captain of New Zealand, raised no objection so the incident occasioned no rancour. But it was not until 1951 that a declaration was permitted as in Law 14.1 "at any time during a match, irrespective of its duration".

Declarations are designed to bring a game of cricket to life and there have been many exciting matches because of the adventurous attitude of captains. Some have misfired, one way or the other, but they have brought about vital victories and have gone a long way towards the winning of championships. What at times causes ill feeling, certainly a fair amount of unrest amongst spectators, is when one side bats on to a stage which completely excludes the opposition. At the same time it must be borne in mind that when a captain does this he is backing his own side to bowl out the opposition twice. It is his prerogative, and it requires sound judgment to decide how much time he needs to do this. My own version is: "If you are not prepared to lose, you don't deserve to win."

There are, and have been, some captains who were known for making what are known as "generous" declarations and the story goes that Essex players once locked Keith Fletcher in the toilet to *prevent* a declaration until another 40 runs had been added. As I understand it, England's players by consensus declared on the last morning of the Second Test in New Zealand in 1978 when Geoffrey Boycott couldn't make up his mind.

A declaration can be made at any time in a game, and if it happens when players and umpires are on the field it causes no problems. We have to check whether an application of a roller is required, if so of what size, and how long the rolling should take. And then, of course, we have to ensure that the captain's wishes are observed. If any problems do arise it is when the declaration is made during an interval or before play starts on any day. Groundstaff, who pride themselves on seeing that all their duties are carried out before play resumes, may sometimes not be immediately available and there is a certain bustle of activity around the place. If a captain delays his declaration until there is insufficient time for the opposition to have the required rolling time, or if anything unforeseen occurs to prevent sufficient rolling time, then the umpires will allow the required time to be taken out of normal playing time. This also applies when a forfeiture of an innings takes place.

When a declaration takes place, the captain of the batting side must tell not only his opposite number but the umpires as well. If he fails to do this it can cause a lot of problems – as it certainly did one morning in 1990 during the match between the TCCB's Under-25 side and the Indian touring team. On the first day, India batted and scored 290 for six wickets; there was no hint of a declaration the following morning. My colleague and I observed the rolling of the pitch which took place at the correct time and the two of us were walking to the middle at 10.55 am when we heard an announcement over the public address system: "Please welcome the Indian side led by Ravi Shastri." And, looking round, we saw the Indian team filing on to field. No one had said a word to the umpires.

We had with us the old ball and the appropriate spares; as far as we knew the pitch had been rolled that morning on the instructions of the Indian captain. It was time to inquire what was going on. It seemed that Shastri had informed the Under-25 captain, John Stephenson, of his decision to declare while he was having a net at about 10 am. John had then asked the groundsman, who was nearby, for the heavy roller to be used on the pitch after 10.30 am. But no one had thought to inform the umpires. So we had a situation where the pitch had been rolled in accordance with the Laws, but there was still a delay of about 6 minutes for the Indians to go back to the pavilion to select a new ball with which to start the Under-25 innings. Some have said the interval should have been 10 minutes, but I can't agree with that: the pitch had been correctly rolled in accordance with the Laws. Others say we should have started immediately, using the ball already in use (the previous day), but I can't agree with that either, since Law 5.3 states "either captain may demand a new ball at the start of each innings". All the argument and confusion could have been prevented if the captains had fully observed the Law.

Another Indian touring team were involved in a slightly different type of incident at Sheffield in 1967. Freddie Trueman, skippering Yorkshire, has always insisted that he enforced the follow-on in a proper manner. The Nawab of Pataudi, leading India, said at the time that he had *not* been invited to bat again. And so the two sides started to come out to field at the same time, almost side by side!

There was a moment of hilarious confusion, followed by an unscheduled delay because a couple of batsmen had to go back and pad up, but who was really to blame? Well, that was never sorted out in terms of a public admission, but I think we should consider just two factors: (1) Fred took an inordinate pride in skippering Yorkshire when Brian Close was not available and made no secret of the fact; (2) the "Noob" was a practical joker of the most wicked kind, from his undergraduate days to his time as an international captain. Make up your own minds!

In a Second XI match at Westcliff-on-Sea, which I umpired, there was one of the most unusual declarations ever. The match was between Essex and Sussex and Ray East was the captain of the Essex side. It was the match which saw Angus McKay play his first game for Essex; he was a boy whom I had met in Zimbabwe upon my first trip to that country and I had recommended him to Essex. I am pleased to say that he took seven wickets in one innings in that match. With the Essex innings in full swing and a good score on the board, a phone call was received in the pavilion, which at a conservative estimate was situated some fifty yards from the boundary line. One of the Essex players went out on to the balcony and shouted to another Essex player, who was watching the match from a seat very near to the boundary line, and as he did so he raised his arms into the air and clapped his hands. All he was doing was trying to attract the attention of the person who was in receipt of the call. The two batsmen, seeing this and thinking that a declaration had taken place, left the field; I and my colleague lifted the bails and followed the players into the pavilion. When the batsmen walked into the dressing-room, there was the captain resting on the bench and in reply to his question of, "What the hell are you doing in here?" they stated that the declaration had been made. Those who know Ray East can probably imagine what Ray's next remark may have been!

LAW

15

START OF PLAY

1. CALL OF PLAY

At the start of each innings and of each day's play, and on the resumption of play after any interval or interruption, the umpire at the bowler's end shall call "Play".

2. PRACTICE ON THE FIELD

At no time on any day of the match shall there be any bowling or batting practice on the pitch.

No practice may take play on the field if, in the opinion of the umpires, it could result in a waste of time.

3. TRIAL RUN-UP

No bowler shall have a trial run-up after "Play" has been called in any session of play, except at the fall of a wicket, when an umpire may allow such a trial run-up if he is satisfied that it will not cause any waste of time.

T he start of a match, as opposed to the ball coming into play and the first ball of an over being bowled, is effected with the utterance of one simple word, "Play". When that is spoken by an umpire the match has started.

Players of both sides must be ready and prepared to play. If not, they are at risk (on appeal) of infringing Law 15. They must also be prepared to play until the match reaches a conclusion. The call must be loud and clear so that both sides know play is about to begin. In the 1755 Code of Laws the call of "Play" was made three times but now it is made only once.

One major point to be noted before we pass on to the main burden of this Law – before the umpires allow play to start they must be sure that the scorers have taken up their positions. Indeed, it is one of the umpires' duties to ascertain this before calling "Play". I know of a couple of occasions when matches have begun without the scorers in position and I have waited, on a number of occasions, when the scorers have run around or across the ground to get into position. There is usually a problem of a pressing, personal nature if they are late and, with very rare exceptions, they are both waiting for a wave from the umpires, which they acknowledge, and off we go. (See Law 4.)

"Play" is called not only to start the match but at the start of each day's play and also at the start of each innings if it doesn't coincide with the start of a day's play. The call is also made on a resumption of play after an agreed interval and to re-start play after an interruption (e.g. for rain or bad light). I have rarely heard "Play" called after a drinks interval but it is, in fact, an agreed interval and the call should be made.

There are times when the actual start is delayed after "Play" has been called. For instance, the bowler may find his run-in is not quite right before delivering the ball, or a sudden glint of sunshine distracts a batsman by reflecting off a car's windscreen. If there is a delay for this sort of incident, it is advisable that the call of "Play" should be made again.

There must be no practice, either batting or bowling, on the pitch, nor can there be practice of any description on the field of play if it wastes time. After "Play" has been called for any session, no bowler is allowed a trial run-up except at the fall of a wicket and then only after requesting permission of the umpire at the bowling end. This will only be given if the umpire is satisfied there will be no waste of time.

At the same time, it is difficult to stop a bowler who has embarked on a trial run-up. The umpire is often occupied in giving his guard to the batsman. He has his back to the bowler and does not see him until it is too late to do anything about it. If he *does* see the bowler, or perhaps if he only *hears* him approaching, what is he to do? Block the way with his body, perhaps causing an injury to either or both parties? Does he throw out an arm, risking an accidental blow to the bowler's face or throat? That would mean the red card in other games! The umpire takes neither of these actions unless he is officious or plain stupid. He hopes players know something about the provisions of Law 15. But there are ways a bowler can get round this restriction if he is determined to do so. For instance, he can perform his run-up and whole approach in reverse, by starting it from the crease. There is nothing illegal in that. In the last analysis, the duties of an umpire are too important for him to want to get involved in personal recrimination with a bowler over this point.

Before the 1980 Code of Laws came into operation a *match* could be awarded under Law 17 (which has now been replaced by Law 15) if a batsman took longer than two minutes to come out to the wicket. This is now not so and the point is covered in Law 31 (Timed Out) with only the incoming batsman dismissed.

Law 15 and the following Laws 16 (Intervals) and 17 (Cessation of Play) – certainly the latter two – have become very important since the 1947 Code of Law was introduced, so much so that they now form three separate Laws in the 1980 Code. Under the 1947 Code they were simply lumped together as Law 17 (Start and Close of Play and Intervals).

LAW

16

INTERVALS

1. LENGTH

The umpire shall allow such intervals as have been agreed upon for meals, and 10 minutes between each innings.

2. LUNCHEON INTERVAL – INNINGS ENDING OR STOPPAGE WITHIN 10 MINUTES OF INTERVAL

If an innings ends or there is a stoppage caused by weather or bad light within 10 minutes of the agreed time for the luncheon interval, the interval shall be taken immediately.

The time remaining in the session of play shall be added to the agreed length of the interval but no extra allowance shall be made for the 10 minutes interval between innings.

3. TEA INTERVAL – INNINGS ENDING OR STOPPAGE WITHIN 30 MINUTES OF INTERVAL

If an innings ends or there is a stoppage caused by weather within 30 minutes of the agreed time for the tea interval, the interval shall be taken immediately.

The interval shall be of the agreed length and, if applicable, shall include the 10-minute interval between innings.

4. TEA INTERVAL – CONTINUATION OF PLAY

If, at the agreed time for the tea interval, nine wickets are down, play shall continue for a period not exceeding 30 minutes or until the innings is concluded.

5. TEA INTERVAL – AGREEMENT TO FOREGO

At any time during the match, the captains may agree to forego a tea interval.

6. INTERVALS FOR DRINKS

If both captains agree before the start of a match that intervals for drinks may be taken, the option to take such intervals shall be available to either side. These intervals shall be restricted to one per session, shall be kept as short as possible, shall not be taken in the last hour of the match, and in any case shall not exceed 5 minutes.

The agreed times for these intervals shall be strictly adhered to, except that if a wicket falls within 5 minutes of the agreed time, then drinks shall be taken out immediately.

If an innings ends or there is a stoppage caused by weather or bad light within 30 minutes of the agreed time for a drinks interval there will be no interval for drinks in that session.

At any time during the match the captains may agree to forego any such drinks intervals.

NOTES

(a) Tea Interval – One-day Match
In a one-day match, the specific time for the tea interval need not necessarily be arranged and it may be agreed to take this interval between the innings of a one-day match.

(b) Changing the Agreed Time of Intervals
In the event of the ground, weather or light conditions causing a suspension of play, the umpires, after consultation with the captains, may decide in the interests of time-saving to bring forward the time of the luncheon or tea interval.

I n 1744 the interval between the innings was, as it is now, of 10 minutes' duration; but in 1774 it was increased to 15 minutes – a much more sensible break in my view. But in 1840 the interval reverted to 10 minutes, and I would love to know the reason for the change. With all the accoutrements of modern batting, 10 minutes is an awfully short time to gird up the loins, and other parts of the anatomy, ready for the fray. I have actually seen opening batsmen sprint from the field to get ready in time. And I am sure spectators would love the 5 minutes' extension. A quick beer or a comfort stop can be more conveniently achieved in 15 minutes, especially when one may have to queue for both.

I am also aware that a pitch at one time could be rolled for 10 minutes rather than 7 minutes as it is now. It is not easy to trundle out the roller, effect a 7-minute application and wheel it away again, all within that 10-minute interval, and I am sure groundstaff would appreciate a longer break. It amazes me that though the maximum rolling time of 7 minutes was not inserted into the Laws until 1931, for the previous 91 years (i.e. since 1840) the time between innings had only been 10 minutes. In short, the time between the innings was the same as the time allowed for rolling! There may have been an experimental Law in force but I do not think so.

In 1980, when the new Code of Laws first applied, the luncheon interval could have been 10 minutes plus the agreed duration of the interval. This was because if an innings ended within 10 minutes of the interval, whatever time remained before the agreed interval would be added on to that interval. In other words, the luncheon interval was being augmented by the time, or some of the time, between the innings.

But many years before 1980 an experimental Law had been formulated which provided for the agreed length of time of the luncheon interval to apply, even if an innings closed within 10 minutes of the interval. It was obvious that an attempt was thus being made to rescind the section of Law 16 which permitted an extension of the luncheon interval. I was surprised that the experiment was not incorporated into the 1980 Code and even more surprised when it was not included in the second edition of the Laws in 1992. It was, and still is, an eminently sensible inclusion. To my knowledge it has operated for more than 20 years and it works well.

The tea interval (or, as it is known in the trade, "the movable feast") is relatively easy – but not always in first-class cricket. Let us take 4.10 pm as the agreed time of the tea interval. If an innings closes within 30 minutes of this time, or if the players have to leave the field for any other reason, tea is taken immediately, and for the duration of an interval previously agreed, which is usually 20 minutes. Tea could then have been taken, and the game resumed, before the agreed time for tea had actually been reached! I have known this to happen many times. Then again, if at 4.10 pm nine wickets have fallen in an innings, play continues for another 30 minutes and so tea is taken at 4.40 pm. But if the last wicket falls *before* 4.40 pm, tea is taken immediately. I have been guilty of a momentary lapse on occasions and seen some of my colleagues similarly slip up. With eight wickets down and the last over before tea being bowled, a wicket has fallen to the last ball of the over. My call of "Over and Time" was immediately followed by, "No, it isn't." We had to go on for another half-hour or until the tenth wicket fell.

Confusing, but not terribly bad. How about this one, though? A county championship match at Bristol: we are operating under first-class regulations which state, "Tea will be at 4.10 pm or when 40 overs or less of the day's allocation remain to be bowled." At 3.40 pm, nine wickets had already fallen and if the last one had gone from the very next ball we would have taken tea. The last pair continued their stand and at 4.10 pm they were still together, and so we had to go on for another half-hour. Now just before 4.40 pm I glanced at the scoreboard and saw that 41 overs had still to be bowled to complete the day's (minimum) allocation and I realised that here was a situation I had never encountered before. Moreover I was sure it had never occurred before. I consulted my colleague and we were agreed we would take tea at the end of the next over, with 40 remaining, which we did. It was 4.43 pm. There was no complaint from anyone. We had continued for 30 minutes after 4.10 pm because there were nine wickets down and 40 overs precisely now remained to be bowled in the day. All the requirements, it seemed, had been complied with. But no.

In my match report to the TCCB I stated the facts and received a prompt reply which told me that we had been right to judge the tea interval time as 4.43 pm but we should not have taken tea at that time. We should have continued for a further 30 minutes from that time, with 40 overs remaining of the day's allocation to be bowled; and if, then, the last wicket had still not fallen, we could have taken tea.

To say that this surprised me is putting it mildly. On the one hand, we might well have taken tea at 3.41 pm if the last wicket had fallen; on the other, we might have found ourselves starting the tea interval at 5.13 pm. And if the last wicket had fallen at any time between those two, we would all have gone in for our break. No wonder it is called the movable feast! That is, if the feast is ever taken at all.

The tea interval can actually be dispensed with altogether if both captains agree. I have only once had *a request* from a captain who wanted to forego the break – it was at Lord's – but as the other captain did not agree we all enjoyed tea and scones provided by the admirable Nancy. Umpires have no direct jurisdiction in this matter at all; it is entirely a matter for the two captains.

Only once, as I have said, have I been asked if the tea interval could be dispensed with but I have, in fact, suggested myself that it might be done on one occasion. This was in a match at Luton in 1992 between an England Amateur XI and the Pakistan touring team. The England XI had to follow on, and with eight wickets down in the second innings they were some way short of making Pakistan bat again. It was the last day, and tea was due to be taken at 3.40 pm. With one over to be bowled at 3.38 pm I was asked by the captains if we could read the situation as nine-wickets-down, rather than eight, because one batsman was injured and would not bat. This would have permitted play to continue for another 30 minutes, and I obviously could not agree. I did, however, suggest to the captains that if *they* agreed we could forego the tea interval altogether. They accepted this and the final wicket fell in the first over of what would otherwise have been the tea interval. Everybody was happy.

In the notes of Law 16, it is pointed out that the interval times can be varied with the agreement of the parties concerned (umpires, captains, and I include the ground authorities, especially the tea ladies) in the event of rain, bad light or anything unforeseen; this will ensure the maximum time for play to take place, a common-sense provision.

This brings to mind a lovely story about H.D. Bird at Bury St. Edmunds. He was umpiring a NatWest Trophy match there a few years ago when players left the field, believing that the tea interval time had arrived. Well, it may have done; and I am sure that if it had, the umpires would have been correct in their interpretation of the interval. But, as the umpires entered the pavilion, they were confronted by a somewhat irate tea lady who required to know why they were coming into the refreshment room. When Harold told her that it was the tea interval, she told him in a very forthright manner that it was not ready at that juncture and he could buzz off and get on with the game until it was: *she* would let him know when he could come in for tea. Never upset the tea ladies.

Drinks intervals in this country are usually agreed upon just before they are taken. This is completely against the Law . . . but we don't tell anyone! In Law, only one drinks interval per session is permitted, but in many countries local regulations allow more than one such interval because of the heat and humidity. Indeed, in one part of Zimbabwe (Triangle) they have *three*. After half an hour there is a 5-minute break for water; after another half-hour there is a break of 20 minutes for cups of tea; and then after 30 more minutes' play, more water is taken on board. After a further half-hour's play there is a break of one hour for lunch. What a civilised way of playing cricket in a hot climate!

In applying this part of Law 16 I have had to insist, more than once, on the right of batsmen to have a drink if they want it. Once drinks have been agreed upon by the captains, the option to take one applies to both sides and not just to one of them. On occasions, the fielding side may decline to take drinks; but if the batsmen are wanting refreshment I allow them to take a drink. If, of course, both captains decline, then there is no drinks interval. In England, "drinks" can be anything. I have had all sorts of *cold* drinks as well as tea and even Oxo on very cold days. I have also known other types of drinks brought on to the field – but certainly not to be drunk by the umpires during hours of play!

Drinks intervals should never be allowed at any time during the final hour of a match and this is well covered in Law. One can see the reason for this, though it may not be so obvious at first-class level, where it would rarely if ever apply: there must be no waste of playing time.

In the third Test in which I "stood" as an umpire, England v. Australia in 1981 at Lord's, Australia needed 232 to win on the last afternoon and just before the final hour began they were 17 for the loss of three wickets. Shortly after the start of the last hour I saw Graeme Wood signal for a drink, and the 12th man tried to bring it on to the field. I refused to let it happen. Graeme asked why, and I told him. He seemed a bit surprised. Feeling that common sense should be applied (Wood was in a backs-to-the-wall situation), I relented to the extent of telling him he could have a drink brought out if a wicket fell. One did, so all was well. The match ended in a draw with Australia at 90 for four and Wood was 62 not out. After we had all showered and changed and were enjoying a beer in the Australian dressing-room, Fred Bennett the manager approached me to say: "You were quite right, Don. We've looked up the Laws and it says 'No drinks in the last hour.'" Now that surprised *me*. Why had they had to check such a well-known feature of Law 16? And I then learned why Graeme had looked surprised, and why the manager had looked up the Law: in the Australian regulations, drinks are forbidden in the final session of play . . . *until* the last hour. Exactly the reverse of the Laws of Cricket.

All intervals, as far as umpires are concerned, are necessary, precious and too short. I have often wondered why the luncheon break could not be 45 minutes instead of 40 and the tea interval 30 minutes instead of 20. This could be achieved without any loss of playing time by starting at 10.45 am instead of 11.00. I don't think it would hurt anyone to arrive and start operations a quarter of an hour earlier. I would, however, draw the line at accepting the suggestion of a catering manageress I encountered in Essex in 1985. The provision of meals was being undertaken for the first time by a firm of outside caterers who clearly didn't know the ropes. Umpires and scorers, sitting at their table together as usual, were treated in such a cavalier fashion when they went in for lunch that we barely managed a bowl of soup and an apple before we had to return to duty on the field. The following morning, before start of play, I paid a visit with both scorers to the manageress and pointed out as forcefully as possible that umpires and scorers had less time to take lunch than the players and it was imperative that we were served first. Obviously the lady was under the impression that the needs of the players were of paramount importance. I thought I had managed to dispel this impression when she gave the matter some considered thought, but I had absolutely no answer when she came up with her solution to the problem: "We'll certainly be glad to serve you four before the players ... if you can come in 30 minutes before they do." Since then, I am happy to say, the Essex Secretary, Peter Edwards, has improved matters but it was a story which did the rounds and caused a lot of smiles.

I expect that the most unusual interval in play took place in 1981 at Cambridge, when I along with Nigel Plews took the players off the field on 24 April at 12.45 pm. The reason was that we both considered the conditions not only unreasonable but also very dangerous. I am tempted to say that as it was Nigel's first match as a "Reserve Panel" umpire, he had a fiery baptism; but that would be really stretching the point – but perhaps not; see Law 32 and a further story with regard to Nigel in his very next match, two days later. Much was written about the conditions of extreme cold, and I can tell you that the day had a temperature of 2 degrees, and with the chill factor of the wind it was minus 3 degrees. Those figures came from the local meteorological office. What finally decided us to approach the two captains, Keith Fletcher of Essex and Derek Pringle of Cambridge University, was that a ball hit back towards the bowler, David Ackfield, along the ground, bruised his hand, fingers and wrist so badly that he was in extreme pain. Derek Pringle, who was batting, was almost unable to see as his eyes were watering so much and his contact lenses were floating around in his eyes. On top of this, the Essex team were wearing overcoats, balaclava helmets and gloves on top of track suits, which again were on top of their cricket clothes. I spoke to my colleague, and I then asked both captains if either of them thought any useful purpose was being served by us remaining on the field of play at that present time. They both dearly wished to go off but did not think the situation could be catered for. I said, "It can: leave it to me." When we were approached by the Press as to the reason for our leaving the field, all I did was to tell them the truth, as I saw no point in trying to "pull the wool over their eyes". They not only accepted the fact, they treated us well in their copy over the following days.

LAW
17

CESSATION OF PLAY

I. CALL OF TIME
The umpire at the bowler's end shall call "Time" on the cessation of play before any interval or interruption of play, at the end of each day's play and at the conclusion of the match. See Law 27 (Appeals).

2. REMOVAL OF BAILS
After the call of "Time" the umpires shall remove the bails from both wickets.

3. STARTING A LAST OVER
The last over before an interval or the close of play shall be started provided the umpire, after walking at his normal pace, has arrived at his position behind the stumps at the bowler's end before time has been reached.

4. COMPLETION OF THE LAST OVER OF A SESSION
The last over before an interval or the close of play shall be completed unless a batsman is out or retires during that over within 2 minutes of the interval or the close of play or unless the players have occasion to leave the field.

5. COMPLETION OF THE LAST OVER OF A MATCH
An over in progress at the close of play on the final day of a match shall be completed at the request of either captain, even if a wicket falls after time has been reached.

If, during the last over, the players have occasion to leave the field, the umpires shall call "Time" and there shall be no resumption of play and the match shall be at an end.

6. LAST HOUR OF MATCH – NUMBER OF OVERS
The umpires shall indicate when one hour of playing time of a match remains according to the agreed hours of play. The next over after that moment shall be the first of a minimum of 20 six-ball overs (15 eight-ball overs), provided a result is not reached earlier or there is no interval or interruption of play.

7. LAST HOUR OF PLAY – INTERVALS BETWEEN INNINGS AND INTERRUPTIONS OF PLAY

If, at the commencement of the last hour of the match, an interval or interruption of play is in progress or if, during the last hour, there is an interval between innings or an interruption of play, the minimum number of overs to be bowled on the resumption of play shall be reduced in proportion to the duration, within the last hour of the match, of any such interval or interruption.

The minimum number of overs to be bowled after the resumption of play shall be calculated as follows:

(a) In the case of an interval or interruption of play being in progress at the commencement of the last hour of the match, or in the case of the first interval or interruption, a deduction shall be made from the minimum of 20 six-ball overs (or 15 eight-ball overs).

(b) If there is a later interval or interruption, a further deduction shall be made from the minimum number of overs which should have been bowled following the last resumption of play.

(c) These deductions shall be based on the following factors:

(i) The number of overs already bowled in the last hour of the match, or in the case of a later interval or interruption, in the last session of play.

(ii) The number of overs lost as a result of the interval or interruption allowing one six-ball over for every full 3 minutes (or one eight-ball over for every full 4 minutes) of the interval or interruption.

(iii) Any over left uncompleted at the end of an innings to be excluded from these calculations.

(iv) Any over left uncompleted at the start of an interruption of play to be completed when play is resumed and to count as one over bowled.

(v) An interval to start with the end of an innings and to end 10 minutes later; an interruption to start on the call of "Time" and to end on the call of "Play".

(d) In the event of an innings being completed and a new innings commencing during the last hour of the match, the number of overs to be bowled in the new innings shall be calculated on the basis of one six-ball over for every 3 minutes or part thereof remaining for play (or one eight-ball over for every 4 minutes or part thereof remaining for play); or alternatively on the basis that sufficient overs be bowled to enable a full minimum quota of overs to be completed under such circumstances governed by (a), (b) and (c) above. In all such cases the alternative which allows the greater number of overs shall be employed.

8. BOWLER UNABLE TO COMPLETE AN OVER DURING LAST HOUR OF THE MATCH

If, for any reason, a bowler is unable to complete an over during the period of play referred to in (6) above, Law 22.7 (Bowler Incapacitated or Suspended during an Over) shall apply.

T his Law is often referred to simply as "Time" because that is the call used by the umpire to inform players that a match, a day's play or a session of play has ended. If that end comes suddenly, because of rain or a bad light decision, an umpire is still expected to apply the call.

When some particularly hurried exits have taken place I have seen the bails inadvertently left on top of the stumps and, before the 1980 Code of Laws applied, this could have meant the dismissal of a batsman long after everyone had left the field. Now this cannot happen because Law 27 (Appeals) applies.

As an interval approaches, the umpires give each other a sign to indicate whether that over is to be the final one of that session. Just occasionally there may be a slight doubt about whether the time for the interval has arrived. It is then decided by the time at which the square-leg umpire completes his walk to the bowler's wicket. If it is before the scheduled time for the interval, even fractionally, then another over must be started, and completed, unless a wicket falls, or unless we leave the field for any other reason within two minutes of that scheduled time. "Any other reason" may include (unlikely though it may be), for instance, a batsman retiring. A final over which starts very close to "Time" being called is something of a trial because it will be eating (no pun intended!) into the luncheon or tea interval. If a wicket falls in the last over of *a match*, whether it is within 2 minutes or not of the scheduled close, the over may be completed if, for any reason, either captain wants this to happen. Indeed a wicket could fall after time has been reached and again if either captain had a desire for the over to be completed, this would happen.

All that we have said so far about Law 17 has been based on considerations of *time*. When, however, we reach the final hour of a match we come, virtually, to an *overs* situation. During that last hour a minimum of 20 overs have to be bowled and if 20 have not been completed the game continues until they have.

From time to time in this book I have mentioned parts of Laws which, from their inception, have (in my view) been good for the game and this part of Law 17 has probably been the best. The framing of it arose from a match in 1967 between Warwickshire and Yorkshire at Edgbaston, something of a *cause célèbre* which led to a tremendous public outcry at the time. An MCC sub-committee afterwards found that Yorkshire had used delaying tactics in the later stages of the game, which constituted unfair play, and they held the

Yorkshire captain Brian Close entirely responsible for the tactics. To put matters in perspective Close, at the time and ever since that date, has consistently denied that his tactics were unfair. However, the incident prompted the law-makers to introduce Part 6 of Law 17.

In principle, it stipulates that a minimum of 20 overs must be bowled in the final hour as long as the players do not leave the field for any reason. Bear in mind that the operative word there is *minimum*. If, before the final hour has elapsed, 20 overs have been completed, the game continues until the time agreed for the close. There have been times when this has happened and more than 20 overs have been bowled; one of them caused complications for me, but more of that later.

If there are stoppages for rain or bad light during that last hour those 20 overs will be reduced by one over for each full 3 minutes of play which are lost. If there is more than one stoppage, then each is judged separately. For example, if we have three stoppages of 10 minutes, 10 minutes and 8 minutes, the overs deducted will be three, three and two – a total of eight overs. In TCCB-organised cricket it is not quite the same. Let us take the regulations governing county championship matches. If, at 5 pm on the last day, the minimum number of overs *to be bowled in the day* (i.e. 82) have not been bowled, there will not be a last hour, in effect, as far as the minimum 20 overs is concerned. The match will simply continue until the required 102 overs *in the day* have been bowled or until 6 pm, whichever is the later.

If, however, *more than* 82 overs have been bowled at 5 pm the "last hour" will be signalled and a further 20 overs will be bowled; but should there be any reason for a deduction of overs for stoppages there is now a variation of the time–overs ratio. One over will be deducted for every 3½ minutes lost. Taking the example I gave in the previous paragraph of three stoppages lasting 10 minutes, 10 minutes and 8 minutes, the reduction of overs now becomes two, two and two – total six overs.

There is another slight variation in the regulations applying to Test Matches. On the last day a minimum of 75 overs must have been bowled by 5 pm; if not, the match will continue until 75 overs *have* been completed and *then* a final hour's play will begin. In that final hour a minimum of 15 overs must be bowled or the game will continue until they have. Why 15? Well, in 1992 the authorities decided that this figure was more in keeping with the average over-rate throughout a day's Test cricket. This is correct as 11 am until 5 pm, of which 60 minutes for lunch and tea, equals 5 hours' playing time; 5 x 15 = 75 overs. Deductions for stoppages in this period became one over for each full 4 minutes of playing time lost for rain or bad light; 4 x 15 = 60 minutes.

In matches between the tourists and county sides there is another slight variation. In this case the number of overs to be bowled by 5 pm is 80 and if they have not been completed at 5 pm the game will continue until they have. Then, a final hour will start with a minimum of 16 overs to be bowled. The rate of deductions of overs for stoppage time is one over for 3¾ minutes of play. Remember: a full 3¾ minutes – again correct and sensible maths and regulations.

When a situation arises which involves a change of innings (end of one, beginning of another) in the last hour we can have some interesting situations. Under the Laws, as opposed to first-class playing regulations, the umpires have to make two quick calculations. One of these I call "the overs situation" and the other "the time situation". The calculation which allows the most overs to be bowled will be the one which applies. Let's try an example taking a straightforward change of innings in the last hour of a game, between 5 pm and 6 pm. After four overs and five balls the last wicket falls at 5.15 pm. The first thing to be done now is forget about these five balls as if they had never been bowled and make our calculation on the basis of four overs only having been bowled. There is then a 10-minute interval before the start of the new innings, giving us a deduction of three overs. That takes up seven of the minimum 20 final overs, leaving 13 when play resumes at 5.25 pm. That is the *overs* calculation – right? Now let us consider the *time* calculation. With 35 minutes' play possible before 6 pm and allowing one over for every full 3 minutes or part thereof of time we arrive at a figure of 11 overs, plus one more for the two "spare" minutes: 35 divided by 3 = 11 + 1. Total 12. As the *overs* calculation allows 13 still to be bowled as opposed to the *time* calculation, which gives us 12, the former is the one which will be adopted in this example.

This was the system which applied in Test and county championship cricket in this country for several years, but not in 1992. As I have said, in championship cricket the start of the last hour will depend on whether the minimum number of overs *in the day* have been bowled by 5 pm. If they have, then the two calculations would apply if a change of innings took place during the last hour.

This may well appear almost incomprehensible to the "lay" follower of the game but it is essential to describe in detail the many different types of regulation a first-class umpire must study and get clear in his mind, quite apart from having a full and complete knowledge of the Laws themselves. There is, you may now think, something more to "standing" than counting up to six, holding a sweater or two and lifting a finger now and then!

The regulations for the 1992 season in Test cricket have really gone back on the theme of providing a minimum number of overs to be bowled in a day in certain situations. Take, for instance, any of the first four days of play when the minimum number of overs to be bowled is 90, the hours of play 11 am to 6 pm and the side bowling first dismiss the opposition at 5.50 pm – but they have done so in only 78 overs and there have been no stoppages for any reason. In such a case it would be close of play at that time, *despite* the bowling of only 78 overs. As the TCCB applied the regulations in previous years, there would still have been ten more overs to be bowled (two having been deducted for the interval between the innings): $78 + 2 = 80$ from 90. Under the 1992 Regulations, however, the new innings would be due to start at the scheduled close-of-play time and play could not start after that time. Not for the first time one is left to ponder that the paying public are not getting value for money; but this is not a case where one can fault the TCCB. It was the tourists who would not agree to a sensible regulation.

Let us now return to Law 17 as it applies to club and friendly cricket. If during a final 20 overs a bowler is injured or suspended from bowling for any reason, another member of the fielding side must complete the over, bearing in mind that no player may bowl consecutive overs or a part of one. If it occurs during a game *before* the final hour the over need not be completed. If, however, it happens in Test, championship or any limited-overs competition the over *must* be completed for the simple reason that there is a requirement for a certain number of full overs to be bowled in a day's play or during an innings.

Let me revert now to the last-hour incident which caused complications for me. It occurred at Trent Bridge (Notts v. Middlesex) on 30 June 1981, and I verify the times by turning up a copy of my official report to the TCCB.

At 4.57 pm, 3 minutes before the scheduled start of the last hour, and off the final ball of an over, Eddie Hemmings top-edged a ball into his face, causing a bad cut around the mouth. He was bleeding badly and semi-conscious. While I was applying first aid I noticed that the time had reached 5 pm and mentioned to my colleague that we should officially be starting the last hour, but suggested we wait until we had resolved the problem of Eddie's injury. At that point Mike Brearley, the Middlesex captain, asked what we would do about the time lost in the final hour and I replied that we would address that matter when Eddie had been treated.

It was after 5.05 pm when he was led from the field by the Notts physiotherapist and after a discussion between Mike Brearley, the two batsmen (Hemmings having been replaced) and my colleague, it was decided the last hour would now be signalled and play would continue until 6.05 pm. No one disagreed, and indeed it seemed a just and fair way of dealing with the situation. If there had been no injury there would certainly have been time for one more over before the last hour was signalled to the scorers. Without our extension to 6.05 pm it would have meant only 55 minutes' play instead of a last hour – something the Law had been framed to avoid. As no one except Eddie had left the field (to have the blood staunched) we were not legally allowed to deduct any overs, even if anyone had asked for that.

So, rightly or wrongly, and in the absence of any objection from any quarter, we played a last hour which was due to end at 6.05 pm. It was then that Sod's Law intervened to confound all our best intentions. In 55 minutes up to 6 pm precisely, 20 overs had been bowled! At 6.03 pm, off the first ball of the 22nd over, the last Notts wicket fell. And all hell broke loose. I cannot blame spectators or ground authorities for being angry – they did not know what had been decided out in the middle and there had been no opportunity to inform them. It may be that our interpretation of the situation was not strictly correct; but I do insist that our motive was entirely pure in that we were trying to be fair to all parties. The players immediately involved were all informed of our decision, taken purely and simply for the good of the game, and none of them offered any objection.

Nevertheless, it led to a certain unpleasantness, and if that was my responsibility, then I can only apologise. Would I take the same course if presented with an identical set of circumstances? Perhaps not. But if I put my hand on my heart I simply cannot say that what we did was *totally* incorrect by the wording of the Law. Not could I ever agree that our decision was in anything but the best interests of the game.

A final word on that incident. It was ironic that for the last match of that 1981 season I should find myself "standing" once more at Trent Bridge. Notts had to win in order to secure the county championship, which would be their first success of any description for 52 years. When my colleague and I emerged from the pavilion I received some comments from the locals which, I admit, I certainly expected. None of them was abusive; in fact I could describe them as good-natured. Whilst during my career I like to think that I have got little incorrect, what I have done has always happened at Trent Bridge. I remember giving Clive Rice "out" caught by the wicket-keeper when he certainly did not hit it. What happened, and I have seen it on video so I can prove it, was he aimed a cut at a short ball and the chain which he wore around his neck came up and hit his visor. That was the noise I heard.

The one thing I can say about the Notts players and public is, whatever I may have done which they felt was not correct, they never held it against me, at least not for long, and I am pleased to say that I have numerous friends at "The Bridge". They won the match and the championship and I doubt that anyone will remember how the winning run was made. It came from a "No ball!", signalled by myself, for a second short-pitched delivery in the over – yes, I am that strong!

LAW

18

SCORING

1. A RUN

The score shall be reckoned by runs. A run is scored when:

(a) So often as the batsmen, after a hit or at any time while the ball is in play shall have crossed and made good their ground from end to end.

(b) When a boundary is scored. See Law 19 (Boundaries).

(c) When penalty runs are awarded. See (6) below.

2. SHORT RUNS

(a) If either batsman runs a short run the umpire shall call and signal "one short" as soon as the ball becomes dead and that run shall not be scored. A run is short if a batsman fails to make good his ground on turning for a further run.

(b) Although a short run shortens the succeeding one, the latter, if completed, shall count.

(c) If either or both batsmen deliberately run short the umpire shall, as soon as he sees that the fielding side have no chance of dismissing either batsman, call and signal "dead ball" and disallow any runs attempted or previously scored. The batsmen shall return to their original ends.

(d) If both batsmen run short in one and the same run, only 1 run shall be deducted.

(e) Only if three or more runs are attempted can more than one be short and then, subject to (c) and (d) above, all the runs so called shall be disallowed. If there has been more than one short run the umpires shall instruct the scorers as to the number of runs disallowed.

3. STRIKER CAUGHT

If the striker is caught, no run shall be scored.

4. BATSMAN RUN OUT

If a batsman is run out, only that run which was being attempted shall not be scored. If, however, an injured striker himself is run out, no runs shall be scored. See Law 2.7 (Transgressions of the Laws by an Injured Batsman or Runner).

5. BATSMAN OBSTRUCTING THE FIELD

If a batsman is out Obstructing the Field, any runs completed before the obstruction occurs shall be scored unless such obstruction prevents a catch being made, in which case no runs shall be scored.

6. RUNS SCORED FOR PENALTIES

Runs shall be scored for penalties under Law 20 (Lost Ball), 24 (No Ball), 25 (Wide Ball), 41.1. (Fielding the Ball) and for Boundary allowances under Law 19 (Boundaries).

7. BATSMAN RETURNING TO THE WICKET HE HAS LEFT

If, while the ball is in play, the batsmen have crossed in running, neither shall return to the wicket he has left even though a short run has been called or no run has been scored as in the case of a catch. Batsmen, however, shall return to the wickets they originally left in the cases of a boundary and of any disallowance of runs and of an injured batsman, himself, being run out. See Law 2.7 (Transgression of the Laws by an Injured Batsman or Runner).

NOTE

(a) Short Run
A striker taking stance in front of his popping crease may run from that point without penalty.

I n any game of cricket the hitting of the ball by the striker with the bat has always been the major source of making runs. This, plus the taking of wickets by the fielding side, has been, in essence, the game as we have known it for almost 250 years. There are, of course, other methods of adding to the score but these have evolved through the framing and implementation of other Laws over the years. It may not be generally known that at one time any run credited to the batting side had to be achieved by the striker and his partner covering the 22 yards (minus 8 feet). There was no such thing as a boundary and so the reasons for framing Law 20 (Lost Ball) become clearer.

In his interesting and intriguing book, *Next Man In*, Gerald Brodribb recalls some of the unusual incidents which occurred before 1884 (where we find the first reference to boundaries) under Law 18. He mentions a number of sources of six runs from one stroke without any of the runs resulting from overthrows and he even finds a couple of sevens. One of these occurred on the wide open spaces of The Oval and one was off the last ball of a match, which I imagine was a capitulation. Personally, I have experienced only a five. But it is really not surprising, in these days when playing areas are, in general, not as large as those of a century or more ago, while fielding standards have improved out of all recognition over the past 50 years, that high-scoring shots have diminished in number.

Gerald Brodribb also mentions the high proportion of boundary strokes in individual innings, and while I have not researched my own records in such great depth I have one game in which I officiated which is perhaps worthy of inclusion in *The Guinness Book of Records*. During the 1991 Scarborough Festival I "stood" in the game between West Indies and the Rest of the World in which 1,415 runs were scored, including 26 sixes, 2 fives and 187 fours. That comes to a total of 914 or 64.59 per cent of the aggregate. I am not sure whether that was a record but there was most certainly some spectacular hitting and my arms were rather tired at the end of it all!

As we have seen, the crediting of four runs for a boundary has been in operation for well over 100 years but the award of six runs, for strikes pitching *over* the boundary line, only came into existence in 1910. I would suggest that the boundary award originally evolved from the fact that in the early days of cricket, only four runs were awarded for a "lost ball" (Law 20). And before 1910, a ball had to be hit completely out of the ground for a six to be awarded. When the ball was hit into a hedgerow bordering the ground, or into undergrowth, or long grass, or perhaps a copse, a frantic search ensued so a boundary line was agreed and any stroke passing beyond it was credited with four runs. Six, for a ball pitching over this boundary line, followed in 1910 so it is interesting to speculate how many more runs W. G. Grace would have amassed if it had applied in his day. He had to hit the ball right out of The Oval, or Lord's, to be credited with six.

Before moving on to some of the bigger hits I have seen, it is as well to bear in mind that a striker may *not* be awarded a six for clearing the boundary at some smaller grounds. Cricket is played on some tiny enclosures and ground regulations may state that a smaller number of runs is credited (than six) for clearing the boundary. The reason for this may be to discourage those who hit the ball a long way and perhaps cause damage to property.

Having said that, I have seen some tremendous blows struck by batsmen, at least two of which linger in the memory. In 1977 (during the match in which John Edrich completed his hundred hundreds) at The Oval, Ashley Harvey-Walker, of Derbyshire, scored 0 not out in the first innings and 101 not out in the second. One shot of his landed high in the very top deck of the pavilion and whilst I know there has been a hit which *cleared* the pavilion, I am sure he will remember his shot long after the not-out century has faded from his mind.

It was in 1975, though, that I witnessed probably the longest hit square with the wicket I have ever seen with a cricket bat. Again it was at The Oval and the batsman was Clive Lloyd – who else? And it came off one of the best bowlers and real professionals I have had the pleasure of knowing in my career – Robin Jackman. Picture the scene: the bowling from the pavilion end, the pitch well over to the gas-holder side of the square, the batsman a left-hander. I was standing at square-leg and Robin bowled a ball which was a trifle full-of-length and, I imagine, round about the line of the leg stump. Clive just swung into his stroke and the ball passed slightly to my right. I turned to watch it soaring away; was it going to be four or six? Then I noticed a spectator (who turned out to be one of the ground staff) stand up in the top row of seats on the "popular" side of the ground. I remember thinking, "He's going to catch it", but his gaze was still directed upwards. Then he turned, obviously still following the flight of the ball. It had certainly crossed the boundary line!

It was obviously a talking-point when the day's play was over but I was not thinking about it when I arrived at the Oval at 9 o'clock the following morning. I was met by Warren Silletoe, the Surrey CCC Secretary, the member of the ground staff I thought had intended to catch the ball, and three other gentlemen. Mr Silletoe asked if I would accompany them on to the ground because they wanted to measure the distance of Clive's hit. Once more I stood at square-leg as they ran a tape from the centre of the batting crease, past my right leg and out to the boundary line. The measuring then continued up to the wall which encircles the playing area, through the seating area to the outside wall with the "spectator" directing us, after which we went outside the ground and carried on in a direct line. On a low wall beyond the opposite pavement we found the mark of a cricket ball. It had carried 146 yards 8 inches. I don't know if it constituted a record but it is a hell of a long way to hit a cricket ball.

I have seen Ian Botham clear the river at Taunton with the ball finishing in a timber yard; Graham Stevenson put the ball over the stand and on to the rugby field at Headingley; and "Bundu" Waller send it over a 20-foot high wall which is 20 yards beyond the boundary line at Bulawayo, in Zimbabwe. One hit which I did *not* see but which is well documented was Cec Pepper's six into Trafalgar Square at Scarborough. I have, however, had the pleasure of officiating with Cec on that very same ground during his umpiring career (1964-79) and he was never – shall we say? – reluctant to recall the occasion. Those who did not see it (though thousands did) can scarcely credit the size of the hit; those who have visited the ground have difficulty in believing the story. It was not just the distance the ball covered, but the height to which the ball soared to clear the multi-storeyed boarding houses on the north side of the Square as well, which makes one gasp. And this from a man not considered good enough to play for Australia although (forgetting his big hitting) he was a leg-break and googly bowler of awesome ability. Like most Aussies he was a bit brash and his sometimes caustic comments as an umpire irritated and offended some players. One of his proud boasts was that "he had taken Bradman's wicket so many times that he had lost count". And if it was not entirely true, nor was it *merely* a boast.

How else can runs be scored? Overthrows, or "buzzers" as they are sometimes known (discussed under Law 19), and boundary overthrows will always cause a bit of excitement, laced with humour. During one of my trips to Zimbabwe a four was credited to a striker from one hit but all of them came from four separate overthrows. I have also seen an "eight" from an all-run four followed by a fielder's indiscretion propelling the ball over the boundary line for four overthrows.

There are, of course, other ways in which runs may be scored as in the award of a penalty. No ball and wide ball bring one-run penalties unless further runs are scored by other means (Laws 24 and 25). Illegal fielding of the ball (Law 41) incurs a five-run penalty plus any runs which have already been credited and "lost ball" (Law 20) will bring an immediate addition of six runs to the total. If more than six have been run before the call, then that number will be credited to the score but *not in addition* to the six. In the case of a fielder deliberately kicking a ball over the boundary, the boundary allowance will be credited plus any runs which have been completed, or which the batsmen have crossed upon, as the kick took place. In the two latter instances, I have never figured as a player or umpire but in the others, I have. In fact I can recall four instances of illegal fielding in which I have been involved. One has been discussed under Law 41 in some detail and in two others which I have mentioned it was a straightforward penalty of five runs because no runs were being attempted at the time. It is just a little unusual that although an odd number of runs goes on to the score, the batsmen remain at the same ends. In just one instance of awarding a five-run penalty the circumstances were rather unsavoury. I shall not refer to them in further detail. I owe too much to the game to want to write of cricket, or of individuals who play, in a derogatory fashion.

There are times when a run will *not* be credited. One is when a striker is caught, even though the catch was effected after the completion of the run. If either batsman is run out (Law 38) the run which was not completed will not be scored but all others completed before the dismissal will count if completed in a correct manner. In the case of obstructing the field (Law 37), runs completed before the obstruction occurred will count, except when the obstruction prevents a catch being taken. In that case, none will count.

I figured in one such instance as a player, on a club ground on the outskirts of Hull. While I was fielding at deep point, a ball was going just wide of my left hand, but I got across and stopped it. The non-striker decided to "take me on" and went for a second run. My throw was on its way and he looked like being *out* by several yards but as the ball was about to pass him he swung his bat and whacked the ball away, passing safely for the second run. As it was a club match, words were exchanged but no appeal was made. Had one *been* made, the non-striker would have been *out* under Law 37 and if I had been the umpire I would have allowed only one run. While the batsmen had certainly crossed for the second run, the obstruction had occurred before it was completed. There is no way I would have allowed the second run. A moot point, perhaps, but wait . . .

"Batsmen shall be returned to the wicket which they have originally left in the case of a boundary-hit being scored, an injured batsman using a runner himself being run out, and also for any *disallowance of runs*." Under this latter part of Law 18 I would allow one run, disallow the second one, return the striker to the non-striker's end and send the non-striker to the pavilion.

If a batsman, in haste or perhaps carelessness, fails to ground the bat while it is held in the hand behind the line of the batting crease, or if during the process of making a run he drops his bat and then fails to ground some part of his person beyond the batting crease before starting on another run, it is known as a "short run". When the ball is "dead" a signal is made to the scorers and at the same time the umpire will verbally tell the scorers how many runs are to be deducted.

In one match I was umpiring at Lord's the batsmen embarked upon two runs. The striker, returning to my end, failed to make it and on the appeal from the fielding side I gave him *out*. This was immediately followed by my colleague's calling and signalling "one short". What a waste of effort, I thought – a sprint of just short of 39 yards and the result of it was one batsman given out and no run to count!

At Bradford an incident occurred which was a bit unusual. In fact I don't think it was noticed by anyone but my colleague – certainly I didn't notice it – and it was not until we were discussing the day's events, later, over a beer, that he said, "I made a mistake over that run out today but I was concentrating on the decision and forgot the other bit." The "other bit" was a short run. The batsmen had taken one run (or so it seemed to everyone on the ground) and turned back for a second. The batsman then at my colleague's end had been sent back, failed to make his ground and been given out. But what no one else had noticed was that before turning he had failed to ground his bat behind the batting crease. My colleague, recalling the incident a few hours later, confessed that he should have given the man *out*, then called and signalled to the scorers, "one run short" – unusual!

One other case is worth recalling. It happened during a Notts Second XI match at Retford, and Derek Randall was the non-striker. His partner hit the ball to deep mid-off and the pair of them took a gentle single at barely walking pace. As Derek approached the wicket-keeper's end he spotted a piece of loose earth on the pitch and after checking with a glance over his shoulder that no one was trying to run him out he stopped, picked it up and threw it away. Meanwhile the ball had been returned to the bowler. Derek then took stance about 12 inches in front of the batting crease to receive the next ball, steered it down to third man and took a single.

At no time from the moment he had started to run a single from the previous ball to the time he completed a run from the next one had he made good his ground at the wicket-keeper's end. All this was observed by yours truly from the square-leg umpire's position but I did not call "one short". Why? Because it is the batsman's failure to make good his ground before turning for a second run which governs whether a "one short" decision is made. But it's an interesting point.

There is just one other reason for not allowing runs, even if some have been legitimately scored, and that is when the umpire is certain a batsman has deliberately run short. In 1975 at Tunbridge Wells I had to take action. Before naming the players concerned let me make it clear that I have always regarded both as friends of mine and they have always shown respect for the umpire's role.

Kent were playing Leicestershire, who were going hard for the county championship. Kent, too, were well placed (in fact they finished in fifth position) so it was always going to be an exciting contest. Kent were batting fourth when Mike Denness came in to join Asif Iqbal with things going reasonably well for them. Mike nudged a ball down to third man and Asif from my end set off like Linford Christie from his starting-blocks, then flew back. As he approached the crease I had taken up a position square-on and looking straight down the batting crease. It seemed to me that Asif sent a quick glance in my direction, as if to say, "Are you watching?" before he grounded his bat, turned and set off for the third run. He must have been about three yards short when he looked at me and was certainly still short when he grounded his bat before embarking on a third. As soon as he set off I knew what action I was going to take when the ball was dead . . .

I walked over to my colleague and asked, "Were the runs all right at your end?" He said, "Yes", and I then told him I would disallow all three because in my opinion Asif had deliberately run short. I turned to the scorers and called, "No runs to be scored." With that, the occupants of the Press Box, situated above the scorers' position, almost fell out of it! Asif tried to insist that he had not run short but his captain told him to get on with his batting.

At close of play I asked both captains if they would come to the umpires' room and as Mike Denness and Ray Illingworth came in I placed the Law book on the table and said, "Law 19, Note 3, part 3. Please, will you read it?" They did so. Ray nodded; Mike commented, "No more needs to be said." This was the 1947 Code of Laws, bear in mind.

Now to be totally, cast-iron certain of my ground, and because Asif's bat had left a mark on the well-grassed square (beside the pitch on which the game was being played), I measured the distance from that mark to the batting crease. It was 6 feet, one inch short. By that fact alone I was quite justified in my decision. There was the usual media attention but neither my colleague nor I wanted to be accosted straight after the day's play. One reporter, however, waited and then approached us in the correct manner. He got the interview and the explanation and produced the most accurate report of the incident. He was Dudley Moore, now of *Kent Sport*, previously known as *Medway Press*.

There was a sequel to this three years later when I was umpiring at Leicester. At the end of a lunch interval Ray Illingworth leaned over my shoulder as he was about to pass and asked, "Do you remember Tunbridge Wells?" Rather fervently I replied, "For ever."

"Well," said Ray, "I thought you might like to know this. I was talking to Alan Knott during the winter and that topic came up. Alan said Asif had told him he *had* deliberately run short. He was trying to get as much of the strike as possible as Mike had just come to the wicket. Asif also said something else: he didn't think any umpire was brave enough to take the action you did."

My final judgement on it all is this: I felt it was professionalism taken to the extreme – by all the parties concerned.

LAW

19

BOUNDARIES

1. THE BOUNDARY OF THE PLAYING AREA

Before the toss for innings, the umpires shall agree with both captains on the boundary of the playing area. The boundary shall, if possible, be marked with a white line, a rope laid on the ground, or a fence. If flags or posts only are used to mark a boundary, the imaginary line joining such points shall be regarded as the boundary. An obstacle, or person, within the playing area shall not be regarded as a boundary unless so decided by the umpires before the toss for innings. Sightscreens within, or partially within, the playing area shall be regarded as the boundary and when the ball strikes or passes within, or under, or directly over any part of the screen, a boundary shall be scored.

2. RUNS SCORED FOR BOUNDARIES

Before the toss for innings, the umpires shall agree with both captains the runs to be allowed for boundaries, and in deciding the allowance for them the umpires and captains shall be guided by the prevailing custom of the ground. The allowance for a boundary shall normally be 4 runs, and 6 runs for all hits pitching over and clear of the boundary line or fence, even though the ball has been previously touched by a fieldsman. Six runs shall also be scored if a fieldsman, after catching the ball, carries it over the boundary. See Law 32 (Caught), Note (a). Six runs shall not be scored when a ball struck by the striker hits the sightscreen full pitch if the screen is within, or partially within, the playing area, but if the ball is struck directly over a sightscreen so situated, 6 runs shall be scored.

3. BOUNDARY

A boundary shall be scored and signalled by the umpire at the bowler's end whenever, in his opinion:

(a) A ball in play touches or crosses the boundary, however marked.

(b) A fieldsman with ball in hand touches or grounds any part of his person on or over a boundary line.

(c) A fieldsman with ball in hand grounds any part of his person over a boundary fence or board. This allows the fieldsman to touch or lean on or over a boundary fence or board in preventing a boundary.

4. RUNS EXCEEDING BOUNDARY ALLOWANCE

The runs completed at the instant the ball reaches the boundary shall count if they exceed the boundary allowance.

5. OVERTHROWS OR WILFUL ACT OF A FIELDSMAN

If the boundary results from an overthrow or from the wilful act of a fieldsman, any runs already completed and the allowance shall be added to the score. The run in progress shall count provided that the batsmen have crossed at the instant of the throw or act.

NOTES

(a) Position of Sightscreen

Sightscreens should, if possible, be positioned wholly outside the playing area, as near as possible to the boundary line.

T his Law is one of a number which I shall deal with in two parts to give a clearer understanding of the points raised. There are two distinct types of boundary demarcation: (1) white line on grass, rope or edge of grass (i.e. a boundary when the ball runs off the grass on to concrete, tarmac, or into a gulley); (2) boundary boards. The allowance in one case or the other can be quite different and – believe it or not – on one county ground they have *all five* of the different boundary markings applying in the same match! That's not too easy for the umpire.

Let's deal first with all the situations except when boundary boards mark the playing area. The marking which prevails on most cricket grounds around the world is a white line painted on the grass but this has been outlawed for many years in TCCB-organised matches. All umpires realise how difficult it is to see from 70 or 80 yards' range when a ball has reached, or just failed to reach, a thin white line on the grass, especially on grounds which are not absolutely flat and there are ridges and hollows. In 1981 the TCCB insisted that a rope should mark the boundary and not a painted white line and this is a great help. I am also delighted to see that on the better standard of club grounds they try to apply this type of boundary marking. The big advantage of the rope is that when the ball reaches the boundary it skips into the air. And with a rope it is easier to see when the ball pitches directly over it, or just short. Conversely, if a gulley marks the boundary line, the ball disappears off the grass.

Forgetting, for a moment, any unusual customs on individual grounds, any ball reaching line, rope or gulley will be signalled a boundary four. If it pitches directly on to a line or rope it is still only four runs, but if the ball lands directly in a gulley then it is six because, of course, it has *cleared* the boundary line before pitching. I have often umpired on grounds where

95

football is played in winter, and when the summer game comes along the groundsman nips round the field marking the boundary line with the machine he uses in winter to mark out the football field. The lines have thus been five inches wide, giving the summer batsman another five inches to clear before he can claim a six!

A fielder with the ball in contact with any part of his person must not have any other part of his person touching or grounded on or over a designated boundary line, otherwise a four is signalled. I know that in several parts of Law 19 it states "with ball in hand", and I know a number of umpires who feel this should be applied literally. But it is wrong, for instance, for a fieldsman to be allowed to "save" a four while sprawling with most of his person over the boundary line and stopping the ball with, say, a foot which has somehow been left in the field of play. That is why I was pleased to be instrumental in a clarification of this part of Law 19 which, from the beginning of the 1992 season, deleted the words "with ball in hand". If, of course, the fielder in the course of taking a catch, or attempting to take a catch, comes into contact with the boundary line whilst he is at that time in contact with the ball, then the boundary allowance will be six runs.

Boundary ropes come in all shapes and sizes. I have seen them as thick as hawsers for mooring the *Queen Mary* to as thin as a piece of twine. This was really of no use at all but I suppose it *could* have been worse – it could have been green twine! I have seen continuous runs of parachute-cord as a boundary rope, and this was not uncommon in my own county years ago when Lincolnshire had rather a lot of airfields. And I have also seen an electric cable used as a boundary mark – with a modest current running through it at night to discourage the beasts of the field from crossing and fouling the playing area. It is said that one day,when the home side were asked to field first, their opening bowler was late in arriving. Unfortunately, he was also the groundsman and therefore the man who switched off the current. As they took the field, the sparks were literally seen to fly when the players, with metal studs, stepped on to the boundary line. The punsters might have been tempted to describe the fielding as "electrifying".

Of the more unusual types of boundary marker I have seen around the world, two in Zimbabwe come to mind. At Mutare the outer edges of the playing area are indicated by tree trunks, split lengthways, and placed end-to-end around the ground. A ball rolling against the logs comes to an abrupt halt – a bonus for out-fieldsmen – and if a big hit lands directly on to a log the sound indicates clearly to the umpire that he should signal a four and not a six.

The lovely ground at Harare South is unusual in a number of ways. In fact I use a photographic slide of it to illustrate my lectures. The ground is ringed by a white picket fence, but 5 or 10 yards inside the fence is a ring of white-painted stones to indicate the boundary line. They are sizable stones, each about as big as a bucket, and they stand at about 15-yard intervals in a rough circle. Unfortunately they are not linked up except by an *imaginary* line and it makes it a bit difficult for a fieldsman, making a desperate, boundary-saving effort, to say whether the ball has crossed the "line" or not. On the same ground are some huge trees with branches which reach over parts of the field of play. These are also shown on my slide, which is very useful as an educational aid. Each time I show it I am prompted to advise aspiring umpires to do something I have undertaken all through my career – to "walk the ground", to observe all the potentially difficult areas. It's also as well to remember what I have mentioned under Law 20 (Lost Ball).

Possibly the worst thing one finds on walking the ground, especially on some small grounds, is that the sightscreens are inside the field of play and cannot be moved to a position outside the boundary. Any screen which is on, or partly within the field of play will be considered a boundary if it is hit by the ball – either running over the ground or on the full – and the allowance will be four runs. If a ball is hit over the top of a sightscreen placed within the marked boundary it is immediately signalled as a six. It therefore follows that the striker cannot be caught out in this area of the ground behind the screen because the ball has already passed the boundary. There are many other unusual situations which can occur involving catches close to a sightscreen, and I advise all umpires to make a close study of this part of Law 19.

There can be other obstacles within the field of play apart from sightscreens, some of which are permanent fixtures, such as the famous tree on the Canterbury ground and the tree I mention in discussing Law 20. An umpire must, before the start of a game, ascertain what ground customs apply in such cases. If the tree at Canterbury is hit by the ball it carries an allowance of four runs – much to the disgust of Keith Miller, the great Australian all-rounder. In one game he played there the tree was just inside the boundary line and several of his big hits just clipped the topmost branches. Thus he was credited with four for each of them, even though the ball landed 40 yards beyond the boundary line!

There is a tree (mentioned in discussing Law 20) on a London club ground which is not, by ground custom, regarded as a boundary – this makes life interesting for umpires. I have seen such things as broken-down rollers within the playing area, huge trees felled by a gale and even a jet fighter plane which had slid off the end of a runway! It is usual to agree with the captains that such objects should be regarded as a boundary four if the ball makes contact with any part of the obstruction, even when hit on the full. And, of course, if it is a boundary, then no catch is valid if the ball is afterwards held by a fielder.

There are other obstacles of a temporary nature which come on to the playing area from time to time, such as stray dogs. Spectators have been known to amble across part of the playing area and indeed to run on to it before the end of a game. A ball which is obstructed by any such "foreign body" temporarily within the field of play should be agreed by the umpires as an award of four runs boundary allowance. In 1989 the TCCB instructed all their umpires that if a spectator ran on to the field and "took charge" of the ball in any way which influenced the result of the match, the umpires, acting together, should make such allowance of runs as they deemed would have been scored if no interference had taken place. This is the sort of thing which we expect to happen only in the final stages of an important and very close match. Some may think that four runs are awarded automatically but if a fielder was about to retrieve the ball when the intervention occurred and only two runs had seemed likely, the umpires could rule in favour of two runs. It has not yet happened in controversial circumstances and I hope it never will. It would be a very difficult position for the umpires.

In New Zealand, at the Hagley Oval, Christchurch, they have grounds with overlapping boundaries and an umpire at square-leg in one game can find himself inside the boundary of another match! It is unusual, but not unduly disconcerting because a fielder chasing the ball from the neighbouring match usually gives a shout of warning! I know it causes some confusion among players not used to this situation, but I find myself taking the view that to see about eight games taking place in an area which in England might accommodate two matches is a sight worth seeing.

Boundaries which result from an overthrow by a member of the fielding side should be signalled to the scorers, and the umpire should make a point of confirming to them the *total* runs scored if others have been run by the batsmen. In the case of extras, they will be credited to the side but not to the striker. The criterion used to decide the total runs from an overthrow is: where are the two batsmen at the moment the ball leaves the fielder's hand? If they have crossed, then that run will count: one, plus four overthrows = five. If they have not crossed at all, then only the four will be credited. If, of course, they have completed one or more runs and have embarked on a further one when the overthrow takes place, then the total will be completed runs plus another if the running batsmen have crossed when the throw is made +4. The ends occupied by batsmen for the next delivery will be governed by their position when the overthrow was made. They will stay at the wicket to which they were closest when the throw was made, whether they had crossed or not. Umpires, therefore, must be careful to note exactly where the batsmen were when the throw was made.

Now we turn to the second part of the boundary allowance awarded under Law 19 – boundary boards. This is a reasonably rare situation and it usually occurs on some of the Festival grounds, parks and some of the smaller grounds where Sunday League cricket is played. One or two which spring readily to mind are Cheltenham College, Queen's Park at Chesterfield, Colchester and Heanor. I have not personally seen any *club* ground with boundary boards but I have seen short lengths of wood, 4 to 6 inches high, each about 6 feet long, placed at intervals to mark the boundary line. The ball must clear these for an allowance of six to be scored. If it strikes the boards by running over the grass, or on the full, it will still count only as four.

The significant difference between a boundary board and a rope (or line or gulley) lies in the fielding or catching of the ball. A fielder can crash into, lean against or slide into a board whilst in contact with the ball, either to effect a catch or field the ball, and no boundary will be scored. He is not able to do this if the boundary is a rope, line, edge-of-grass or gulley. He must not touch any of these, otherwise a boundary will be scored.

At Cheltenham a Middlesex fielder caught a big hit, then crashed against the boundary boards, slid down and finished up sitting on the grass ... but holding the catch. I signalled to the striker that he was out – and some of the crowd began to boo the player who had taken the catch! I hope they read this book. At Chesterfield, from the final ball of an over, a batsman hit the ball high to mid-wicket where it landed full pitch on the boundary board. I signalled four to the scorers, called "Over", and walked to my position at square-leg. I then saw a man in the crowd close to where the ball had landed, jumping up and down with arms held high to indicate a six. I hope *he* reads the book, too.

At Colchester in 1992 I had an unusual situation with regard to boundary boards. John Childs of Essex chased a ball, stopped it by hand then slid his feet into the boards. The ball could clearly be seen in his hand and had never been within 6 feet of the board. As John got to his knees he indicated a boundary four, but no way was I going to give the same signal to the scorers. The two batsmen had stopped in mid-pitch, so I turned and stated to them, "I am not awarding four." At first I do not think they believed me, but as the ball was returned to the middle someone shouted "Run him out!" and they fled to their ends. I did advise them that it is the umpires who will make the appropriate signals to the scorers – nobody else. Some time later, John, quite crestfallen, apologised to me and said, "I should have known it was not a boundary. I played at Cheltenham long enough, another ground with boundary boards."

One little story against myself: it happened at Lord's in a Sunday League match. Five or six MCC Young Cricketers are used as ball-boys in matches there, sitting at intervals around the boundary. I was standing at the pavilion end when the striker glanced a ball to fine leg, and I saw the young ball-boy get off his seat and station himself at the point where the ball would cross the rope at the Nursery end. He bent down with his hands cupped to receive the ball and then he stood up as if he had fielded the ball. I turned and signalled "four" but, fractionally too late, I noticed that the fielder who had been chasing the ball was now lengthening his stride. He had seen what I had not; that the ball had come to rest just short of the line. That was why the ground staff "fielder" had stood up. Meanwhile the batsmen, seeing my signal, had stopped in the middle of the pitch for a chat. There was nothing I could do (apart from feeling a fool) but allow the boundary to stand and apologise to the fielding captain. I like to think Mike Brearley understood my predicament and appreciated my confession that the mistake was entirely mine.

And one final thought on overthrows. At Headingley in 1976 (England v. West Indies) Alan Knott was credited with a *seven* in the course of scoring 116, for a single, two overthrows and four overthrows.

LAW

20

LOST BALL

I. RUNS SCORED

If a ball in play cannot be found or recovered, any fieldsman may call "lost ball", when six runs shall be added to the score; but if more than six have been run before "lost ball" is called, as many runs as have been completed shall be scored. The run in progress shall count provided that the batsmen have crossed at the instant of the call of "lost ball".

2. HOW SCORED

The runs shall be added to the score of the striker if the ball has been struck, but otherwise to the score of byes, leg-byes, no-balls or wides as the case may be.

W hilst I shall only make brief reference to points of law in writing about Law 20 (Lost Ball), it is only because of the fact that this Law is almost extinct in these days, because playing areas have undergone such a dramatic improvement over the past 50 years, even at minor club level. The writing and use of Law 20 (Lost Ball), as we know, dates back to days when games of cricket were played upon any field. If it had been grazed by sheep things were not too bad, apart from what the creatures left behind; but if the game, as I remember playing it, took place in a field of uncut meadow grass, then many times we were searching for the ball whilst the batsmen ran numerous times between the wickets. No one had ever heard of the call of "Lost Ball" or indeed the Law itself.

In more than 25 years as an umpire I have never figured in a match in which either I or my colleague has heard a call of "lost ball". I expect there are others, more senior than me, who have never received such a call and I have never met an umpire who has. However, I have seen situations, both as an umpire and as a spectator, when such a call *could* have applied once, in fact, I was waiting for it. In the main, what follow are incidents in my career in relation to this Law.

There are parts of the Law which must necessarily be fully understood by umpires, nevertheless. The first of these is that the lost ball must be inside the field of play before six runs can be added. In the slightly more unlikely event of the ball being "unable to be recovered", this too, must be a situation inside the field of play.

If more than six have already been run when "lost ball" is called, those runs will be credited to the batting side's total, though not "plus six". If fewer than six have been run, then the total added when the call is made will still be six. Remember, too, that if the batsmen have run, say, seven and have crossed on the eighth, that last run will count as well – eight in all. In a worthy book on the Laws of Cricket which is widely read, fieldsmen are advised not to make such a call until the batsmen have crossed on their sixth run. I would go just a little further (if only to give the fielders a chance to find the ball and perhaps effect a run-out) and advise waiting until just before the batsmen cross for the seventh time. Even if six runs have already been scored it is surely worth giving your side the satisfaction of a chance of dismissal. The fielder may think not even then, if he is in the act of retrieving the ball and feels that he can effect a "run out" during that seventh run. If he achieves this then only six will be scored – and I think that some of the allowance may be felt to have been retrieved, if it means a wicket has fallen.

How then are the runs registered in the scorebook? As the Law says, they go to the striker if the ball has been hit; otherwise, as byes, leg-byes, no balls or wides as the case may be. I must also point out that the moment "lost ball" is called, the ball (wherever it is!) becomes "dead" as far as wicket-taking or run-scoring is concerned.

In 1971 I was umpiring in a Lincolnshire League match on the sports ground of a local firm. It had a nice playing area, a good square and reasonably well-prepared pitches. But like most sports grounds of its type it was also used for winter games, in this case association football. The posts and crossbar had been removed for the summer months but the base where the uprights had stood – let's call it a "sleeve" for want of a better word – was still in place. It is usual to cover the opening of this "sleeve" with a lid, perhaps a bit of plywood nailed into place, but in this case it had not been done.

The boundary line for the cricket match ran between where the posts stood for football so that one "sleeve" was 10 feet or so inside the field of play – and uncapped. I was standing in the square-leg position when the ball was struck over wide long-on, and rolled towards the boundary. And disappeared! The mid-on fielder, who had chased the ball, was then seen on his hands and knees and my colleague, at the bowler's end, assumed he had slipped in his pursuit, so he signalled "four" to the scorers. In his position I would probably have done the same.

Laughter from the spectators, however, quickly indicated that this was no straightforward matter of a four being scored. But the ball was left in the sleeve while the game continued, four having been added to the total, and as far as I know the ball remained in the sleeve until the soccer season came around. It is advisable for umpires, before a game on some grounds, to walk the boundary taking note of the position of overhanging branches of trees, with a special look at areas where football is played in winter! I was horrified to find in Sri Lanka, during an umpiring and lecturing tour in 1991, that a set of rugby posts appeared overnight at one end of the ground where I was actually officiating. Up to that point I didn't even know that rugby was played in Sri Lanka. A check of the other end of the rugby pitch (which was within part of the playing area currently in use) revealed that sacking had been rolled up and slotted into the base for the rugby posts. I never did ask if the same practice had been used at the other end where the posts were already in position but that evening I admonished myself in front of about 20 umpires and lectured on the pitfalls of such a situation.

One of my most unusual experiences occurred during one of my trips to Zimbabwe and I was coaching at a school well "up country" where the pupils were all members of the indigenous population. The playing fields ran down to the bank of a river which was heavily infested with crocodiles and I noticed three or four huge reptiles sunning themselves on the bank. "What happens," I asked one of the masters, "if the ball is hit close to one of the crocs?" "Not much," was the laconic reply. "The boys will throw stones at them and that quickly sends them back into the water. Cricket balls are not easy to get up here so we can't afford to lose one."

In my 1980 tour of New Zealand I did hear one amazing story of a call of "lost ball". I can't vouch personally for the truth of it but I was assured in Christchurch that it had actually happened. We were discussing the highest number of runs any of us had seen from one hit (without overthrows) and I said I had known nine scored – and in a county match, too. "Ah," said one of the group, "but we had a ten here in Hagley Park. We are not saying it was correctly scored but it was certainly what the umpire ordered."

In the match when this call was made, an inexperienced umpire was "standing" and it was in the season prior to my visit. I admit that I have never seen for myself such an incorrect interpretation of the Law and I know that there are many good umpires in New Zealand, particularly in Christchurch, who have a thorough knowledge of the Laws. I was assured that this story was true but I often wonder if someone was just trying to go one better.

Hagley Park is a lovely spot in a lovely city and has one of those wide open spaces where several club matches are played simultaneously. They occur all over Britain, of course – Knavesmire, in York, and The Forest, in Nottingham, are two which spring quickly to mind, and obviously the London parks. The perimeter of Hagley Park is a walkway three or four yards wide and forms the boundary for some of the matches. Beyond the walkway is a thick undergrowth of plants, trees and shrubs and it was into this that a ball ran after a batsman hit it. The fielder who chased the ball came back fairly quickly to announce that the ball was lost, whereupon the umpire awarded ten runs – four for the boundary and six for the lost ball! Remember, for an award under Law 20, the ball must be lost within the field of play.

THE RESULT

1. A WIN – TWO-INNINGS MATCHES
The side which has scored a total of runs in excess of that scored by the opposing side in its two completed innings shall be the winner.

2. A WIN – ONE-INNINGS MATCHES
(a) One-innings matches, unless played out as in (1) above, shall be decided on the first innings but see Law 12.5 (Continuation after One Innings of Each Side).
(b) If the captains agree to continue play after the completion of one innings of each side in accordance with Law 12.5 (Continuation after One Innings of Each Side) and a result is not achieved on the second innings, the first innings result shall stand.

3. UMPIRES AWARDING A MATCH
(a) A match shall be lost by a side which, during the match (i) refuses to play or (ii) concedes defeat and the umpires shall award the match to the other side.
(b) Should both batsmen at the wickets or the fielding side leave the field at any time without the agreement of the umpires, this shall constitute a refusal to play and, on appeal, the umpires shall award the match to the other side in accordance with (a) above.

4. A TIE
The result of a match shall be a tie when the scores are equal at the conclusion of play but only if the side batting last has completed its innings.

If the scores of the completed first innings of a one-day match are equal, it shall be a tie but only if the match has not been played out to a further conclusion.

5. A DRAW
A match not determined by any of the ways as in (1), (2), (3), and (4) above shall count as a draw.

6. CORRECTNESS OF RESULT

Any decision as to the correctness of the scores shall be the responsibility of the umpires. See Law 3.14 (Correctness of Score). If, after the umpires and players have left the field in the belief that the match has been concluded, the umpires decide that a mistake in scoring has occurred which affects the result, and provided time has not been reached, they shall order play to resume and to continue to the agreed finishing time unless a result has been reached earlier.

If the umpires decide that a mistake has occurred and time has been reached, the umpires shall immediately inform both captains of the necessary corrections to the scores and, if applicable, to the result.

7. ACCEPTANCE OF RESULT

In accepting the scores as notified by the scorers and agreed by the umpires, the captains of both sides thereby accept the result.

NOTES

(a) Statement of Results

The result of a finished match is stated as a win by runs, except in the case of a win by the side batting last, when it is by the number of wickets still to fall.

(b) Winning Hit or Extras

As soon as a side has won, see (1) and (2) above, the umpire shall call "Time" and the match is finished and nothing that happens thereafter other than as a result of a mistake in scoring (See (6) above) shall be regarded as part of the match.

However, if a boundary constitutes the winning hit – or extras – and the boundary allowance exceeds the number of runs required to win the match, such runs scored shall be credited to the side's total and, in the case of a hit, to the striker's score.

T his Law is one which should have no complications whatsoever in an age when there are many good, competent and enthusiastic scorers at all levels of the game. There should be no repetition of the mild panic which is said to have occurred at Leyton in 1932 when Yorkshire scored 555 for the first wicket with Herbert Sutcliffe getting 313 and Percy Holmes 224 not out. This beat by one run a partnership by another Yorkshire pair, Brown and Tunnicliffe, 34 years earlier and Sutcliffe, anticipating his captain's declaration, then deliberately lost his wicket. There was, consequently, consternation when the scorers, checking their totals, discovered the score was actually 554 and not 555. It was some time later that they realised they had not noted a no ball during the innings!

There were the days when the result of a game of cricket was determined simply by one side scoring a greater number of runs than the other, but today we have several different kinds of match. There are the one-day games with each side having a limited number of overs – and in some instances, one side may have more overs than the other! There are, of course, matches of more than one day with two innings available to each side in which one side may need only one of their innings (Law 13, Follow On). It is, I think, very rare for a one-innings match to be made into a two-innings affair these days and it usually only happens when one of the sides wants to indulge in batting practice.

Law 12.5 states that the captains may agree to continue play if, in their opinion, there is a prospect of carrying the game to a further issue in the time left. Let us say that it is a club friendly fixture with an 11 am start and the side batting first are bowled out for 50 in 70 minutes. The side batting second then score 51 runs for victory in a short time, say 45 minutes, without losing a wicket. It's all over by the lunch interval. But it is now a lovely, warm June afternoon and everybody is geared up to a full day of cricket. What a pity to waste it. It would be sensible, and probably mutually desirable, for the captains to agree to play on in the afternoon. The side batting second could continue their innings and declare at a score of, perhaps, 160 for seven wickets. The side which batted first would take their second innings and they in turn would declare at 200 for nine wickets, a lead of 90. This would mean that the side who batted second would require 91 to win the match; but in their second innings they were all out for 75. In such a case the result would be a win for the side who had batted first on the day, by 15 runs, despite looking to have lost the match after the first innings. If no definite result were achieved, the side batting second would have won the one-innings game by ten wickets. And everyone, it is to be hoped, would have enjoyed a good and full day's cricket.

If one side refuses to play or concedes defeat, and again if the batsmen or the fielding side leave the field of play without the umpires' permission, the game *shall* be awarded to the other side – but only on appeal by that side.

A tie is a rarity in a cricket match, particularly in a two-innings-a-side game. For it to happen, each side must have scored the same aggregate of runs in their two innings and the side batting last must have lost all their wickets, or at least the innings must have been completed. Those last nine words are added in case someone points out that a member of the side batting last might be injured and unable to come to the wicket. But if the *ninth* wicket of the side batting last was to fall on the last ball of the match and an injured player was unable to bat, the result would be a draw. It would not matter whether the injured man was in the dressing-room, on the ground, or in hospital where he was likely to remain for a week or more. The result can be no other than a draw: the injured man has no need to be in attendance on the ground. It is not a tie and certainly not a win for the bowling side.

In TCCB limited-overs competitions which are knock-out affairs (Benson

& Hedges Cup and NatWest Trophy) another factor is taken into consideration in getting a result if the scores are equal at the end of the match. Victory then goes to the side which has lost fewer wickets. In my time I have officiated in several matches which have finished level and thus had to be decided under the wickets-lost regulation. These have included three semi-finals in consecutive years, the most famous of which was at Lord's in 1983. Middlesex scored 222 for nine wickets and were beaten by Somerset who finished with 222 for the loss of eight wickets.

Who else but Ian Botham could have been the Man of the Match in a game like that? The scoreboard read "43–4" when he came in to bat and shortly afterwards it became 52–5 with the departure of Viv Richards. He was caught by Wayne Daniel who, I remember, had almost completed a lap of St John's Wood before his joyful team-mates caught up with him. With 170 still needed and half the side out, Botham was then involved in a partnership of 104 in 30 overs with Nigel Popplewell and 62 in 13 overs with Vic Marks until the end of the 59th over arrived with the scores level and eight Somerset wickets down. As I walked away to square-leg, Ian came after me and asked, "Don, what happens now?" Looking up at the scoreboard, I replied, "You require one run." "No," countered Ian, "what happens if we don't get it?"

I said, "Two hundred and twenty-two for eight beats 222 for nine. But if you or Trevor Gard [Ian's partner] is out, you might well lose. Their score at 30 overs was far better than yours." (This was a reference to a further regulation which decrees that if the scores are level and each side has lost a similar number of wickets, the decision goes to the side scoring most runs after the first 30 overs of the innings.) Ian commented grimly, "I shan't get out and Trevor will not face." And so it proved. Every ball of John Emburey's last over was studiously blocked, with a broad bat and immense concentration.

It is worth bearing in mind that Botham played out that last over without attempting to score a run of any kind when he was on 96. The temptation to complete his hundred and to give Somerset a clear-cut arithmetical win must have been tremendous.

One part of Law 21 with which I am not in full agreement is Section 6, which states that the correctness of the scores shall be the responsibility of the umpires and in a cross-reference to Law 3.14 it lays this responsibility on the umpires not just at the conclusion but *throughout* the match. I can just guess what I would be told if I stopped a match and queried the score – something like, "You get on with your job and leave us to get on with ours", although I am sure it would be more politely phrased. But I wouldn't really blame a scorer who took umbrage. An umpire who tries to score a match as well as adjudicate is a fool. He then could not do either job properly. Umpiring, as I hope we are seeing throughout this book, requires total concentration, and I'm quite sure scorers need to concentrate hard as well. I feel this part of the Law is a bit of an insult to all scorers and I hope in due course to have it changed.

Obviously, if players and umpires leave the field believing a match has been concluded, then they learn that runs are still required to achieve a result, a resumption must be made if time is available. If no time is available, the result must stand and captains be informed, which would be a very sorry state of affairs. I do not see that Law 21.7 (Acceptance of Result) could then really apply, at least to one of the captains. How on earth could he agree that he had lost the match when he had not been at fault in any way?

LAW

22

THE OVER

1. NUMBER OF BALLS
The Ball shall be bowled from each wicket alternately in overs of six or eight balls according to agreement before the match.

2. CALL OF "OVER"
When the agreed number of balls has been bowled and as the ball becomes dead, or when it becomes clear to the umpire at the bowler's end that both the fielding side and the batsmen at the wicket have ceased to regard the ball as in play, the umpire shall call "Over" before leaving the wicket.

3. NO BALL OR WIDE BALL
Neither a no ball or a wide ball shall be reckoned as one of the over.

4. UMPIRE MISCOUNTING
If an umpire miscounts the number of balls, the over as counted by the umpire shall stand.

5. BOWLER CHANGING ENDS
A bowler shall be allowed to change ends as often as desired provided only that he does not bowl two overs consecutively in an innings.

6. THE BOWLER FINISHING AN OVER
A bowler shall finish an over in progress unless he be incapacitated or be suspended under Law 42.8 (The Bowling of Fast Short-pitched Balls), 42.9 (The Bowling of Fast High Full Pitches), 42.10 (Time-wasting) and 42.11 (Players Damaging the Pitch). If an over is left incomplete for any reason at the start of an interval or interruption of play it shall be finished on the resumption of play.

7. BOWLER INCAPACITATED OR SUSPENDED DURING AN OVER
If for any reason a bowler is incapacitated while running up to bowl the first ball of an over or is incapacitated or suspended during an over, the umpire shall call and signal "Dead ball", and another bowler shall be allowed to bowl

or complete the over from the same end, provided only that he shall not bowl two overs, or part thereof, consecutively in one innings.

8. POSITION OF THE NON-STRIKER

The batsman at the bowler's end shall normally stand on the opposite side of the wicket to that from which the ball is being delivered unless a request to do otherwise is granted by the umpire.

I t strikes me that in the very early days of the game bowlers had a pretty easy time of it. The over consisted of only four deliveries and a bowler could only change ends once in an innings. In 1870 the Laws were amended to allow him to change ends twice in an innings, but no more, and he could not, of course, bowl two overs in succession.

In 1889 the number of deliveries which constituted an over was increased to five and a bowler could now change ends as often as his captain desired – again, the bowler could not operate in two consecutive overs. It was not until 1900 that an over was increased to six balls and that is now generally accepted throughout the world. Bowlers of old did not have long approaches to the wicket, nor did they deliver the ball with the great speed of more recent years.

After the bowler has delivered the prescribed number of balls, "Over" is called by the umpire at the bowler's end. This was laid down in the very earliest Code of Laws but for some reason was omitted from the 1774 Code. It was not until 1835 that this instruction returned to the Laws. The omission may simply have been an oversight and probably the umpires carried on calling "Over" after the prescribed number of deliveries. If an umpire today omitted to call "Over" the consequences might well be serious, for it is one of the actions that makes the ball dead.

An increase to eight balls in an over was adopted in Australia in 1922 after trials. New Zealand experimented with the eight-ball over in the 1920s but quickly went back to six balls. South Africa changed to eight balls an over in 1937-38 and an MCC tour of that country in 1938-39 was played under that regulation. It was tried in England in the 1939 season but after the Second World War cricket resumed with an over of six balls. As recently as 1977-78, with England on tour in Pakistan, the eight-ball over was used in Tests, and when Bob Willis, with his 40-yard approach, was no-balled four times in one over it made it a very long one indeed! In some league cricket in this country the eight-ball over is still used for certain limited-over competitions. The Northern League, for instance, has one of 30 eight-ball overs a side, and there is a local knock-out competition of 16 eight-ball overs each side which I have umpired many times.

I think it is pretty well known that a ball which is judged by the umpire to be a wide or a no ball will not count in the over and this can lead to some very long overs indeed. I have "stood" for overs of ten or eleven deliveries and in the 1991 season at Scarborough I stood at square-leg when the bowler delivered 14 balls before my colleague at the other end could call "Over". In fact I rolled up a sweater, used it as a pillow and lay down for a moment though this was, needless to say, in the more relaxed atmosphere of a Festival match rather than a county championship game. At Old Trafford in 1934, Gubby (Sir George) Allen bowled a first over of 13 deliveries when he was "called" for three wides and four no balls, and in 1975 Jeff Thomson, the Australian fast bowler, bowled an over which went on for nearly 18 minutes.

A bowler who starts an over must finish it unless he becomes ill or is injured and incapacitated, and in certain other special circumstances. One of these is if he is suspended for time-wasting, but to the best of my knowledge this has never been invoked. Another is for bowling high full pitches and I don't think this has ever applied either, though it almost did in a match in which I "stood", Northants v. Warwickshire at Northampton in 1990. The bowling of fast, short-pitched deliveries has been penalised a few times but the one transgression of Law 22.6 which has caused an umpire to remove a bowler from the fray many times is for damaging the pitch, which is something we shall discuss more fully under Law 42.

I should at this point confess to a slip on my part, at Cardiff some years ago. The last ball of an over was delivered and I was certain I had seen it smack into the wicket-keeper's gloves so I called "Over" and started to move away. It was then that I heard the non-striker shout "Run" and both batsmen set off. I turned back to see one of the slips chasing in pursuit of the ball some 20 yards behind the wicket-keeper. It had in fact slipped through his hands and I hadn't seen this. All I could do was apologise to all the players, return both batsmen to the wickets from which they had run and make sure that no runs were credited at all. I did not call and signal "Dead ball" because my shout of "Over" – premature as it actually had been – had had the effect of making the ball dead.

Under Law 3 I have listed the many articles which I take out with me to the middle but apart from one's knowledge of the Laws, and the regulations applying to any particular match, the most important item to take is a small notepad and a pen. Not to do so is something I regard as unprofessional. There are many things that have to be noted in the course of a game and one of the most important of these is the time at which a player leaves the field of play (Law 2.8). When overs have to be deducted from the minimum number bowled in a day under the present first-class regulations because of stoppages for rain and/or bad light, the time of leaving the field, and the time at which play is resumed, must be carefully noted. At each interval we must note which batsman will face the first ball to be bowled on the resumption, at which end that batsman will be standing and which of the 11 members of the fielding side will *not* be allowed to bowl that over.

It may be that we all have to dash off in the middle of an over with torrential rain sweeping over the ground, perhaps, and just as the batsmen have completed a single. It will be at your peril that you fail to note this, or how many balls remain to be delivered in the over. Remember, too, that it is not just the umpire at one end who should make these notes; both should do so. At Bristol in 1978 (Gloucestershire v. Worcestershire), my colleague Barrie Meyer was rushed into hospital for an operation during the night after the first day's play. The following morning I had to get play under way at the end from which the bowling would begin, even though I had been standing at the bowling end when the previous day's play ended. I could well have been in some predicament had I not taken notes on the previous evening.

Two consecutive overs standing at the bowling end? Let me explain. When we realised that Barrie would be unable to continue on the second morning the TCCB contacted Dave Halfyard (the former Kent and Notts bowler) who had been appointed to the first-class umpires list the previous year and who was without a fixture on that day. Dave lived in Cornwall, which some people think is just round the corner from Bristol but is, in fact, a long drive away.

On this occasion, it took some time to contact him and he was then asked to get to Bristol "as soon as possible". Meanwhile, the Gloucestershire club had called in a second-team umpire to "stand" with me until Dave arrived. In such a case, the TCCB-appointed official is required to take the bowling end continuously until the other official umpire arrives, and as my colleague did not appear until around 4 pm it made it an awfully long day for me . . . the pressure seems to increase far more than two-fold when, for most of the day, you are standing at the bowling end. Then you really have to know your Law *and* to have your wits about you. Some may think that all of the difficult decisions arise and are judged upon by the umpire at the bowling end: not so. There are many important decisions which must be adjudicated upon by the umpire at the striker's wicket. I perhaps may have had quite a serene morning, only a couple of "No balls", two appeals for lbw, not even close, and a catch which was taken easily by square-leg fielder, but the "substitute" umpire may have had a couple of close "run out" decisions, one out and one not out. Perhaps a great decision for a stumping on a lift of the striker's back foot, short runs upon two occasions and having to call "No ball" because of three fielders behind the line of the batting crease on the leg side. That lot would make any umpire gulp, and I consider that the umpire at the striker's wicket is just as important as the one at the bowling wicket.

There have been a few instances when the correct procedure after an interval has not been applied, and while I have never been directly concerned in any of these I came very close to it on one occasion at The Oval. Close of play on Saturday saw me at the bowling end and after calling "Over" and "Time" I made my notes. Sunday was occupied by a limited-overs match at another venue and when the first-class game resumed on the Monday I positioned myself for the first ball of the day at square-leg. As my colleague called "Play" it suddenly occurred to me that the wrong batsman was facing the bowling. My hand flew to my notebook in the top pocket and just in time I called "Dead ball". The bowler was a few paces from his delivery stride. The batsmen then rather sheepishly changed ends.

Another incident of a most unusual nature occurred in a weekend game at Edgbaston. I am sure the umpires had made their notes, but what happened gave them little time for reflection. Again it was a case of a game resuming on Monday after a one-day match had been played on the Sunday. After the first five balls of the opening over the bowler was injured and, after receiving attention, limped from the field. Bob Willis, captain of Warwickshire, asked, "How many left?" and was told, "One ball." He then stated, "I will bowl it" and duly completed the over. It was not until some time later that it was realised that Bob had bowled the final over on Saturday night from the opposite end around 40 hours earlier – a complete contravention of Law 22.5 had occurred.

Yet another incident involved a match in which Sussex were playing. It was a three-day game, and little play had occurred on the first two days because of rain. In fact the umpires and everyone concerned had been on and off the field innumerable times. The third day's play began, and for some reason which has never been satisfactorily explained the first ball was bowled to the batsman who had received the last one of the previous day, with no run scored from it. There is nothing which can be done in such circumstances – unless it is the umpire reminding himself that failure to note all relevant matters leaves him open to the possibility of making a mistake. I expect that in the last few years of my career some of my friends will try to see that I do so, in the nicest possible way of course, especially after reading this book.

For several years we have heard grumbles about slow over-rates and I agree that if a match is still going on at 8 o'clock at night, with the required minimum of overs to be bowled in the day still to be reached, a certain lack of interest does manifest itself. That certainly applied in the early eighties and since then the TCCB have taken steps to ensure that overs are bowled at a quicker rate. On the other hand, I have looked at my diaries for my first season as a first-class umpire, 1975, and they show that on 18 June, at Edgbaston (Warwickshire v. Yorkshire), 133.2 overs were bowled in the day and a total of 376.4 overs during the three days of that match. At Ilford, 7-10 June (Essex v. Lancashire) 376 overs were bowled and during that season I had 17 days on which more than 120 overs were delivered and that was irrespective of wides or no balls bowled, stoppages for the weather and intervals between innings.

The time it takes to bowl an over is also interesting, and I can claim to have been involved in the setting up of a world record in this respect. It happened at Taunton on 9 September 1983, the last day of a match between Somerset and Kent. Some sort of deal must have been struck by the captains (as an umpire, one doesn't want to know about such things) for in the 30 minutes (4.30–5 pm) no fewer than 33 overs were bowled – less than one minute per over! and the men who achieved it were Chris Cowdrey and Neil Taylor, neither of whom could be described as a "non-bowler".

LAW
23

DEAD BALL

I. THE BALL BECOMES DEAD
When:
(a) It is finally settled in the hands of the wicket-keeper or the bowler.
(b) It reaches or pitches over the boundary.
(c) A batsman is out.
(d) Whether played or not, it lodges in the clothing or equipment of a batsman or the clothing of an umpire.
(e) A ball lodges in a protective helmet worn by a member of the fielding side.
(f) A penalty is awarded under Law 20 (Lost Ball) or Law 41.1 (Fielding the Ball).
(g) The umpire calls "Over" or "Time".

2. EITHER UMPIRE SHALL CALL AND SIGNAL "DEAD BALL"
When:
(a) He intervenes in a case of unfair play.
(b) A serious injury to a player or umpire occurs.
(c) He is satisfied that, for an adequate reason, the striker is not ready to receive the next ball and makes no attempt to play it.
(d) The bowler drops the ball accidentally before delivery or the ball does not leave his hand for any reason, other than in an attempt to run out the non-striker (see Law 24.5 – Bowler Attempting to Run Out Non-Striker Before Delivery).
(e) One or both bails fall from the striker's wicket before he receives the delivery.
(f) He leaves his normal position for consultation.
(g) He is required to do so under Law 26.3 (Disallowance of Leg-byes).

3. THE BALL CEASES TO BE DEAD
When:
(a) The bowler starts his run up or bowling action.

4. THE BALL IS NOT DEAD

When:

(a) It strikes an umpire (unless it lodges in his dress).

(b) The wicket is broken or struck down (unless a batsman is out thereby).

(c) An unsuccessful appeal is made.

(d) The wicket is broken accidentally either by the bowler during his delivery or a batsman in running.

(e) The umpire has called "No-ball" or "Wide".

NOTES

(a) Ball Finally Settled

Whether the ball is finally settled or not – see 1 (a) above – must be a question for the umpires alone to decide.

(b) Action on Call of "Dead Ball"

(i) If "Dead ball" is called prior to the striker receiving a delivery the bowler shall be allowed an additional ball.

(ii) If "Dead ball" is called after the striker receives a delivery the bowler shall not be allowed an additional delivery unless "No ball" or "Wide" has been called.

T his, in my opinion, is the most important of all the 42 Laws of Cricket. Any umpire who has failed to undertake a full study of Law 23 will find himself, at some stage of his career, in all kinds of difficult situations.

When I became a member of the TCCB's first-class panel of umpires in 1975 and saw various instances of strikers interfering with the ball, which had been played and was stationary in front of them, I feared and dreaded an appeal from the fielding side, bearing in mind the provisions of Law 23. Mercifully, the first-class game in England is played to an unwritten code of ethics which is of the very highest standard. No one would dream of appealing against a striker who, having played a ball down on to the pitch and seen it stop, then raked it back with his bat as an aid to the wicket-keeper coming round from behind the stumps to retrieve it. But if anyone did appeal
. . .

The umpire would be in the invidious position of having to consider the appeal for, obviously, "Hit the Ball Twice" (Law 34) and as the ball was not dead he would be obliged to give the striker *out*. I imagine that if a young professional were to make such an ill-advised appeal, it would be withdrawn by his captain and the villain of the piece would have his backside metaphorically kicked around the dressing-room for the remainder of the season.

Once again, this is a Law which I shall deal with in two sections. First, let us look at what we might describe as an "automatic" dead ball situation, when something occurs which has the effect of making the ball dead without a call or signal from the umpire. Secondly comes the situation where the umpire *has* to intervene with a call and signal of "Dead ball" for any number of reasons.

Many times I am asked to explain what exactly is meant by "dead ball", what is meant by the ball being "live" and to clarify the split second at which the ball becomes dead. From the moment a ball becomes dead, no runs can be scored from it and no wickets taken. When the ball is live, runs can be scored and wickets taken. The ball becomes live when the bowler takes the first pace of his approach to the wicket to deliver the ball, or, in the case of a bowler who takes no run at all, from the moment he begins his bowling action. As for the split second when the ball becomes dead, I think it will become clear as we go through all the provisions of Law 23, that the moment is as immediate and instantaneous as someone clapping their hands together. The moment when our notional hand-clap occurs is indicated below by the word in italics.

So (1) the ball made "dead" without call or signal from umpire: while the Law states "when the ball finally settles in the hands of the wicket-keeper", and the operative word there is "finally", I take it a stage further and say "when the wicket-keeper, after taking the ball, *discards* it to another member of his side as long as there is no chance of a dismissal". An umpire should never consider the ball to be finally settled and therefore dead when it is taken by the wicket-keeper either from a delivery by the bowler or a return to him from the field by a member of his side so long as there is a chance of dismissing either batsman. Nor should we consider the ball dead upon being discarded from the wicket-keeper's glove if he has spotted that the non-striker is out of his ground and he throws the ball in an attempt to run out the non-striker.

If the bowler gets back the ball while standing some distance down the pitch and as he starts to walk back to his mark the non-striker decides to move out of his ground to do a bit of "gardening" it is no use removing the bails from his wicket and appealing for run out, because the ball has been made dead once the bowler has taken his *first pace* – even though it has been taken in front of the wicket. He does not have to be behind the wicket for it to count as a pace back to his mark.

(2) The ball also becomes dead when it becomes *lodged* in the dress or equipment of either batsman or either umpire. Many people think the only position of *lodgement* is behind the flap of the striker's pad. Not so. It can become *lodged*, for example, between the striker's arm and body, under the armpit, between the thighs or even a bit higher, in the nastiest of all places. I have even seen the ball *lodged* between both pads of the striker, about shin-high, and in all cases the ball is dead. It would be unusual if the ball hit the non-striker and *lodged* in any of those positions I have quoted as examples but if it did, again the ball would be dead. I have seen a ball *lodge* in a striker's

protective helmet, in which case it is dead, and I have actually seen a ball hit by the striker which bounced off the helmet of the non-striker! If it had *lodged*, instead of bouncing away, it would have been dead. It does not matter if the ball *lodges* only temporarily – it is still dead. At the same time, umpires must be careful in deciding what is a temporary *lodgement*. It must be clear to the umpire that the ball has become stationary and is not merely running slowly down body or equipment. Also the "clamping" of the ball by two or more parts of the body must have been the result of a reflex action, or an appeal under Law 37 (Obstructing the Field) could be sustained. If the ball has made contact with the bat before becoming *lodged* and is then extracted by a fieldsman, no catch will be valid, for the *lodgement* has made the ball dead.

(3) The ball is dead as soon as the call of "Over" or "Time" has been made. In the 1947 Code of Laws the bails also had to be removed from both wickets after the call of "Time". If they were not, a batsman could, in theory at any rate, find he had been given *out* while eating his lunch! That is no longer applicable.

Whilst a *call* of "Over" makes the ball dead, any attempt to effect a dismissal after that *call* will not be allowed. But anything that has happened *before* the *call* to effect a dismissal may be allowed. For instance, a bowler delivers the final ball of an over and the *call* is made by the umpire who then walks off towards square-leg: he is joined by the bowler who says, "I think the striker hit that last ball I bowled and the wicket-keeper caught it. How's that?" If the umpire is of the same opinion he is within his right to give the batsman *out*. Indeed, he must do so, provided the bowler at the other end has not begun his approach to the wicket or (if he doesn't take a run) commenced his bowling action. If he has, such an appeal will be nullified because the ball has again become live.

(4) The ball is dead as soon as either batsman is dismissed, and by that I mean when the umpire, whichever one is involved, has *signified* by raising his finger that the batsman is *out*.

(5) The ball is dead if it becomes *lodged* in the protective helmet worn by any member of the fielding side and I do mean "any". More than once I have seen a wicket-keeper wearing such a helmet. It must be remembered that the ball has to be *lodged*. If it merely *strikes* the helmet it is not dead. To clarify that point – no catch is valid from such a contact with the helmet but the ball, bouncing off the helmet, can be taken by a fieldsman and a run-out effected. In the umpire's bible, *Cricket Umpiring and Scoring*, at the top of page 134, mention is made that if a ball lodges in the protective helmet of a fielder, wicket-keeper or non-striker a call and signal of "Dead ball" is required from the umpires: not so, the ball is automatically "dead".

(6) The ball is dead immediately when illegal fielding *takes place* (Law 41.1) and dead immediately a *call* of "Lost ball" is made by any member of the fielding side (Law 20).

The author at six

ABOVE LEFT: *Passing the time of day with Clive Lloyd*

ABOVE RIGHT: *Another interruption in play*

BELOW: *The hardest workers of all*

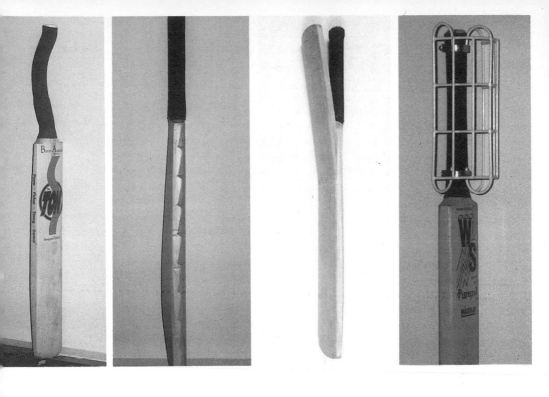

Each of these bats is illegal, except the one with a bent handle. Although the extended face bat conforms with Law 6, the MCC decided that it did not conform to the recognized structure of the bat. All the other bats would inflict damage on the ball. ABOVE: *bent handle, serrated edge, extended face, metal hand guard;* BELOW: *plastic hand guard, aluminium, holes in blade*

Two respected captains: (ABOVE) *Mike Brearley (umpire – Kenny Palmer) and* (BELOW) *Ray Illingworth (umpire – Lloyd Budd)*

TOP: *Pakistanis in full cry during their 1992 tour of England*

ABOVE: *Two balls used in the same match in 1992, one by each side in their first innings. One has been used, while the other would appear to have been abused*

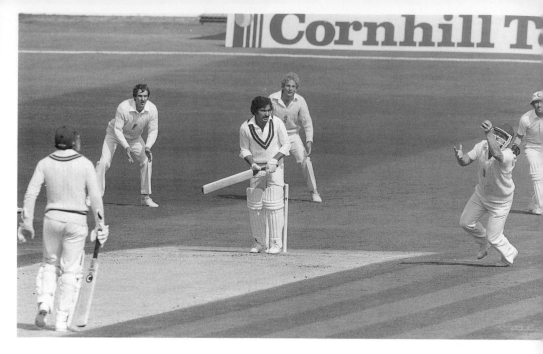

Great catches by Gatting (ABOVE) *and Brearley* (BELOW)

RIGHT: *Different boundaries* (LEFT TO RIGHT): *overhanging trees, a gully and edge of grass, a boundary rope, the famous Canterbury tree, boundary boards, and the difficult one – a boundary board and rope within inches of each other*

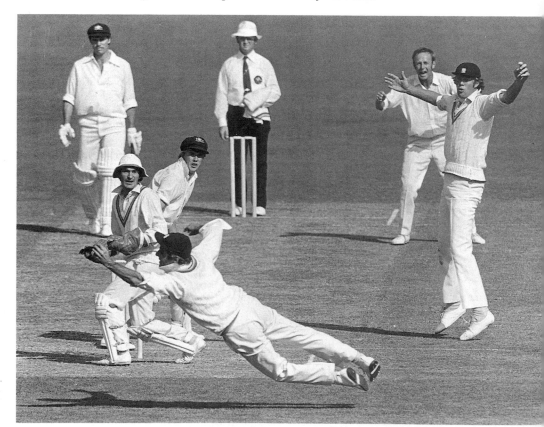

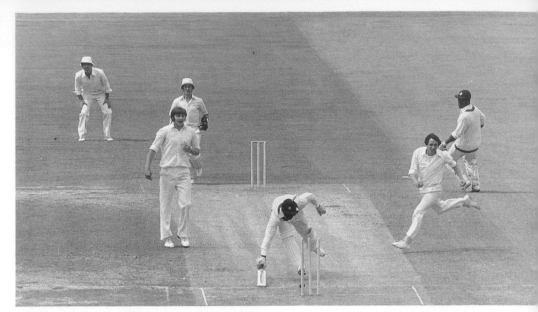

TOP: *A brilliant run out by Derek Randall*

ABOVE LEFT: *Did it go for six or did it carry the boundary lines? Ian Botham in stirring form*

ABOVE RIGHT: *A ball legally kept in good condition by Worcestershire CCC. Used for 144.4 overs in one innings*

RIGHT: *The bail does not have to fall completely to the ground in order for an "out" decision to be given (Law 28). The fact that it has been dislodged from the top of the stumps is what makes it "out"*

(7) The ball is dead when it *reaches, hits* or is *carried over* a boundary, however marked (Law 19).

In all of these seven instances it is the occurrence, the happening, the incident, which has made the ball dead. The only reason for the umpire calling and signalling "Dead ball" is to make sure certain people are aware of the fact, the most important being the scorers. In the event of any runs having been scored when the ball becomes lodged (as explained in Points 2 and 5), these will be allowed, as will another if the batsmen have crossed. For a dismissal under Law 33 (Handled the Ball), or Law 37 (Obstructing the Field), any runs which have been scored will be credited but only those scored prior to the offence.

I can think of a couple of instances of confusion over when the ball is or is not dead. On what I regard as the loveliest ground in the world, the Triangle Country Club in Zimbabwe, I was "standing" at the bowler's end when a ball was bowled, taken by the wicket-keeper and immediately volleyed to the square-leg fieldsman. But it was not kicked very accurately, because the ball flashed past the fieldsman who had to chase 20 yards or so towards the boundary to retrieve it. After this football act took place, the batsmen decided to take a single, but as the ball had been automatically rendered dead by the taking and disposing of it by the wicket-keeper, albeit in an unusual manner, I returned the batsmen to their original ends and disallowed the "run". Whilst this is an occasion when the ball is automatically dead upon the discard, it is also a situation when it is wise just to turn to the scoring position and to signal "Dead ball". At all times you must endeavour to be of help to your colleagues in the score box, as they will always be ready to help you.

The other instance of confusion was at Cambridge and this was one that worked against the fielding side and in favour of the batsmen. I was standing at square-leg. A ball delivered by the bowler bounced off the pad of the striker and ran to gulley. The fieldsman there tossed it to a slip fielder who in turn threw it to the man at mid-on. He held on to the ball until the bowler was almost back to his mark and then threw it to him. For some reason or other the bowler looked away at that precise moment and the ball passed him and rolled on to the boundary edge where a spectator threw it back to the bowler. My colleague, at the bowler's end, had not seen mid-on's throw to the bowler or what happened after that – it took place behind his back – but as some time had elapsed he turned, in time to see the ball back in the bowler's hand. As neither batsman had moved he saw no cause to take action and was about to let play continue when I walked over to him, explained what had happened, and he immediately signalled four runs – leg-byes. That is a prime example of working together. At no time had the ball become dead, prior to its crossing the boundary line.

(8) The ball is dead when it is finally settled in the hands of the bowler, but not immediately he receives it from a member of the fielding side if there is

still a chance to effect a dismissal. A bowler makes it dead when he has taken the *first pace* back to his mark to bowl the next ball.

Early in 1979 Sir George (Gubby) Allen was kind enough to ask me to look through the draft new Code of Laws to operate from the start of the 1980 season and to suggest any changes I thought might be necessary. I suggested two, one of which was accepted, the other not. The change which was agreed was to Law 23.1 (d) which, in the draft, stated that a ball lodged in the clothing or equipment of the batsmen would only be regarded as dead if the umpires called and signalled it as dead. I advised that if the umpire had not observed the ball becoming lodged, or was not very quick in making his call, we could have a situation where fielders rushed in to grab the ball which had made some contact with the bat before lodging in the batsman's clothing or equipment and claiming a catch. On the other hand, we could have batsmen capering about the ground, trying to dislodge the ball before the "catch" was completed. In short, it could result in a comic-opera situation which wouldn't do much for the image of the game. I am glad to say the law-makers returned this aspect of "dead-ball" to one of being automatic when the ball lodged.

Now we come to the sections of Law 23 where either umpire is *required* to call and signal "Dead ball". His call and signal will have the effect of stopping any action which might take place at that moment. I should say at this point that in section 7 of my clarifications (below) the umpire at the striker's (i.e. square-leg or point) end most certainly will not make the call and in section 3 he would be most unwise to do so. In all other cases the call and signal can be made by either umpire.

(1) Intervention in the case of unfair play. I have taken this course on a number of occasions, but as far as I can recall they have all been of an innocent nature. In a match at Derby the striker played a ball down in front of him and was about to push the ball to the wicket-keeper, as a helpful gesture (in fact his bat was touching the ball), when the non-striker came running down the pitch, calling for a run. The striker then set off and the run was completed. There were certain rumblings from the fielding side and I took the view that the run constituted unfair play. I called and signalled "Dead ball", returned the batsmen to their original ends and made sure that no runs were credited. The view may be taken in some quarters that I should not have taken this action. My reply is this: I knew there was not going to be any appeal under Law 34 (Hit the Ball Twice) but if there had been, my reply would have been *not out*. I had seen the interaction between striker and wicket-keeper which amounted to an unspoken dialogue: "Shall I knock it back to you?" "Fine. Thanks." To me, it was the taking of the run which was unfair.

We are also empowered to intervene if obstruction of a batsman by any member of the fielding side takes place. In 1991, during a match between Surrey and Gloucestershire at Guildford, Alec Stewart was run out after clearly being obstructed but not in any way deliberately. I was at the bowling end and Alec was the non-striker. The striker played a ball from David Lawrence about four yards down the on side of the pitch and set off for a quick run. David followed through to pick up the ball and throw down the wicket at the other end while Alec was trying to beat the throw. He was always a pace behind the bowler and it is not easy to get round a man as big as "Syd" at any time. He virtually ran up Lawrence's back! But he still didn't beat the throw. An appeal rang out and I thought my colleague, Bob White, the former Middlesex and Notts player, handled the situation brilliantly. As he walked towards the broken wicket he glanced at me and I set off to meet him. Bob then asked the Gloucestershire captain, "Do you wish that appeal to stand?" and he was told, "Yes." He then asked, "Don, did you see anything in that obstruction as deliberate?" I assured him that I did not. Bob then indicated to Alec that he had been run out. I don't think Alec was very pleased, but I am quite sure the decision was absolutely correct because the obstruction had not been deliberate.

If either umpire had been of the opinion that deliberate obstruction had occurred we would have considered the ball dead from the moment the obstruction took place. The response to the appeal would have been *not out*, and one run would have been credited to the striker, even if the batsmen had not crossed. This is the only occasion that a run can be credited if the batsmen have not crossed in running and if "Dead ball" has been called before their crossing. They will then go to the opposite ends for the next ball to be bowled.

(2) When a member of the fielding side, or either batsman, suffers a serious injury or his fellow-umpire is injured or ill.

At Bradford, in 1978, I had not only to call "Dead ball" from the bowling end but to render aid as well! It was a Yorkshire–Middlesex game; David Bairstow was batting and Wilf Slack was in the forward short-leg position, wearing a helmet. David pulled a ball with ferocious power and it went between the bars of the visor. This was in the days before helmets had been improved to the extent of being really effective and the ball could go between the two bars which were supposed to protect the face. Even so, what the outcome might have been if he had not been wearing any protection at all, I hate to think.

I was actually on my way to Wilf as I called "Dead ball", and without labouring the point I saw there was a lot of blood and broken teeth around. The important thing, as I saw it, was to get him back to the pavilion and to medical attention, as soon as possible. I simply did what I thought was necessary; but it was rather nice to be told later, in a letter from the TCCB, that Mike Smith, the captain, and the Middlesex team had appreciated my efforts. However, the incident made me realise that I ought to know much more about first aid, and the following winter I spent every Wednesday evening at the St John Ambulance Brigade headquarters in Grimsby, with Bill Stockwood and Dr John Birch. What I learned there has served me well.

Whilst I have had to call "Dead ball" for injuries many times, unfortunately the worst accident I have ever seen was at Southampton (Hants v. Warwickshire) in 1982 when Mark Nicholas ducked into a ball from Gladstone Small. He was wearing a helmet but one without a visor and the crack was terrible to hear. The ball had smashed Mark's cheekbone so badly that there was a dent in his face – but 48 hours and a delicate operation later he was back on the ground. Some of these boys are really tough individuals.

Another story to prove how tough cricketers are: in the NatWest semi-final in 1992, Leicestershire v. Essex, Mike Garnham, the Essex wicket-keeper, very late in the match was shaping to take a ball as the batsman got a little edge to it. The crack as the ball hit him in the eye could be heard all around the ground, and there was a lot of blood as we carried him off. That was on a Thursday, yet on the following Tuesday, with a great number of stitches around his eye, he was again donning gloves in a match at Colchester.

One thing an umpire must watch is not calling "Dead ball" so quickly that it denies the fielding side a chance of taking a wicket. I have seen a ball hit a fielder and ricochet high into the air, giving an obvious chance of a catch. In the days before helmets there was the occasion when a ball struck hard on to Brian Close's forehead at short leg was caught by Philip Sharpe at slip! Should the umpire call "Dead ball" while the ball is in the air the "catch" will be invalidated. So to delay the call for a second or two while the ball is in the air is sensible, even if the injury subsequently turns out to be serious. One has to take the view that a couple of seconds are not going to make too much difference and that help will already be on its way to the injured player.

(3) When the umpire considers the striker was not ready to receive a delivery. This is the part of the Law where I recommend that "Dead ball" is only called by the umpire at the bowling end. To my mind, the umpire standing square with the striker's wicket is not really in a position to see whether the striker is ready or not. The bowling-end umpire, on the other hand, is looking at the striker from the front-on position and can see the slightest move of the man at the wicket, usually a raising of the hand and a murmured "Sorry". While it is a bit disconcerting for the bowler to be stopped in full cry, and can sometimes result in a pulled muscle, it has traditionally been accepted by the bowler in good spirits as one of the hazards of his calling.

What the umpires have to ensure is that the striker withdraws from his stance position for adequate reasons. Almost invariably his reason is someone walking, or moving, behind the bowler's arm which, from time to time, includes a few spectators passing in front of the sightscreen at the bowling end. On some (fewer) occasions it occurs because of reflections from car windscreens or windows. I have seen "Dead ball" called when a bowler has got so close to the wicket as he delivers the ball that he has removed not only the bails but a couple of stumps as well. And as the stumps went careering down the pitch towards the striker it was undoubtedly a great distraction!

The striker, when withdrawing from his stance position, should not make any attempt to play the ball if it has already been delivered by the bowler. No runs can be scored and no wickets taken once the ball has been called "dead". I have personally called "Dead ball" when the ball has still been delivered and more than once it has hit the striker's wicket. In a club match at Cleethorpes in 1973 I actually did not have time to call "Dead ball" as the bowler delivered it and the striker pulled out of the way with a hurried "Sorry". Naturally enough, it was a talking point afterwards because I had told the bowler, "Not out. The ball was dead", and I was asked for an explanation. I replied that I did not have time to make the call of "Dead ball" as there was a split second between the striker's movement and the ball hitting the wicket. There may not be total agreement with me but if, as in that case, I felt it to be for the good of the game, I would not be shaken from my view.

(4) When the ball is dropped by the bowler or if it fails to leave his hand for any reason. Often it is the umpire at the striker's end of the pitch who makes this call, for when the ball is dropped by the bowler it is usually behind the back of the bowling-end umpire. I feel that another part could be added to Law 23 at this point and it should read, "'Dead ball' should be called if the ball leaves the bowler's hands but not in the correct manner." In practice, I know that all umpires believe they operate this already but as Law 23 stands at present it is not specified in so many words. One bowler, Simon Base, of Derbyshire, has really caused problems – for me and some of my colleagues – at times because for some reason no one has managed to explain the ball has flown out of hand, backwards, when he was actually in his delivery stride. Umpires have actually been hit and it has proved rather disconcerting. When it happens it is, of course, a case for calling and signalling "Dead ball". That is, if the ball is not stuck in the umpire's open mouth!

(5) When a bail falls from the striker's wicket. This usually happens when a strong wind is blowing, but it can be a most hazardous call for an umpire to make. Under Law 35 (Hit Wicket), the striker is in danger of being dismissed from the moment the ball becomes live (i.e. from the first step of the bowler's approach). If the striker accidentally removes even one bail during the bowler's approach, so long as the ball is actually delivered an appeal for dismissal should be sustained. The ball, of course, must be a fair delivery. A striker cannot be given *out* for a no ball. But if there is a strong wind blowing, how are we supposed to judge whether the fallen bail is the responsibility of the striker, or the elements? I believe that so long as it is clear that the bail has been removed by some other agency than the striker's bat, or person, then the call of "Dead ball" should be made. Of the two umpires, the one at the striker's end is in a position to have the best view and he should be at his most alert and observant in such conditions. If he observes that the bail has been removed in an illegal manner he says nothing and hopes that his colleague also stays quiet. When an appeal is made it is for that umpire at the striker's end to give a decision for "Hit wicket".

(6) When it is necessary for the umpires to consult. If this happens, I believe it should not take place until the ball has been made dead automatically. If there is ever an occasion for the umpires to consult each other while the ball is live, then one or other of them must first make it dead by calling and signalling. We would look fools if we were both chatting in mid-pitch when, say, the wicket-keeper removed the bails and appealed for a decision. We would not only have failed in our duty to observe the Law but neither of us would be in a position to decide a "run out" or "stumped" decision.

(7) When there is a disallowance of leg-byes. This must be a matter for the bowling-end umpire alone. How on earth can anyone think there would be an occasion when this part of Law 23 could rest in the hands of the umpire at the striker's end? The bowling-end umpire is the only person on the field who can decide if a shot has or has not been played at the ball.

Whilst in the seven instances we have considered, the Law demands a call and signal, there are many times when the call alone will meet the requirements of the situation. However, in these circumstances, the umpire should ensure that everyone knows exactly what is going on – especially the scorers.

Instances of situations when the ball is not dead are stated in the Laws but I'd like to give one illustration of something which happened in a one-day international and the umpire made a mistake in interpreting Law 23.4(b). It was a televised game, so some readers may remember the occasion. The ball was thrown at one of the wickets, the bails were removed and an appeal was shouted for "Run out". The decision was *not out* and it looked to be correct. But the ball then ran down the length of the pitch, past the other batsman who had not yet made his ground and broke the wicket to which he was running. "How's that?" came the cry and "Not out" was the umpire's reply. This amazed everyone, for the umpire concerned was one of the best around and continued to be so for several years after that. But when we discussed the matter, only a couple of weeks later when "standing" together, he confessed, "Honestly, Don, I thought the ball was dead once that first wicket had been broken." That umpire had not only my respect but that of all connected with the game of cricket. The fact that he had turned to me, "the new boy", for clarification of his decision showed that I had been accepted into an elite band.

On page 104 of *Cricket Umpiring and Scoring* it states that once a ball has passed the striker's wicket it is no longer available to the striker. It also adds that the striker should not be allowed to play a ball which has passed the wicket and is out of his reach. Whilst I accept all other points made in the paragraph, there is no way I can agree with or follow that particular recommendation, as the following story illustrates. (It takes some believing but it is actually true.)

In a match at Leicester, Brian Davison was batting and he went on to the back foot to a ball which "bounced" a little, from a length. The ball hit Brian on the inside of the upper arm, almost in the armpit, and it then rose about ten feet in the air and, in a gentle arc, it fell about five yards behind the stumps and roughly ten yards in front of the wicket-keeper. Now just how it happened – from spin imparted, or the ball hitting some kind of obstruction behind the stumps – I just don't know, but the ball ricocheted back, past the stumps, and rolled to a position almost halfway back down the pitch, where it was retrieved by the bowler. Everyone was amazed. The spot where the ball had landed behind the stumps was scrutinised by those near enough to do so and it was seen that there was a heel-mark there, but whether the ball had actually struck it was something no one could actually say. But the point is this: if the striker had seen the ball ricocheting back, he would have been entitled to defend his wicket, because if it had struck and dislodged the bails he would have been *out*, bowled, irrespective of the direction from which the ball was coming.

While I have written a lot in my efforts to impart and explain the correct clarifications of all parts of Law 23, I do have a set of 36 photographic slides, which to my mind show this Law to great effect. It is a Law which lends itself to the visual aid, and one which I never fail to include in my lectures worldwide. I have dealt at some length with Law 23, but I hope this is justified because in my opinion, as I said at the start, it is the most important of the 42 Laws.

24

NO BALL

1. MODE OF DELIVERY

The umpire shall indicate to the striker whether the bowler intends to bowl over or round the wicket, overarm or underarm, right- or left-handed. Failure of the bowler to indicate in advance a change in his mode of delivery is unfair and the umpire shall call and signal "No ball".

2. FAIR DELIVERY – THE ARM

For a delivery to be fair, the ball must be bowled, not thrown – see Note (a) below. If either umpire is not entirely satisfied with the absolute fairness of a delivery in this respect he shall call and signal "No ball" instantly upon delivery.

3. FAIR DELIVERY – THE FEET

The umpire at the bowler's end shall call and signal "No ball" if he is not satisfied that in the delivery stride:

(a) The bowler's back foot has landed within and not touching the return crease or its forward extension; or

(b) Some part of the front foot whether grounded or raised was behind the popping crease.

4. BOWLER THROWING AT STRIKER'S WICKET BEFORE DELIVERY

If the bowler, before delivering the ball, throws it at the striker's wicket in an attempt to run him out, the umpire shall call and signal "No ball". See Law 42.12 (Batsman Unfairly Stealing a Run) and Law 38 (Run Out).

5. BOWLER ATTEMPTING TO RUN OUT NON-STRIKER BEFORE DELIVERY

If the bowler, before delivering the ball, attempts to run out the non-striker, any runs which result shall be allowed and shall be scored as no balls. Such an attempt shall not count as a ball in the over. The umpire shall not call "No ball". See Law 42.12 (Batsman Unfairly Stealing a Run).

6. INFRINGEMENT OF LAWS BY A WICKET-KEEPER OR A FIELDSMAN

The umpire shall call and signal "No ball" in the event of the wicket-keeper infringing Law 40.1 (Position of Wicket-keeper) or a fieldsman infringing Law 41.2 (Limitation of On-side Fieldsmen) or Law 41.3 (Position of Fieldsmen).

7. REVOKING A CALL

An umpire shall revoke the call "No ball" if the ball does not leave the bowler's hand for any reason. See Law 23.2 (Either Umpire Shall Call and Signal "Dead Ball").

8. PENALTY

A penalty of one run for a no ball shall be scored if no runs are made otherwise.

9. RUNS FROM A NO BALL

The striker may hit a no ball and whatever runs result shall be added to his score. Runs made otherwise from a no ball shall be scored no balls.

10. OUT FROM A NO BALL

The striker shall be out from a no ball if he breaks Law 34 (Hit the Ball Twice) and either batsman may be run out or shall be given out if either breaks Law 33 (Handled the Ball) or Law 37 (Obstructing the Field).

11. BATSMAN GIVEN OUT OFF A NO BALL

Should a batsman be given out off a no ball the penalty for bowling it shall stand unless runs are otherwise scored.

NOTES

(a) Definition of a Throw

A ball shall be deemed to have been thrown if, in the opinion of either umpire, the process of straightening the bowling arm, whether it be partial or complete, takes place during that part of the delivery swing which directly precedes the ball leaving the hand. This definition shall not debar a bowler from the use of the wrist in the delivery swing.

(b) No ball Not Counting in Over

A no ball shall not be reckoned as one of the over. See Law 22.3 (No Ball or Wide Ball).

T his Law has probably caused more problems for the law-makers, over the years, than any other. No sooner has one aspect of it been clarified than trouble has developed in another. I would like to deal with three separate aspects of Law 24: (1) incorrect positioning of the arm for the delivery of the ball from the hand; (2) incorrect foot placement during the delivery-stride and (3) other reasons for the call and signal of "No ball".

In the earliest Code of Laws it was all very simple: an umpire would call "No ball" if the bowler delivered the ball with his back foot over the bowling crease. In fact to be strictly accurate the wording used was a bit of more colourful English: the *hinder* foot! It attracted no penalty in those earliest days and the ball was considered "dead". No runs could be scored, therefore, even if the striker hit the ball.

(1) Position of the arm. It was not until 1864 that the bowler was allowed to deliver the ball with the arm raised above shoulder-height although a number had, in fact, been using this method (quite illegally) for several years. Since 1775 bowlers generally, however, had been delivering with what we would call today an "underarm" or "lob" action. A statement around 1811 made it clear that the ball had to be delivered with the hand below the elbow. About the same time the striker was allowed to score runs by hitting a no ball, and the only way in which he could be dismissed was "run out". It was not until 1829 that a penalty was introduced in favour of the batting side if runs had not otherwise been scored from the no ball.

It was about this time, too, that a number of bowlers began to cause problems for umpires by using what we call a "round-arm" method of delivery and it was this that finally forced on the law-makers a change, allowing the arm to be raised to shoulder-height in 1835. Again, there were bowlers who abused this Law and despite action taken by some of the stronger-minded umpires, another Law was passed in 1864, to allow what is now known as "overarm" bowling. It was no doubt thought that this would end the wrangles, that there were no remaining problems to be ironed out. Alas, no. By 1880 umpires were beset by the difficulties of "overarm" bowlers now throwing the ball, rather than bowling it. Fortunately, there were umpires who were, so to speak, prepared to stand up and be counted and subsequently, by a combination of strong umpires and MCC and TCCB legislation, those who deliver the ball unfairly have almost completely been eradicated. In my time as a first-class umpire I have seen a bowler who most certainly threw and I have reported two others I thought to have a "suspect" action. Both were filmed and it was found that in the course of certain deliveries they certainly did not comply with Law 24.2. The name of one of those two would certainly be viewed with amazement.

(2) Position of the feet. It was into the 1970s before the bowling crease ceased to be mentioned as a factor in judging the fairness of a delivery as far as the feet were concerned. There are some supporters of the game who believe it should still hinge on the position of the back foot rather than the front. Indeed, in 1991, Sir Donald Bradman submitted a paper, accompanied by a personal plea, for a return to the "back foot" ruling. Those who have seen the photographs of Rorke of Australia bowling will realise why we must

not go back to the "back foot" ruling. With his long drag he was only 18 yards from the striker, and he still had the ball in his hand; and that is considered fair? NEVER.

A sub-committee was set up by MCC, of which I was a member, and I spoke against the proposal from Sir Donald. To my delight, though I must say also to my surprise, so did Trevor Bailey, and from what has happened since then it would appear that we carried the day. While it would be a brave, perhaps foolhardy man who disregarded or argued with anything spoken or written by Sir Donald Bradman on the game of cricket, there were a number of aspects of his paper with which I could not agree, the main one being as follows: the call and signal of "No ball" is based mainly on the position of the front foot (leaving aside for the moment the question of the return crease) and it was said that the umpire could not utter the call quickly enough to give the batsman the opportunity to take advantage of the unfair delivery.

The call and signal of "No ball" is not, and never has been, to enable the batsman to have a "free" hit to the boundary. The sole purpose of the call is to prevent the bowler being credited with a wicket from an unfair delivery.

Trevor Bailey had other reasons for opposing a change which were not only valid but well thought-out. Mr Bailey's extremely important point to the sub-committee was that in all other sports a line is drawn which the participant must not cross. The front-foot rule gives us that. The Association of Cricket Umpires sent out a questionnaire to members and the greater number of replies were *against* a return to the back-foot rule. It is not as easy to adjudicate upon (as the front-foot) and, in my opinion, it brings with it a danger of bowlers using suspect actions. The front-foot rule requires that foot to be in a particular place at the moment of delivery (i.e. some part of it behind the batting crease), whereas the back-foot rule was bedevilled by the *drag* of the bowler's rear foot. It enabled some bowlers, in fact, actually to get further down the pitch before letting the ball go and it also led to greater damage to the pitch by the bowler.

To judge whether a delivery is fair I say to myself: "Front foot, front line: back foot, side line (return crease)." As long as the bowler, in his delivery-stride, places his back foot inside the return crease (i.e. nearer to the stumps) and no part of his back foot is touching that crease, its forward extension or its extension to the rear of the bowling crease and at the same time some part of his front foot is behind the batting crease, then there is no cause for a call of "No ball" by the umpire at the bowling end.

It will be seen that when a bowler is in his delivery-stride, so much concentration is required from the umpire at the bowler's end on the bowler's foot placement that he is not able to observe the bowler's arm at the same time. In any case, it is a physical impossibility for him to do so. Fortunately in 1899 a Law was framed so as to allow *either* umpire to call and signal "No ball" for any transgression of Law 24. We seldom have a call for a ball being projected unfairly these days and the umpires, working as a team, can jointly prevent it.

Under the earlier Law the only method of dismissal from a no ball was "Run out", but a batsman can now be dismissed off a no ball under Law 33 (Hit the Ball Twice), Law 34 (Run Out), Law 37 (Handled the Ball) or Law 38 (Obstructing the Field). Under Laws 34, 37 and 38 both striker and non-striker can be given *out* but only the striker can infringe Law 33 (Hit the Ball Twice).

In all standards and classes of cricket there are bowlers who regularly commit themselves to bowling a no ball by an incorrect placement of the foot in the delivery-stride. The start of the delivery-stride is when the bowler's back foot hits the ground and it ends, a split second later, when the front foot hits the ground. Nothing which happens before (or indeed after) that will constitute a no ball under Law 24.3.

It was in 1974 while umpiring one of my club's friendly fixtures that the full meaning of the words "delivery-stride" was graphically brought home to me. Martin Maslin, a distinguished Minor Counties cricketer who that year won a Gillette Man of the Match award for Lincolnshire v. Glamorgan, was bowling for Cleethorpes from the end at which I was "standing". And pitch end "covering" against the weather had not been quite so effective as it might have been in a first-class match. In came Martin, down went the back foot, closely followed by the front one which landed with the heel fully behind the batting crease. But he had landed on a damp spot! His front foot then slid forward about 15 inches as he let go of the ball – which the batsman could, nevertheless, only play down in front of him with some difficulty – and as I shouted "No ball". There for all the world to see was the slide-mark, the point at which he had released the ball ... the evidence that my call was correct. However, it was most certainly *not* correct. The slide of the foot had taken place after the completion of the delivery-stride, when the front foot hit the ground.

As we have seen, there are four Laws under which a wicket can be taken after a call of "No ball". If the batsman is ruled *out*, the one-run penalty still counts unless runs are made in another manner. It will also count if neither batsman is *out* or if the ball has not been struck. If the no ball has been hit by the striker and the batsmen are, say, embarking on their fourth run when one of them is run out, then the first three runs will be credited to the striker, but not in addition to the one-run penalty.

(3) Other reasons for a call and signal of "No ball" by the umpire: the two most common instances of this are under Law 41.2 when the umpire square with the wicket (either square-leg or point) sees there are more than the permitted number of fieldsmen (two) behind the line of the batting crease at the moment the ball is delivered, and under Law 41.3 which penalises a fieldsman encroaching on the pitch, either by foot placement or having part of his person extended over the pitch. Both points are dealt with in more detail in considering Law 41 but it should be noted here that the call of "No ball" in the case of an encroaching fieldsman will be made, for obvious

reasons, by the umpire at the bowler's end. When this Law came into operation it was called "Incommoding the Striker", as delicate a piece of phrasing as you could hope for!

There are other, less familiar, occasions for calling "No ball". One of them, though obscure, is in fact one which I have had to apply: a bowler failing to notify his intention of changing his mode of delivery. If a bowler has been operating, for instance, right-arm over-the-wicket, and suddenly changes to round-the-wicket without telling the umpire, there should be a call of "No ball". It is no use the bowler saying, "But I told the striker I was going to change." He may well have done so but if the umpire was not aware of it how can he *know* the striker is aware? No. The bowler must notify the umpire of the change and then the umpire can inform the batsman.

In Calcutta, in 1982, a Test between India and England was drearily heading towards a draw and Graham Gooch, who is a good mimic of other bowling styles, decided to entertain the crowd by bowling for England after the fashion of the Indian bowlers: Kapil Dev (right-arm quick), Madan Lal (right-arm medium), Shivlal Yadar (right-arm off-spin) and then Dilip Dashi (slow left-arm). For the Dashi impression, Gooch even went down to the boundary and borrowed a pair of spectacles from an England supporter and delivered a passable couple of left-arm balls. But as all the impersonations took place in the space of 12 deliveries it is doubtful whether he informed the umpire of each change in style though no one seemed to mind, or to question it (although he would only have had to give notification of a change in the mode of delivery upon one occasion).

Next we come to the wicket-keeper who encroaches, or has some part of his person or dress in front of the stumps at the moment of delivery. Whilst I have never called "No ball" for an infringement of Law 40.1 I know of umpires who have. There are, I am afraid, officials who firmly believe that anything written in the Laws is as if it were inscribed on the tablets of stone and carried down from the mountain. They should remember that some of these tablets were cracked in Moses' descent and refrain from calling "No ball" if they think the peak of the wicket-keeper's cap is a shade forward of the stumps. Common sense should prevail. I do feel that the old Law 43 was better in this respect than the present Law 40. It said that "if any such infringement contributed in any way to the dismissal of the striker then a call and signal of 'Dead ball' must be made". If the encroachment did not in any way contribute to the dismissal, then the umpire would be justified in disregarding it – a much better clarification, in my view, for the free running of the game.

The umpire will call and signal "No ball" should the bowler throw the ball, but there are several types of throw and two of them, obscure parts of Law 24, take place more or less behind the back of the bowling-end umpire, so it is the square-leg umpire who calls. But only in *one* instance: in the other there is *no* call of "No ball". (1) If the bowler throws at the striker's wicket in an attempt to run him out (as when the batsman "gives him the charge") it is a no ball, simply because the delivery has not conformed with Law 24.2. The umpire then has to decide whether the batsman was unfairly trying to steal a run. If not, then he gives the striker *not out* (always assuming, of course, that the throw hits the stumps) and ensures that a run is credited to the total as a "No ball". This point is again covered in Law 42.12 and I do not know that such an incident has taken place in the course of a game.

It is point (2) which I have never known to occur but presumably it must have done at some time to give rise to Law 24.5, which deals with a throw at the non-striker's stumps. The first thing one must hope for is that this throw does not hit the bowling-end umpire! The square-leg umpire will not call "No ball" in this case, because the ball has not been projected at the striker's wicket. The batsman, therefore, is in no need of protection from being dismissed. If any runs result from such a throw, how are they to be scored? They will go into the book as no-ball extras, even though "no ball" has not been called and signalled, simply because there is no other way of crediting them. This is rather unusual.

Recalling for a moment that the two instances of throwing which we have just discussed both begin with preventing the batsmen from stealing a run, a bowler has only to hold on to the ball – i.e. not deliver or throw it – and as soon as the batsmen have crossed the umpire will call and signal "Dead ball" because the batsmen are indulging in an unfair act. The temptation to effect a dismissal, I suppose, is strong; but the bowler must be prepared for the consequences of his action if his throw misses the stumps and runs result.

When I am conducting a seminar I am often asked if I have seen every possible incident in a cricket match which can occur. In fact, while I have seen many unusual and obscure occurrences, I have never been aware of either of the two we have just mentioned.

We sometimes see and hear a good sharp signal and call from an umpire as he sees the bowler's front foot hit the ground just beyond the batting crease only for the bowler to *realise* he is over-stepping and hold on to the ball. There is a general smile when the bowler then waves the ball in front of the umpire's nose as if to say, "What are you shouting about?" All right. It's nice to have a smile all round. But there is nothing for the umpire to feel ashamed about. On the contrary, it shows how alert and "on-the-ball" he is. He should share the smile, perhaps, and then signal "Dead ball" to the scorers, thus revoking his call of "No ball".

At this point I should mention that what we will call the bowling of too many short or full-pitched deliveries can result in a call and signal of "No ball" – and a warning to the bowler as well – but that penalty occurs under Law 42.8. I am astonished that there is no mention of this in Law 24 and I feel it must be the result of an oversight. We shall deal with the matter in context when we come to Law 42.

In the game at county level there are one or two other reasons for the call of

"No ball", and I suppose the best known of these is when there are not the required number of fieldsmen within the fielding circle radius of 30 yards from the stumps when the ball is delivered. The "circle" was first introduced into the Benson & Hedges Cup competition in 1981 with the object of making the contest more interesting for spectators. It was then introduced into the other one-day competitions and is now a feature of all domestic, limited-overs contests. The regulation states that at the moment of delivery by the bowler, no fewer than four fielders, plus bowler and wicket-keeper, must be within a radius of 30 yards from the pitch. The demarcation line is achieved by taking a semi-circle of 30 yards behind each middle stump to a point square with the stumps on both leg and off sides, then joining up the ends of both semi-circles with a line drawn parallel to the pitch itself.

A mistake usually occurs when a fielder who has been on the boundary for a right-hand batsman forgets to move inside the circle for a left-hander, and vice-versa. It's pretty certain that most umpires standing at the striker's end have had to call "No ball" at one time or another because there were only three fieldsmen inside the "circle". Umpires are required to look out for such things. I must confess to occasions when, as the bowler was running in, I have said from square-leg quite audibly, and deliberately, for the benefit of any fielder within earshot, "How many in the circle?" The fieldsman has then stopped the bowler before he has delivered and the field has been adjusted. Not everyone will agree with this course of action, of course, but to me it is more important to get on with the game in a good spirit than to score a point by waiting and calling "No ball". Anyway, I do it for all sides.

In the 1992 World Cup we saw strict adherence to the penalising – by a call of "No ball" – of deliveries which passed above the shoulder-height of the batsman standing upright at the crease. While I am in favour of any ruling which sets out to keep fast, short-pitched deliveries to a minimum, I have to say I disagree with the stipulated height of the ball as it reaches or passes the batsman. In Law 42.8 Note (d) the height referred to is "above the shoulder-height of the striker when in a normal batting stance". What bothers me even more is that for the 1992 season's Test and county matches the height was again given as "whilst standing upright" and, even more than that, a bowler would be allowed to bowl one such short-pitched ball at each batsman during every over of the innings. That legislation could have the effect of allowing the fast, short-pitched ball to be delivered more frequently than before, not only at recognised batsmen but at less efficient tail-enders as well. I thought the idea was to cut out as much fast, short-pitched bowling as possible, but the legislators have opened up the possibility of our seeing, in a championship game of 110 overs a day, as many as 220 balls of the short-pitched variety. It could lead to some awfully boring days, apart from other considerations.

Earlier I mentioned three bowlers I had seen whose actions seemed to me to be flawed. In 1977, I was "standing" in a Gillette Cup match at

Northampton with Durham (then a Minor County) as the opposition. From square-leg it seemed to me that David O'Sullivan, a New Zealand slow left-arm bowler, at that time with Durham but who had also played for Hampshire, projected every delivery in an incorrect manner. As I had only two years' experience as a first-class umpire I walked over to my colleague, Eddie Phillipson (who had over 20 years' experience and had "stood" in a dozen Tests) and asked if he would stand back, just a bit, and watch O'Sullivan's arm. Eddie smiled, "Try not to let it bother you, Don. He has been bowling like that for years. Hampshire would not re-sign him because of the action but he is still allowed to play." So I followed his advice. I knew that O'Sullivan did not bowl with the deliberate intention of gaining an unfair advantage; it was just that his action was naturally flawed as far as I was concerned.

Four years later when I toured New Zealand I saw him playing for Central Districts and his action had not changed. But before that, and by a coincidence it was within a few months of my experience at Northampton, my collaborator in this book was watching Central Districts play the touring England team in New Plymouth. He was approached by a New Zealand supporter during a luncheon interval and asked what he thought of Geoff Cope's action. Cope, the Yorkshire off-spinner, had had a certain amount of trouble about *his* action and had changed his bowling style completely. The Kiwi supporter was told, "I haven't noticed Cope. I have been too busy watching O'Sullivan."

Now we move forward to the 1979 season and the next bowler I saw and believed he threw was Karson Ghavri, the medium-fast left-armer, who toured England with the Indian team of that year. While umpiring MCC v. India at Lord's I sensed that something was wrong with his action but could not pinpoint anything definite. We had been instructed by the TCCB that if we suspected a bowler threw, in our opinion, we should not "call" him but report the matter and the bowler would then be filmed the next time he played. On 3 June 1979, I ended a report to the TCCB with these words: "You are aware of my visit to you during the tea interval on the third day. Perhaps I shall be the only person who will report on this player's action but should he be filmed at a future date and his action found to be totally fair it will not convince me that I did not observe two deliveries which were performed completely contrary to the first sentence of Law 26." The fact that one of those deliveries went through Mike Brearley's visor and split his nose did not influence me in any way. I had decided long before that Ghavri's action had been suspect in the occasional delivery.

The third bowler I must mention most definitely did *not* throw deliberately. He was a world-class bowler and a lovely man. People may find it difficult to believe but I am convinced that for a short time in his career Bishen Singh Bedi threw. I noticed it during the last match of my first season in 1975 and again, it was more of a *feeling* that something was not quite correct when Bishen was bowling at my end. I spoke to my colleague and he was of the same opinion but neither of us could put it more definitely than "a feeling". I put in my report that "I felt there was something not quite right with the odd delivery." The TCCB decided to film him and – to their amazement, I suspect – there was a delivery when the body fell away to the side and the arm was bent. Bedi was such a good bowler with, normally, a lovely action. What I think happened was that he was shown the film, saw what was wrong and was a good enough cricketer to put it right immediately. Certainly, his performances with the ball suggested he got better and better as the years went by.

There has been a clarification in regard to a certain aspect of this Law with which I am unable to agree. This was contained in the Green Sheet issued by ACU in October 1989, and refers to runs being scored from a "No ball" which is delivered with the scores of the two sides in the match being level. The statement is to the effect that the "No ball" call and signal will not end the match, although it always has been assumed, and correctly so, that this action and therefore the addition of the one run penalty as a "No ball" extra to the batting side's score has won the game. Whilst I do advise the bowling end umpire to immediately call "Time", I feel that this is not really relevant to the issue. Unfortunately the clarification then extends the confusion by stating, that the "No ball" may be hit and any runs scored will be credited to the striker. I know that Law 24.8 and 9 throw the matter into confusion but these two points are not to cover a situation such as the one mentioned.

Only in the case of a boundary hit by the striker, when less than the boundary allowance is required to win the match, or a boundary four credited as extras from a fair delivery will be credited to the score, in excess of the number of runs required to win the match. The clarification then states instances which make things ludicrous. If runs are going to be allowed, then the ball cannot be considered "dead" and I present the following situation. The "No ball" is driven straight back and is touched by the bowler, the ball then crashes through the bowling wicket with the non striker out of his ground, an appeal rings out but the ball is crossing the boundary line. The clarification states, "the non-striker will be 'not out' although the ball is still 'live'," but what about the boundary four – will they be credited? According to the first part of the clarification they should be, as only the crossing of the boundary line by the ball will make it "dead". The umpire's position is surely to help the game run as smoothly as possible and not to cause confusion. I hope that by the time this book is published, I will have taken steps to return some credibility to this issue.

At the Laws Committee meeting held on 12 October 1992 I asked that a reclarification could be considered for the answer on the original Green Sheet to question 34. Question: The batting side require one run to win the match, the next delivery by the bowler is called and signalled "No ball" by the umpire. The striker hits the ball and it crosses the boundary line. Should the match end with the one run penalty for the "No ball" or should the striker and the batting side be credited with the four runs?

Answer: The answer on the Green Sheet was that the batsman would be credited with four runs, also to the score of the batting side, but since then some horrific situations have been put forward which could arise. After long discussions, it was agreed that to stop other situations arising once "No ball" had been called, the match was over. "No ball" and "Time". Some sense at last.

For the 1993 season the TCCB have decided that, in all of their domestic competitions any transgression of Law 24 "No ball" will lead to a credit to the batting side of two runs as a penalty. Added to these will be any runs which further accrue to the batting side. This is probably one of the most radical changes of regulation in the game of cricket to have taken place in this country for many decades.

This in itself may appear easy to implement, but at the Cricket Committee meeting it was also proposed that the two runs would always be a debit to the bowler along with any further runs which are scored by the striker hitting the ball. What will happen to any other runs which come from the ball contacting the striker's person, or from no contact whatsoever?

Despite a very strong lobby from many of the bowlers in county cricket it was decided to stay with the status quo. All runs which may be scored, by whichever method, will be debited against the bowler, these in addition to the two runs for the transgression. Some thought it desirable that if contact had been made by the ball with the striker's person, these extra runs should be debited as "leg-byes" and those from no contact as "byes". If those wishes had prevailed, this would have meant a major change in the umpire's method of signals and there would have had to have been some rapid liaison between umpires and scorers as to the method and signals to be used to inform scorers how any runs should be credited.

The suggestions were upon a signal of "No ball" two runs would be debited against a bowler and that signal alone would suffice if the striker played the ball with the bat and further runs were scored. For any further runs which accrue after the ball has contacted the striker's person, the "No ball" signal, accompanied by the "leg-bye" signal, would be appropriate but the problem occurs when we come to a situation of further runs after the delivery of a "No ball", when no contact is made with the ball whatsoever. It was felt that the only signal would have to be the "No ball" signal, accompanied by the "bye" signal, and this signal would have meant something completely different to that which it has conveyed for the past number of decades.

The penalty of two runs for a "No ball" delivery is a most radical change but if the bowlers had had their way the change would have been even more radical. Common sense has prevailed despite the bowlers feeling hard done by. It is up to all of them to endeavour to eradicate this delivery from their repertoire.

25

WIDE BALL

1. JUDGING A WIDE

If the bowler bowls the ball so high over or so wide of the wicket that, in the opinion of the umpire, it passes out of reach of the striker, standing at the wicket in a normal guard position, the umpire shall call and signal "Wide ball" as soon as it has passed the line of the striker's wicket.

The umpire shall not adjudge a ball as being wide if:

(a) The striker, by moving from his guard position, causes the ball to pass out of his reach.

(b) The striker moves and thus brings the ball within his reach.

2. PENALTY

A penalty of one run for a wide shall be scored if no runs are made otherwise.

3. BALL COMING TO REST IN FRONT OF THE STRIKER

If a ball which the umpire considers to have been delivered comes to rest in front of the line of the striker's wicket, "Wide" shall not be called. The striker has a right, without interference from the fielding side, to make one attempt to hit the ball. If the fielding side interfere the umpire shall replace the ball where it came to rest and shall order the fieldsmen to resume the places they occupied in the field before the ball was delivered.

The umpire shall call and signal "Dead ball" as soon as it is clear that the striker does not intend to hit the ball, or after the striker has made an unsuccessful attempt to hit the ball.

4. REVOKING A CALL

The umpire shall revoke the call if the striker hits a ball which has been called "Wide".

5. BALL NOT DEAD

The ball does not become dead on the call of "Wide ball" – see Law 23.4 (The Ball is Not Dead).

6. RUNS RESULTING FROM A WIDE

All runs which are run or result from a wide ball which is not a no ball shall be scored as wide balls, or if no runs are made, one shall be scored.

7. OUT FROM A WIDE

The striker shall be out from a wide ball if he breaks Law 35 (Hit Wicket) or Law 39 (Stumped). Either batsman may be run out and shall be out if he breaks Law 33 (Handled the Ball) or Law 37 (Obstructing the Field).

8. BATSMAN GIVEN OUT OFF A WIDE

Should a batsman be given out off a wide, the penalty for bowling it shall stand unless runs are otherwise made.

NOTE

(a) Wide ball Not Counting in over
A wide ball shall not be reckoned as one of the over – see Law 22.3 (No Ball or Wide Ball).

"Wides" were not recognised in the 1744 Code of Laws and it was not until around 1811 that a law for wides first appeared. They were then entered in the scorebook along with all the other "byes". I think the definition of a bye is easy enough. For me it is a ball which has passed "bye" (the old English spelling) – a ball which the wicket-keeper has been unable to stop. In 1828, a wide was to be recorded as such, thus exonerating the wicket-keeper from blame for failing to stop it. By 1835 there was a Law which instructed the umpire at the bowler's end to call "Wide ball" as soon as the ball passed the striker. The ball was then considered "dead" and only a one-run penalty would be recorded. It was in 1844 that a Law came into operation under which the ball was no longer "dead" upon the call of "Wide ball" and all runs obtained from such a delivery would be recorded. After this, in both the 1845 and 1947 Code of Laws, clarifications were set out as to the position of the striker and the height and width of the ball. These were matters to be decided "in the umpire's opinion". Obviously, in early matches, the ploy of bowling out of the reach of the striker was unfair and it was penalised then, as it is now.

A striker can be given *out* off a wide ball under Laws 33, 35, 37, 38 and 39. A non-striker can be given out, similarly, under Laws 33, 37 and 38. There are records of dismissals under these Laws going back to the 1850s but it is not clear whether they were dismissals after a wide had been called and signalled.

In modern professional cricket, umpires are instructed to be much more strict in calling and signalling "Wide ball" especially in the several limited-overs competitions. At one time the TCCB instructed umpires to take action if we thought a ball had been bowled deliberately down the leg side. It was referred to as "intent".

Before 1980 a ball which was judged to be a wide could only be called when the ball had passed the striker but in the 1980 Code there was a slight change to Law 25 to the effect that "Wide ball" would not be called until it had passed the striker's *wicket*. Close attention to the new Code saved me from potential embarrassment in a Kent v. Glamorgan John Player League match at Canterbury on 18 May 1982. Barry Lloyd was bowling his off-spin from my end to Asif Iqbal and decided to go round the wicket. He asked me to stand a little further back from the wicket, a position in which I could easily see the swing of his arm and the delivery of the ball. One delivery stuck between his fingers for a split second and when the ball was released it landed about ten yards to the off side of the pitch and carried on rolling. When it stopped, there was no thought in my mind of calling "Dead ball" because the ball had been correctly (if inaccurately) delivered. What I did think was "It's a wide", but only for a second. Only two people were moving – myself and the cover-point fieldsman who was about to pick up the ball. I said, "No, leave it." It was about 16 yards from Asif, but it was between the bowler's crease and the striker's wicket, out to Asif's right. I asked him, "Do you want to take advantage of a free hit?" and after a few seconds' consideration he replied, "No, Don. I don't think so." *Now* I signalled "Dead ball", picked it up and threw it back to the bowler. When I reached my position behind the bowler's wicket, Asif walked down the pitch and said, "Shouldn't we get a wide for that, Don?" "No, Asif," I replied. "I'll explain later."

Kent won the game quite easily with a fine not-out hundred from Chris Tavaré and 56 not out from Asif and afterwards Claude Lewis, the Kent scorer, approached me to ask quietly, "That funny incident when you signalled 'Dead ball', Don ... why didn't you allow another delivery?" I smiled and explained the position, but no wonder he was confused. Scorers would normally expect another delivery to be allowed after one ball has been signalled as "dead" prior to its reaching the striker, but not in this case. If, in fact, the delivery had travelled another 2 feet in distance it would have been called and signalled as a "Wide ball". If the incident had occurred a couple of years earlier it would have been a wide – by 2 feet! There is just one other point of Law worth noting: if Asif had elected to hit the ball when invited to do so, and if he had failed to make contact, I would then have called "Dead ball". The striker can only make one attempt to hit the stationary ball.

I have always been a great believer in umpires working together and helping each other as much as possible, on and off the field. In 1978 I was umpiring with Jack Van Gelovan, the former Leicestershire all-rounder, and during one evening a long discussion took place on dismissals from a wide, and in particular under Law 39 (Stumped). By a coincidence, the following week Jack was umpiring at Bradford, standing at the striker's end, when there was an appeal for a stumping ... just as his colleague was shouting

"Wide ball". Jack gave the batsman *out* and stuck to his guns. A couple of days later he was kind enough to ring me and express gratitude for that discussion we had had. He was one of the many former first-class cricketers who, over the years, have helped me with good advice; it was nice to think I had been able to do something in return.

Gerald Brodribb, in his book *Next Man In*, mentions a wide ball which was once caught by the fielder at third man. At Lord's of all places, I once saw my colleague at square-leg have to take a couple of hasty paces back to avoid a delivery from the bowler at my end. Verily, wides come in all shapes, sizes and widths.

As in the case of a no ball, if either batsman is given out under the appropriate Law from a wide, and no runs have been made otherwise, the one-run penalty for the delivery will stand. An interesting clarification came out of the meeting of the Laws Committee meeting to this Law, which I feel may cause a great deal of comment. As we all know, the striker can be out from the delivery of a "Wide ball" should he hit down his wicket whilst trying to play at the delivery. However if, with the score level, the striker actually accomplishes this indiscretion, on appeal, he will be out but the "Wide ball" will not be credited as an extra to the batting side. It was judged that the hitting down of the wicket happened first and whilst this may not always be the case in practice, that was the decision taken at the meeting. Remember, this is only when the scores are level, not in the ordinary course of events. I am not quite sure why it was decided to allow the run in one case and not in the other, and perhaps further discussion on this matter would be appropriate.

Should an act of illegal fielding take place after a call and signal of "Wide ball", a five-run penalty will be added to the one-run penalty for the wide. That will be recorded as six wides. While Law 24 (No Ball) makes no mention of this, it is axiomatic that both the five runs and the one run are penalties and the runs have not been otherwise scored. What applies in this case from a no ball must equally apply in the case of a wide.

A wide ball can also be judged on the height at which it is bowled above the striker's wicket, and I have seen amusing examples of this on a number of occasions. It tends to happen mostly in hot countries when bowlers' palms are sweaty, allowing the ball to escape from the grasp slightly earlier than expected. In October 1984, I was invited to accompany a number of senior cricketers on a short tour of Barbados and it certainly was hot. Even the Bajan players were feeling it and one of their bowlers delivered a ball which passed, at a conservative estimate, 30 feet over the head of the batsman. This was Mike Gear, a seasoned Minor Counties player, who was to become the first chief executive of Durham CCC in 1992. Umpiring at the bowler's end was David Archer, a most experienced official, but his only action was to call "Over" and he walked off to square-leg. The players looked around, at each other and then at me as I walked in to stand at the bowler's end for the next over. They couldn't understand why there had been no call of "Wide ball". There are times in an umpire's life when something just fails to register in his mind and this must have been one of them, similar to the story I tell against myself in dealing with Law 19 (Boundaries).

It was, incidentally, on that tour that I had the privilege of seeing what may well have been the last innings played by Roy Marshall, Hampshire's West Indian opener. I heard one of the home side ask Mike Gear who he was and Mike, after explaining, added, "But surely you know him. He's in fact from Barbados." The Bajans didn't know him but they very soon learned. Roy, getting on in years at the time, hit one of their bowlers' deliveries (the bowler considered himself a bit quick) so hard and so far that the ball disappeared out of the ground, never to be seen again.

Under Law 2 I have written a short paragraph with regard to David Archer the West Indian "Test" umpire and in this Law I refer to umpiring the last innings which Roy Marshall played, on a tour of Barbados. David in fact was my colleague during that match and it is not only ironic but also sad that in the December 1992 issue of *Wisden Cricket Monthly*, there are the obituaries of both of them; what is more, they died within three days of each other and the age of both was almost identical. Roy remained interested in the county club at Taunton, fighting a long illness with dignity; David umpired a "Test" as recently as April 1992. Both, without doubt, are a great loss to the game.

26

BYE AND LEG-BYE

1. BYES

If the ball, not having been called "Wide" or "No ball", passes the striker without touching his bat or person and any runs are obtained, the umpire shall signal "Bye" and the run or runs shall be credited as such to the batting side.

2. LEG-BYES

If the ball, not having been called "Wide" or "No ball", is unintentionally deflected by the striker's dress or person, except a hand holding the bat, and any runs are obtained, the umpire shall signal "Leg-bye" and the run or runs so scored shall be credited as such to the batting side.

Such leg-byes shall be scored only if, in the opinion of the umpire, the striker has:

(a) attempted to play the ball with his bat or

(b) tried to avoid being hit by the ball.

3. DISALLOWANCE OF LEG-BYES

In the case of deflection by the striker's person, other than in 2(a) and (b) above, the umpire shall call and signal "Dead ball" as soon as one run has been completed or when it is clear that a run is not being attempted, or the ball has reached the boundary.

On the call and signal of "Dead ball" the batsmen shall return to their original ends and no runs shall be allowed.

I n the 1968 season an experiment to this Law was brought into force which is virtually word for word the Law as it exists at present. It emphasised that the striker must have been trying to play the ball with his bat or that he had been taking some action to avoid being hit by the ball. If he was in the process of either of these actions when the ball made contact with his person and runs resulted, they would be legitimate and scored as "leg-byes".

As the Law stands, in many cases it might be from some other part of the striker's person or protective equipment other than his legs that the deflection occurs but any runs resulting will still be scored as leg-byes. There is just one part of the striker's protective equipment which, if so struck, will not result in leg-byes. This is the batting glove(s) as long as the hands wearing them are holding the bat. In any deflection, legal or otherwise, runs will be credited to the striker, and it follows that if the ball is caught by a fielder, then the striker will be dismissed under Law 32.

Before 1965, the striker did not have to play a stroke at a delivery for leg-byes to be credited when there was a deflection from his person. All the umpire had to decide was that the striker did not deliberately deflect the ball with his person. He could allow it to hit him and any runs which accrued from the deflection would be credited as leg-byes. I feel the law-makers have done well for, in my opinion, the Law is now as fair to both sides as it is possible to achieve.

When a bye is scored (from a delivery which makes no contact at all with the striker's bat, person or equipment) it is a matter of disgust to all wicket-keepers who take pride in ensuring that nothing is debited against them. This leads me to a point which many first-class wicket-keepers feel I do not get right because of *their* lack of knowledge of the Laws. Early in my career I am pretty sure that I was "marked down" in captains' reports – certainly by one wicket-keeper captain – because my action in this connection was perfectly correct. I refer to the delivery of a no ball which makes contact with the striker's person and, say, a couple of runs result. These are legitimate. In this case the Law states: "When the ball is dead the umpire will repeat the No ball signal to the scorers accompanied by a Bye signal." I have known wicket-keepers go blue in the face and tell me it should be "leg-byes" and at times question my decision – even my sanity. I am sure I have not been given the marks which my attention to the Law have merited.

Once a no ball, always a no ball; and in the instance I have cited, they will always be credited as such. They will never be credited as "byes" causing the wicket-keeper to feel I am doing him a disservice. The reason for the "Bye" signal is to inform the scorers that no contact was made with the striker's bat, or hands holding the bat, by the ball. The signal also ensures that I do not do the bowler a disservice by having the runs debited against him. To all wicket-keepers I say, "Trust me. I may get an occasional *out* or *not out* decision wrong but I certainly don't get that part of the game wrong!"

Unfortunately, I have to say that very few of my colleagues get this sequence of signals right. Most of them will accompany the "No ball" signal with a "Leg-bye" signal, and a few believe that simply a repeat of the "No ball" signal will suffice.

It is not so bad in the first instance, even though the procedure is incorrect, but those who know their Law will wonder why such a simple set of signals is not being carried out. The second one, when only the "No ball" signal is repeated, passes without comment from the bowler. He sees only the signal but fails to realise any runs which are credited will go to the striker and

143

therefore *against* him if the umpires do not inform the scorers that the ball has not been hit by the bat. The way the umpire does that is to give a signal which wicket-keepers think is a signal for a bye. It is not. It is simply saying to the scorers, "He did not hit it." As I say, once a no ball, always a no ball and this applies equally to a wide ball – although you wouldn't expect a wide ball would ever contact the striker. But it often escapes the attention of the wicket-keeper, who does not feel badly done-by in such a case. A wide is not going to be debited against him, as opposed to a bye.

If the batsmen embark on runs after an illegal deflection of the ball by the striker's person, the umpire will allow just one run to be completed, and then must immediately call and signal "Dead ball". Failure to take this action can lead to serious complications, because if either batsman is out of his ground it must be construed as taking a run. Either can be dismissed before "Dead ball" is called, except the striker in a case of Law 38.2.

After the ball reaches the boundary from any sort of deflection the scorers will be awaiting a signal from the umpires as the ball is automatically "dead". Instead of the boundary allowance signal, they will receive a "Dead ball" signal, which will tell them the boundary is not to be credited as the deflection was illegal. If the batsmen realise a deflection was illegal and make no effort to run I strongly advise a call of "Dead ball" just in case either batsman lays himself open to dismissal by leaving his ground to undertake repair of the pitch or perhaps to have a chat with his colleague. One further matter to which the umpires must pay attention, if there is a contravention of this Law, is to ensure that the batsmen are at their original wickets before the next ball is bowled.

As under Law 36.1(a), the umpire has the responsibility of deciding if an attempt to play the ball has been made – not an easy decision and whichever way you decide it will not necessarily meet with universal approval. But it is a decision which has to be made. If a delivery rears up towards the striker's head and he deliberately knocks away the ball with a hand which is not holding the bat, it will be regarded as a legal act so long as the umpire is of the opinion that the action was instinctive and in defence of the striker's person. Any runs which are taken will be recorded as leg-byes. If, however, that is not the umpire's opinion and an appeal is made, he could consider that Law 33 (Handled the Ball) had been infringed. On the other side of the coin, if the striker is not legitimate in the deflection of the ball by his person and the fielding side commit an illegal act (e.g. illegal fielding) there will not be an award of five runs under Law 41.1 (The Fieldsman) to the batting side who must not benefit from an illegal act.

A number of deep thinkers in the game feel there should be no such thing as an allowance for leg-byes. It is felt to be unfair. I have no fixed views on this, either way, but as a matter of fairness I do ask: "If you are not going to allow leg-byes to the batting side, how can you hope to sustain an lbw appeal in the fielding side's favour?"

If all the 42 Laws were framed as well as this one, equating fairness and justice to both sides in equal proportion, maybe the game would be even better than it is.

LAW
27

APPEALS

1. TIME OF APPEALS
The umpires shall not give a batsman out unless appealed to by the other side, which shall be done prior to the bowler beginning his run-up or bowling action to deliver the next ball. Under Law 23.1(g) (The Ball Becoming Dead) the ball is dead on "Over" being called; this does not, however, invalidate an appeal made prior to the first ball of the following over provided "Time" has not been called – see Law 17.1 (Call of Time).

2. AN APPEAL "HOW'S THAT?"
An appeal "How's that?" shall cover all ways of being out.

3. ANSWERING APPEALS
The umpire at the bowler's wicket shall answer appeals before the other umpire in all cases except those arising out of Law 35 (Hit Wicket) or Law 39 (Stumped) or Law 38 (Run Out) when this occurs at the striker's wicket.

When either umpire has given a batsman not out, the other umpire shall, within his jurisdiction, answer the appeal or a further appeal, provided it is made in time in accordance with (1) above (Time of Appeals).

4. CONSULTATION BY UMPIRES
An umpire may consult with the other umpire on a point of fact which the latter may have been in a better position to see and shall then give his decision. If, after consultation, there is still doubt remaining the decision shall be in favour of the batsman.

5. BATSMAN LEAVING HIS WICKET UNDER A MISAPPREHENSION
The umpire shall intervene if satisfied that a batsman, not having been given out, has left the wicket under a misapprehension that he has been dismissed.

6. UMPIRE'S DECISION
The umpire's decision is final. He may alter his decision, provided that such alteration is made promptly.

7. WITHDRAWAL OF AN APPEAL

In exceptional circumstances the captain of the fielding side may seek permission of the umpire to withdraw an appeal provided that the outgoing batsman has not left the playing area. If this is allowed, the umpire shall cancel his decision.

A n appeal for the dismissal of a batsman under nine of the ten Laws which decree he may be given *out* (I refuse to contemplate the tenth for reasons given in discussing Law 31) is as much a part of the game of cricket as the bat, the ball or a set of stumps. Appeals may be quiet and restrained; they may be vociferous and accompanied by a waving of arms or even jumping up and down. But they must command the respect and sober judgement of the umpire to whom they are addressed. There are appeals of "quality" by some sides and individuals; others are not quite as worthy of the same consideration. Yet from the greatest to the least they must be judged with the same care, attention and impartiality – equally.

An umpire is not able to give a decision unless an appeal is made to him, nor is he required to. I recall a quite amazing incident in a Benson & Hedges zonal match in 1985, Essex v. Combined Universities at Chelmsford. Essex batted first and the last ball of their innings was bowled to Ken McEwan, whose personal score stood at 99. He played the delivery down to the pitch and a run was attempted. Before the non-striker, Keith Fletcher, could complete the run the ball was thrown to the wicket-keeper and the wicket was broken with Keith still about 6 feet out of his ground. There was no semblance of an appeal or a shout or exclamation of any sort.

This, I felt, was an odd situation and some explanation was called for, so I shouted to Rob Andrew, the England rugby international who was captain of the Universities side. His only reaction was to wave his hands in a manner which signified to me, "Leave it", or "Forget it". It was as if the whole side had agreed not to appeal and thus allow McEwan to complete his century. As Essex had scored 333 for four in their 55 overs, perhaps they thought one more run wouldn't make a difference? Certainly it was indicative of the sporting spirit in which most University men play their cricket, notably Rob Andrew. Unfortunately, that was not the way most of the Press (or the TCCB) saw the incident. Some of the headlines read: "It's Always Worth a Shout", "McEwan's Century is a Gift", and "Don's Ton-up Trouble".

I didn't see that *I* had any trouble. I had complied fully with the Laws of Cricket, as I hope I always will. What disturbed me was that none of the reports bothered to mention the matter of sportsmanship. Then I received a letter from Donald Carr, Secretary of the TCCB, which astounded me. He wrote: "I was rather surprised to read of your decision at the end of the recent Essex v. Combined Universities match at Chelmsford, though I am not aware of the precise details. I would be interested to know the facts and the reason for your decision to award a run off the last ball of the Essex innings."

The only comment which could be made was that there was no decision for me to give. I was not asked for one, by anybody. As for "awarding" a run – it was not "awarded"; it was gained by the batting side. I think the best, the most concise account of the incident, appeared in the 1986 *Wisden*: "Off the last ball of the Essex innings Fletcher was 'run out' going for the run which brought up McEwan's hundred but in the absence of an appeal he was not given 'out' by umpire Oslear." Nothing else needs to be said.

An appeal may be made prior to the bowler starting his run-up or bowling action to deliver the next ball or before "Time" has been called. In that Chelmsford match I have often wondered what I would have done if, as I walked off the field, the captain had said to me, "Sorry, but I'm now making an appeal." *My colleague had long since called, "Time"*. Any bets? "Not out".

The umpire at the bowler's end has far more appeals to answer than his colleague at the striker's end. The division is actually 6½ against 2½ (one being judged at either end) but all are equally important. Should an umpire not reply in the affirmative to an appeal which has been made to him another appeal can then be made to his colleague if it falls within his jurisdiction and it is made in time. It may seem strange, but if there is an incident off the final ball of an over without an appeal being made, an appeal will still be in time if it is made before the bowler at the other end starts any action to deliver the first ball of a new over. A full minute may have elapsed since the incident when the umpire who is now in the square-leg position calls and signals that the batsman now in the non-striker's position is *out*. Umpires should note that in such a case the scorers should be made fully aware of what has happened, and the nature of the dismissal.

If an umpire is unsure of certain facts when an appeal is made to him he may consult his colleagues if the colleague was better placed to observe the incident. This rarely happens in first-class cricket because the standard is very high, but no one would shirk the issue if it was necessary. In the 1992 season I found myself in such a situation at Chelmsford. (Why is it always Chelmsford?) A ball was edged low and very wide to the right-hand side of the wicket-keeper. I turned down the appeal but the wicket-keeper was insistent and he looked across at my colleague as though wishing I would consult him. I looked at my colleague, quickly realising that he was at least as far away from the scene as I was and his view of whether there had been a catch was masked by the body of the wicker-keeper himself. He was in no position to see whether there had been a clean catch or not so there was no point in consulting him. I had not, however, thought of consultation. I was satisfied that the catch had not carried to the wicket-keeper's glove and my decision was always going to be *not out*, so there was no point in involving my colleague or allowing the players to think I was unsure of my decision.

Sometimes – in very rare cases – a batsman may think he has been dismissed and leave the wicket when the umpire does not take the same view. In such cases I advise a rapid call of "Dead ball" by the umpire, which will suffice to prevent anything silly happening after that. Consultation may take place by any or all the parties involved and the matter be resolved. One player who tried to ensure that in certain circumstances the umpire was not involved at all was John Jameson, the former Warwickshire and England batsman, and personally I think it showed sportsmanship of the highest calibre. If John (as the striker) was not sure a low catch had been taken cleanly he would ask the fieldsman, "Did you catch it?" If the answer was "Yes" John would leave the pitch and never, throughout the whole sequence, would he look at the umpire. I hope that all the fielders were as honest as John was prepared to be. My advice to umpires who see this sort of thing taking place, is: "Keep out of it." Only if our decision is required should we become involved. We are in a privileged position and we adjudicate on incidents only when asked to do so.

The Law states that if, after answering an appeal, the umpire wishes to change his decision, he may do so but it must be done quickly. I have only once had to take this action – in a match at Headingley. Arnie Sidebottom was bowling and, in answer to his loud appeal for lbw, I was raising my finger to signify *out* when I realised in the last split second that there had been some contact of ball on bat before it hit the pad. I found myself with finger raised saying "That's not out. He hit it." I got a bit of stick from my Yorkshire friends but that was much better than giving someone *out* who was not.

Drafted into the 1980 Code of Laws was the opportunity for the captain of the fielding side to withdraw an appeal if he so wished. This has not often been implemented and most captains are reluctant to do so because they feel they may be usurping the umpire's authority. It usually happens when an *out* decision has been given and the fieldsmen close to the scene of action feel, on reflection, that not only was the decision incorrect; they themselves were not correct in appealing. The action to withdraw an appeal may only be taken by the captain who must make his request to the umpire before the batsman leaves the field of play. My advice to umpires when faced with this situation is: Always accede to the request. You may be a bit embarrassed for a moment but your standing in the eyes of others in the game will be enhanced.

Wicket-keepers often break the wicket and appeal but with no real chance of success (the striker has never looked remotely like leaving his ground) and as the umpire runs in to remake the wicket a muttered apology is often heard. "Sorry." My favourite reply is, "If you never buy a raffle ticket you are never going to win a raffle prize." Again it emphasises: No appeal, no dismissal.

28

THE WICKET IS DOWN

1. WICKET DOWN
The wicket is down if:

(a) Either the ball or the striker's bat or person completely removes either bail from the top of the stumps. A disturbance of a bail, whether temporary or not, shall not constitute a complete removal but the wicket is down if a bail in falling lodges between two of the stumps.

(b) Any player completely removes with his hand or arm a bail from the top of the stumps provided that the ball is held in that hand or the hand of the arm so used.

(c) When both bails are off, a stump is struck out of the ground by the ball, or a player strikes or pulls a stump out of the ground, provided that the ball is held in the hand(s) or the hand of the arm so used.

2. ONE BAIL OFF
If one bail is off, it shall be sufficient for the purpose of putting the wicket down to remove the remaining bail, or to strike or pull any of the three stumps out of the ground in any of the ways stated in (1) above.

3. ALL THE STUMPS OUT OF THE GROUND
If all the stumps are out of the ground, the fielding side shall be allowed to put back one or more stumps in order to have an opportunity of putting the wicket down.

4. DISPENSING WITH BAILS
If, owing to the strength of the wind, it has been agreed to dispense with the bails in accordance with Law 8, Note (a) (Dispensing with Bails), the decision as to when the wicket is down is one for the umpires to take on the facts before them. In such circumstances, and if the umpires so decide, the wicket shall be held to be down even though a stump has not been struck out of the ground.

NOTE
(a) Remaking the Wicket

If the wicket is broken while the ball is in play, it is not the umpire's duty to remake the wicket until the ball becomes dead – see Law 23 (Dead Ball). A member of the fielding side, however, may remake the wicket in such circumstances.

T o my mind, "The wicket is down" can be accomplished by four different methods: it can be bowled down as in Law 30; it can be thrown down by any member of the fielding side throwing the ball at and breaking the wicket, as in Law 38 (Run Out); it can be broken by a fielder with the ball in his hand, again under Law 38; or by the wicket-keeper with ball in hand under Law 39 (Stumped); it can be struck down by the bat or the person, clothing or equipment of the striker as in Law 35 (Hit Wicket).

Let us take, first, what may appear to be the most straightforward way, bowled – it is obviously easier now for a bowler than in the days when it was a two-stump wicket with an overall width of 6 inches. It must have been disconcerting for a bowler to see a perfectly delivered ball missed by the striker but passing between the stumps without touching either of them. This would mean that the bail was not dislodged and in such a case the wicket was not considered to be bowled down. In one match at Hambledon in 1775 the last pair scored 14 runs to win a match while the ball passed between the stumps in this manner no fewer than three times. That led to the introduction of three stumps that year.

I feel that the increased dimensions which have taken place over the years have been fully covered under Law 8. Heaven forbid that we ever have a four-stump wicket with a width of 12 inches, but I have heard it suggested.

Present-day wickets do not allow the free passage of the ball through them, yet umpires must always be vigilant to spot if the stumps are thin enough, or perhaps have a bend in them, leaving a larger gap between them so a ball is able to pass through. Remember, also, the story under Law 8 of the stump at Huddersfield with a groove so deep that the bail would not have been removed to ensure that "The wicket was down".

All that need happen to ensure a wicket being "down" is for one bail to be completely removed from the top of the stumps. Please note that plural: "stumps". I have seen a wicket bowled down, with one bail on the ground but the other balanced across the top of the leg stump. If the bail now on the ground had instead remained in place the decision would have been *not out* as the other bail had only been removed from *the top of* one of the stumps. It must also be a *permanent* removal (note the story under Law 30 of seeing a ball clip the outside of a stump and the bail jumping several inches into the air before landing back in the groove). That is *not out* as the removal of the bail was only of a temporary nature.

However, in some quarters there is the notion that the bail must fall to the ground to ensure that "The wicket is down". This is not so. That wicket is "down" and so the decision is *out* (see picture in photo section).

What I consider one of the most thrilling sights in the game is a brilliant piece of fielding with the wicket being *thrown* down. I have mentioned some of the great exponents of this art in Law 38. Again, all that need happen is for one bail to tumble completely from the top of the stumps after the ball has hit the wicket and before the batsman has made his ground.

Please take note of the following as it is a clarification by the MCC Laws Committee on 12 October 1992. Question: A fielder throws the ball at the wicket with the striker's bat grounded behind the line of the batting crease; the ball hits the wicket and a bail falls off. As the ball ricochets away the batsman lifts his bat and starts to run. At that moment the second bail falls off. How's that? Answer: If we turn to Law 38.1 it says that if the batsman be out of his ground when the wicket is put down, the decision would be *out*. In our hypotetical example, the batsman was not out of his ground when the wicket was put down. Law 38.1 does not say "out of his ground when the wicket is broken". When the second bail fell off, some time after the initial impact of the ball against the wicket, it is not ruled as "putting the wicket down". That would have required a second action by the fielding side and that did not take place. The answer to the appeal would therefore be *not out*.

Should one bail have been removed from the top of the stumps, the removal of the other in the correct manner will constitute a wicket being "put down". Perhaps we might have a situation in which both bails have been removed from the top of the stumps and all three stumps are lying on the ground. I have seen this happen. The ball was being returned to the wicket-keeper, who took it above his head, took a couple of steps backwards and unfortunately "sat" on the stumps. In such a case, all the fielding side has to do is place one of the stumps back in a stump-hole and remove it in a correct manner to establish that "The wicket is down". If the batsman has not made his ground at that end of the pitch he will be dismissed. If both bails are off, the necessary action from the fielding side is to replace one bail and remove it in the correct manner for the wicket to be "down".

If there has been some action which has removed both bails from the top of the stumps and an *out* decision has not been given by the umpire, and the batsmen are still running to and fro on the pitch, there may be no time to replace one of the bails, or perhaps no one thinks about doing so. The fielding side, to effect a dismissal, may, in this case, remove a stump completely out of the ground. This may be done by throwing the ball at, and removing a stump completely out of, the ground; or a fielder, with the ball in his hand, may remove a stump from the ground by pulling it up or striking it down, out of the ground, with his arm – as long as the ball is in the hand, or the hand of the arm which takes such action. It is no good (as I have seen) holding the ball in one hand and pulling up a stump with the other. That is most certainly *not out*.

As stated under Law 39 (Stumped), if we are playing without bails on top of the stumps, it is for the umpires to decide on the facts before them whether "The wicket is down". In such a situation a stump does not have to be struck out of the ground. I carry a set of heavy bails and they usually suffice when there is a high wind. I can recall only two occasions when it has been impossible to keep even this type of bail on top of the stumps. One was in a match at Portsmouth some years ago and the other at Headingley at the start of the 1992 season. The wind was so strong on one day that it blew across the ground a protective helmet which had been placed behind the wicket-keeper. It raced towards the square-leg boundary with a couple of slip-fielders in hot pursuit!

The fourth way in which the wicket is "down" is when the striker hits down his own wicket (Law 35, Hit Wicket) but I have had to give very few decisions under that Law. In the main it is usually the quicker type of bowler who benefits, and more often than not it is some part of the striker's person or equipment which strikes down the wicket, rather than the bat. I have seen a striker lose his protective helmet, which has landed on top of the stumps, removing the bails. One helmet fell to the ground and rolled against the stumps, removing one bail – again an instance of striking the wicket down. A striker getting on to the back foot to play a ball delivered by a quicker bowler, often is so close to the stumps that a bail can be removed by his heel, the side of a pad and even his flannels – in all those cases the wicket is struck down.

This is a much more important Law than might be imagined and should be read in conjunction with all the Laws mentioned in the opening paragraph of my remarks on Law 28.

29

BATSMAN OUT OF HIS GROUND

I. WHEN OUT OF HIS GROUND

A batsman shall be considered to be out of his ground unless some part of his bat in his hand or of his person is grounded behind the line of the popping crease.

This Law is largely self-explanatory. Unless a batsman has some part of his person or his bat held in the hand grounded behind the line of the batting crease (i.e. nearer to the stumps) which he is trying to reach he will be deemed to be "out of his ground". At times, it will seem to those who are some distance away from the wicket that the batsman has made good his ground as his bat is well in front of him whilst he is running, but a spectator taking that view may well have forgotten the golden rule, taught to us from the earliest days of picking up a bat: run it along the ground when taking a run, as far in front of oneself as possible. It will be no use having the bat well in front of him if it is waving about in the air. To have made good his ground, some part of bat or person must be *grounded* behind the batting crease.

At other points in this book you will see an explanation of why I go down on one knee at the striker's end – even, occasionally, at the bowling end – to see if the bat is in contact with the ground behind the batting crease.

I have a number of photographic slides which I use to illustrate lectures. They show very clearly when this contact has *not* taken place. One of them shows a batsman in the non-striker's position actually sitting on top of the handle of the bat while it is in an almost perpendicular position. It can be seen that while the toe of the bat is clearly grounded behind the line of the batting crease, he has still not complied fully with the requirements of the Law because both feet are forward of the batting crease. If the wicket is broken and an appeal made for his dismissal the umpire's decision must be *out*. The bat in this case was not held in hand.

Another slide shows a batsman who has slipped and let go of his bat which is lying on the ground – half the blade behind the batting crease, the other half and the handle well forward of it. The batsman has been able to stretch a leg back and place one foot on the bat-handle. Again, the Law has not been complied with and upon appeal the decision would have to be *out*.

Should the batsmen be taking a run, both will be out of their ground at the same time. I have heard a number of umpires argue that if the batsmen have crossed they will not be allowed to recross if it is the same run, for the purpose of a dismissal under Law 38 (Run Out). That is not correct. They can cross and recross as often as they like in their efforts to make good their ground during the taking of a run. Should the wicket be put down, always apply the criterion as in Law 38: "He who is closer to the wicket which is put down shall be *out*, for he is the one who is 'out of his ground'." I have also covered this point in dealing with Law 38. It is important.

There is one unusual occurrence which will not be classed as "out of his ground" if it happens. This is when a batsman has first made good his ground and then leaves it (in the umpire's opinion) to avoid injury. It is under Law 38.1, and is an addition to the 1980 Code of Laws. Remember: this applies only when the batsman has first made his ground – not before he has made it – and it must be to avoid being injured, not necessarily from the ball. It may be the view of the umpire that if the batsman had remained in a particular position he could have affected the wicker-keeper's taking of the ball and then crashing into the batsman, injuring both of them. It is sensible that the batsman should legally be able to leave his ground in such a case.

BOWLED

1. OUT BOWLED

The striker shall be out *Bowled* if:

(a) His wicket is bowled down, even if the ball first touches his bat or person.

(b) He breaks his wicket by hitting or kicking the ball on to it before the completion of a strike, or as a result of attempting to guard his wicket. See Law 34.1 (Out Hit the Ball Twice).

NOTE

(a) Out Bowled – Not lbw

The striker is out bowled if the ball is deflected on to his wicket even though a decision against him would be justified under Law 36 (lbw).

T he decision of *out*, bowled, is one which very rarely has to be given by an umpire because it is usually clear-cut. I do, however, remember one such decision in a club match at my home ground, in Cleethorpes, when I was required to adjudicate.

The wicket-keeper was standing up to the stumps to a medium-paced bowler, one of whose deliveries passed the bat and just touched the outside of the off stump. The ball then smacked against the wicker-keeper's pads and rebounded on to the stumps. The striker turned to find one bail behind the stumps, one in front; one stump was leaning backwards and one forwards. He didn't know what to make of it. After a couple of seconds, the wicket-keeper appealed to me, at the bowler's end, and I signified that the striker was *out*. It was obvious to me that he had been bowled. But I must stress that great concentration was required to spot that the ball had made slight contact with the off stump and this had caused a bail to be removed from the top of the stumps. Concentration is what umpiring is all about.

In the very early days of the game it must have been disconcerting for bowlers, with only two stumps supporting one bail 6 inches in length, to know there were times when the ball passed between the stumps without making contact and the bail remained in position. The wicket, therefore, was not "bowled down". This led, in 1775, to the third stump being added with no change in the dimension of the wicket. All the lawmakers were doing was ensuring that the ball did not pass *between* the stumps, *through* the wicket. Under Law 8 (The Wicket) I have referred to changes in the dimensions of the wicket. The present dimension has been in operation only since 1931.

There have been many well-documented records and oddities regarding a wicket being "bowled down". The record distance a bail has flown from the top of the stumps (unless it has been broken recently) is 83 yds 1 ft 9 in. – achieved by a player named Burrows during a match in Tasmania. In an English Minor Counties match in 1908 a bail was measured as having flown 70 yards to the boundary edge. I have seen a stump, after being hit, travel 14 yards from its pitched position. There have been cases of all three stumps being left flat on the grass in a case of bowled and instances of off and leg stumps being knocked out while the middle stump remained in position.

During a match at Horsham (the one involving the incident related under Law 37), there was another interesting incident (both occurred during the same session of play). A ball flicked the striker's pad as it passed down the leg side and was well taken by the wicket-keeper who was standing reasonably close to the stumps. Standing at the striker's end, I saw clearly that neither the striker's nor the wicket-keeper's person had made contact with the stumps, but as the ball passed the wicket the leg bail fell off. An appeal was made by the wicket-keeper to my colleague, who said *"Not out"*. During a later discussion he added that he could not see the leg stump but he had seen a deflection off the striker's pad which was, of course, further to the leg side. He was unable to see, or say, how the ball could have made contact with the wicket. We shall never know. But I would love to know how that bail came off!

In order to decide the ultimate winner of all TCCB limited-overs competitions if they are not completed in the allotted time we have a contest of bowling at a set of stumps. This owes its appearance to the Tilcon Trophy, played at Harrogate, or perhaps I may say it owes its origins to my colleague John Holder and myself. On 21 June 1985, the final was due to be played, but it rained. The managing director of the Tilcon Group, Peter Clark, asked the two of us if we could think of a way of deciding the competition other than the toss of a coin.

John had seen something of this sort (bowling at a set of stumps) used to decide a competition in league cricket and I remembered from my early days throwing at a single stump for fielding practice. It was around these two memories that we formulated a quick competition to decide a winner when there was no time left to play a match. Each of the eleven players would bowl two deliveries at a single stump and the side scoring more hits would be the winner. In that year of 1985 we saw Warwickshire beat Notts by five hits to one and with a few modifications the TCCB have now adopted a similar procedure. It has given the game a new expression: "being Tilconed".

Curiously enough, these ad hoc rules had to be put into operation in the

Tilcon Trophy semi-final the following year (1986) and once again I was one of the umpires. That's a personal record, but Norman Gifford holds an even better one. He scored hits for Warwickshire in both those games!

For a decision of *out*, bowled, all that is required is for a bail to be completely removed from the top of the stumps. I am sure we have all seen cases of the bails merely being "disturbed" when the ball has hit the stumps and not removed completely. (See further examples under Law 28, The Wicket is Down.) The set of heavy bails which I carry with me is useful in a very strong wind and I have, on occasions, played for most of the day without bails in place at all. Both my colleague and I have said, on such occasions, how unusual it was to be looking down a pitch at a wicket without any bails. In such cases, a ball has only to make contact with a stump, however slight, to constitute "bowled". Concentration then becomes more essential than ever, if that is possible! I umpired without bails at Portsmouth in mid-August 1979, a day when the winds were so strong that many yachts were lost during the Fastnet Race and a marquee was blown completely across the ground.

The dismissal "bowled" is one which will not follow strictly the chronological order of events. If the ball has first struck the pad in circumstances in which an lbw appeal would have been sustained, then gone on to hit the wicket and remove a bail, the decision will be *out*, bowled – even though the lbw situation occurred first. This is not the only instance (see Law 41).

The striker will be *out*, bowled, if the ball first makes contact with his bat or if there is a rebound from the striker's person after he has hit the ball and the ball breaks the wicket. There are other people in the field, of course, from whom a rebound will not be considered as rendering "the wicket down" under Law 30 (Bowled). An umpire or the non-striker are two cases in point. The Law also states the wicket-keeper, although I think this would be obvious, as the ball had passed the wicket; but do remember the story under Law 23 (Dead Ball) in regard to Brian Davison having the right to defend his wicket.

At a meeting of the MCC Laws Committee on 12 October 1992, a clarification to Law 30 was agreed: "In the case of a ball which has been fairly delivered by the bowler stopping prior to its reaching the striker the striker will be allowed one free hit at the ball. Should such a hit be made and the ball is hit against his own wicket and the wicket broken, upon appeal the striker will be out under Law 30 (Bowled).

31

TIMED OUT

1. OUT – TIMED OUT

An incoming batsman shall be out *Timed Out* if he wilfully takes more than 2 minutes to come in – the 2 minutes being timed from the moment a wicket falls until the new batsman steps on to the field of play.

If this is not complied with and if the umpire is satisfied that the delay was wilful and if an appeal is made, the new batsman shall be given out by the umpire at the bowler's end.

2. TIME TO BE ADDED

The time taken by the umpires to investigate the cause of the delay shall be added at the normal close of play.

NOTES

(a) Entry in Scorebook

The correct entry in the scorebook when a batsman is given out under this Law is "timed out", and the bowler does not get credit for the wicket.

(b) Batsmen crossing on the Field of Play

It is an essential duty of the captains to ensure that the in-going batsman passes the out-going one before the latter leaves the field of play.

T his is classed as the tenth way of being out, but if ever a Law was ridiculous and virtually impossible to enforce, this is it. It was ridiculous, in my view, that it was ever thought necessary to include it in the 1980 Code of Laws at all and unnecessary, I feel, because what most cricketers, at all levels, want to do is pad up and go out to try and score a few runs. As for "wilfully" delaying things – most players find difficulty in waiting for their turn to bat. That is why some batsmen sit "padded up" for hours before they are required.

Having said that, let's look at the Law in detail and try to make clear its application if this ever becomes necessary. It states that the time allowed from the fall of a wicket to the new batsman setting foot on the field of play is two minutes. I think that is a reasonable length of time but there *could be* a considerable delay at some grounds.

There is a famous story of David Steele (then of Northants), when playing for England at Lord's, going down two flights of steps too many on his way out to bat. He then found himself in the MCC Members' toilet area! It was then necessary for him to go back up those two flights and make his way through the Long Room – both areas which are thronged during a summer Test Match – and I bet the second-hand on a few watches had made several circuits of the dial before he reached the gate and stepped on to the field of play.

To digress for a moment, in 1992 the officials of the Cricketers Association negotiated with the TCCB an allowance of 3 minutes, this to be taken into consideration when calculating a side's bowling over-rate, yet Law 31 continued to state that 2 minutes was the time allowed when considering an appeal!

Under Law 31, as in all other dismissals, an appeal is required and if one is not made the umpires are not required to take any action whatsoever even if a considerable time has elapsed since the fall of the previous wicket. Should an appeal be made, the umpires, acting together, must be sure that not only has more than 2 minutes elapsed but that the delay was wilful.

Umpires do not normally note the time of a dismissal and to my mind there is no reason why they should. If the delay is for a noticeably long time they won't need a watch. As for the delay being "wilful" – how ridiculous! Delays can take place for any number of accidental reasons . . . misplaced batting gloves, forgetting to put on a box or another item of protective equipment, and I have known a man to be accidentally locked in a toilet; recently (not an isolated incident) a batsman has arrived at the boundary edge to find he hadn't brought a bat. It happened to Bob Willis once in a Test Match at Edgbaston.

"Definitions" to this Law recommend that if an incoming batsman is on the field when an appeal is made the two umpires should question him on the reason for the delay. This, to me, is another waste of time. Should an appeal under this stupid Law ever be upheld and an incoming batsman dismissed, the time taken to investigate the delay will be added at the scheduled close of the day's play. Once again – how ridiculous!

Let us see what would happen if there was a delay of, say, 15 minutes before a new batsman appeared and the disgruntled fielding side then made an appeal. The umpires agree that more than 2 minutes has elapsed but the new batsman then appears on the field of play, runs to the middle and offers profuse apologies for the delay in his appearance. And the umpires accept his apology and explanation! It is then only 45 seconds since the fielding side appealed, so 45 seconds will be added on at the end of the day. But not the 15 minutes which had elapsed before the appeal was made? Ridiculous! If the time to be added, because of an infringement of Law 31, is on any other day than the last, it is easy: just add it on after the time for the close of play.

If it is a match which requires a minimum number of overs to be bowled in a day and the number of overs have not been bowled when the time of the scheduled close is reached, add the time when the overs have been completed. Should an infringement of Law 31 take place during the final day of the match, prior to the last hour's play starting, the signal for that last hour will be made later than its scheduled time, by the number of minutes which have been taken up to investigate any delay. I am not sure that I agree with this procedure. I feel the time should be added after the final hour, or after the 20 overs have been bowled, if that be later.

It can be seen that this goes some way to prove that the action taken by my colleague and I at Nottingham in 1981, Nottinghamshire v. Middlesex, was correct (see story in Law 17). I know that the circumstances were not exactly the same, but it shows that there can be alterations to the starting time of the final hour of a match. Should an infringement take place during the final hour of the match, the time will be added after the scheduled time of the close of the match, or after the 20 overs have been completed, should this be later.

My good friend, Peter Stevens of Worcester, a prominent member of ACU in respect of the training of umpires and also one of my ex-colleagues from the first-class panel of umpires, suggests to me an even better method. In the final hour, if any infringement of this Law takes place, whatever time is taken to investigate the delay should be apportioned at one over for each three minutes or part thereof. If the time taken is of a four minute duration, then two further overs will be bowled in addition to the final 20. This to me would appear a very sensible and fair suggestion to cover the issue.

Many people have given a great deal of thought to the formation of this Law, but I feel it was framed out of fear – fear that at some future date the old Law 17.1(iii) would have to be applied with the match ending at that point. Isn't it better to lose one batsman than the hours of cricket?

I would love to know more about how this Law was recommended, considered and then included in the 1980 Code. At the moment, while I know how to implement it (and sincerely hope I never have to), I can only say again: what a load of rubbish!

32

CAUGHT

1. OUT CAUGHT

The striker shall be out *Caught* if the ball touches his bat or if it touches below the wrist his hand or glove, holding the bat, and is subsequently held by a fieldsman before it touches the ground.

2. A FAIR CATCH

A catch shall be considered to have been made fairly if:

(a) The fieldsman is within the field of play throughout the act of making the catch.

(i) The act of making the catch shall start from the time when the fieldsman first handles the ball and shall end when he both retains complete control over the further disposal of the ball and remains within the field of play.

(ii) In order to be within the field of play, the fieldsman may not touch or ground any part of his person on or over a boundary line. When the boundary is marked by a fence or a board the fieldsman may not ground any part of his person over the boundary fence or board but may touch or lean over the boundary fence or board in completing the catch.

(b) The ball is hugged to the body of the catcher or accidentally lodges in his dress or, in the case of the wicket-keeper, in his pads. However, a striker may not be caught if a ball lodges in a protective helmet worn by a fieldsman, in which case the umpire shall call and signal "Dead ball". See Law 23 (Dead Ball).

(c) The ball does not touch the ground, even though a hand holding it does so in effecting the catch.

(d) A fieldsman catches the ball after it has been lawfully played a second time by the striker but only if the ball has not touched the ground since first being struck.

(e) A fieldsman catches the ball after it has touched an umpire, another fieldsman or the other batsman. However, a striker may not be caught if a ball has touched a protective helmet worn by a fieldsman.

(f) The ball is caught off an obstruction within the boundary, provided it has not previously been agreed to regard the obstruction as a boundary.

3. SCORING OF RUNS

If a striker is caught, no runs shall be scored.

NOTES

(a) Scoring from an Attempted Catch
When a fieldsman carrying the ball touches or grounds any part of his person on or over a boundary marked by a line, 6 runs shall be scored.
(b) Ball Still in Play
If a fieldsman releases the ball before he crosses the boundary the ball will be considered to be still in play and it may be caught by another fieldsman. However, if the original fieldsman returns to the field of play and handles the ball a catch may not be made.

As fielding was the only aspect of the game in which, during my playing days, I approached a reasonable standard of proficiency, my thoughts on this Law will include more than a few personal recollections. For me, the delight of the game was to field, chase, stop and throw a ball and, most of all, to catch one.

To say that I only dropped two catches in my career would be to invite ridicule from my former team-mates but I have to insist that I dropped only two which I felt I should have held. At the professional level there were – and are – many brilliant catchers of the ball. To my regret I never saw men like Tony Lock, Mickey Stewart and Ken Grieves play and the man I have heard described as "the greatest" was Peter Walker, of Glamorgan. My present boss Tony Brown, ex-Gloucestershire, once took seven in an innings but I did just see him play.

I was, in fact, carrying on a family tradition at Cleethorpes Cricket Club where my brother has now taken over 500 catches for the club, mainly at slip, and my father held hundreds, too. In fact the three of us played together in the same side for a short time and, between us, we must have held over 1,000 catches for that Club.

Catches come in various ways – high and low, quick and slow – and one or two which stick in the mind I shall describe later. For the moment, let us look at the Law. Catches at slip are, perhaps, the ones that fly the quickest and there is no set time for the ball to be held by the catcher. I have often heard talk of a fielder catching the ball and throwing it high in exultation, not caring where it drops after that. And I have heard the claim that such a catch should be disallowed.

I would point to the first sentence of "Definitions" under Law 32 in *Umpiring and Scoring* by Tom Smith, which clarifies this point: "The completion of a catch is defined as the retention of the ball and the power of complete control over its further disposal." The very fact the catcher has "further disposed" of the ball – into the air – proves to me that it was held. It is possible to debate for hours whether a ball was caught, or merely knocked up or juggled with. But a proficient umpire can tell instantly when a ball has been caught correctly. Some catches may not be taken simply in the hands but the catch is still valid if it held to some part of the anatomy – between his thighs, in the armpit, hugged to catcher's body. It is also caught if it accidentally lodges in a sweater worn by the fielder or indeed within a wicket-keeper's pad. All are valid catches and should be given the *out* decision.

Over the past two decades there is one article worn by some fieldsmen which will not merit an *out* decision if the ball is held within it – the protective helmet. I have also seen a wicket-keeper wearing one. More recently, it would not be a catch if the ball had first made contact with a helmet, even a slight contact.

Some of the great catches are those made by a fieldsman diving at full stretch, hand and arm thrust along the turf. A catch of that kind is valid so long as it is not the ball which touches the ground. The ball may touch many things within the field of play and still lead to a valid catch as long as it has not touched the ground, a striker's or non-striker's helmet or even their person, an umpire, another fielder, any obstruction within the field of play if the umpires have not previously agreed on that obstruction being a boundary.

Many outfield catches are spectacular in the extreme but they require consideration as to their validity. For example, the fielder must be within the boundary of the field of play throughout the whole act of taking the catch (i.e. from the moment the fielder first makes contact with the ball to the ultimate completion of the catch). During this time he must not touch any boundary line, rope or gulley whilst in contact with the ball. If contact is made it will be six runs and *not out* as in Law 19.

A fielder, after catching the ball, may realise he is incapable of stopping himself going outside the field of play. In that case he may throw the ball to one of his colleagues. If he does this before encountering the boundary the catch is valid.

At Cardiff some years ago John Hopkins chased towards a boundary, made a great catch, hit the ground and slid over the boundary line. This was ruled as six runs and "not out", much to John's disgust. But it has not always been so. In the 1947 Code (Law 35, Caught), the last paragraph states: "The fieldsman must have both his feet entirely within the playing area at the instant the catch is completed." Any further action by the catcher after that moment, running or sliding over the boundary, would therefore not have invalidated the catch as it did in John's case. A fielder may also lean over a boundary line, rope or gulley in making a catch but he must not touch it. With a boundary board it is different: a fielder may lean over or against a boundary board or fence to complete a catch.

When the 1980 Code came into operation, this point was well clarified. At the time, I thought it was great but after more than a decade of its application

I am not so sure. It may be better, once we know a catch has been completed *within* the confines of the boundary, if the catcher is allowed to end up wherever his momentum takes him. He can even make a circuit of the ground upon a lap of honour, holding the ball aloft.

The first time I saw a ball caught and carried over the boundary was under the old Code of Law and it was still *not out* because in fact the catcher was in mid-air when he caught the ball but he was certainly outside the boundary line when he landed. This was at Denton, near Manchester, in a final of what was known as the President's Trophy, played between the North Staffs and Cheshire League and the South Lancs League. A left-handed batsman pulled a ball to the long-leg boundary and a fieldsman ran round the boundary edge, leapt up and caught the ball in his right hand. As he landed there was a clatter of studs upon tarmac. He had landed on a cycle-track which circled the ground. The edge of the track was in fact the boundary of the cricket field. This match was played on 11 September 1977, and as it was under the old Code I might have had some difficulty in knowing if it had been a legitimate catch but for the clatter of the fieldsman's spikes on the tarmac. In fact I was given an extra bit of help when the fieldsman, exasperated, threw the ball down on to the track where it bounced 50 feet into the air!

The use of a rope for the boundary instead of a white line painted on the grass was at the insistence of the first-class panel of umpires. This method was used, the TCCB making the regulation compulsory in all their competitions for the 1981 season. It it of great help to umpires, and fielders, in catches taking place close to the rope. Umpires are able to see and fieldsmen to feel if they make contact with the rope (i.e. the boundary line) whilst in contact with the ball. This will invalidate a catch. The fieldsman had less chance of knowing when he was standing on a painted white line, and it was equally difficult for the umpire to see where the fieldsman was standing in relation to the white line, at least from a distance of up to 90 yards or so.

Under Law 19 (Boundaries) readers will have seen a story about a catch being taken at Cheltenham by a fielder who then crashed against the boundary boards. This catch was quite legal as long as the fieldsman did not ground any part of his person *over* the board. That, to me, means the board in its raised position. The fielder's contact can make the board lean backwards and if a fielder makes a catch while leaning against the board in the raised position, the catch will still be legal. To my mind, what must *not* happen is for the board to fall, or be knocked flat on the grass and the fielder to sit, or place his foot or any part of his person on that board. That would invalidate the catch and it would be "six and *not out*". My reasoning in this case is that the fieldsman will then have part of his person grounded beyond the natural, upright position of the board and therefore *over* the boundary line.

Many experimental changes have been tried to this Law since 1947. It has swayed between "catch-and-stay-within-the-field-of-play" and "catch-and-be-allowed-to-go-beyond-the-confines-of-the-boundary-line" and I am still not sure which is the better system. What is more puzzling to me is that "a fielder may not touch with any part of his person, while in contact with the ball, any boundary, however marked, except a boundary board". If he does, he will invalidate the catch he has just made. Yet, legally, he can crash into a boundary board which might actually help him stay within the field of play. The catch will still be valid.

My last match of the 1992 season was at Leicester. It was enjoyable, and I felt I had performed reasonably well but at the same time there is a distinct possibility that I may have got a decision wrong. As it was a "caught" decision I place it in this chapter. Joey Benjamin bowled a ball, short of a length, which David Capel shaped to play in front of his chest. To me, the ball hit David's top hand high of the glove and looped to second slip where it was caught. An appeal was made and David did not move, which surprised me because I know him to be a fair-minded player. I was so surprised, in fact, that I did not raise my finger and, probably after a second, I said, "I am afraid that is *out*." David left without any pause so there was no problem, but I *felt* that he was not happy though we did not discuss the matter in any way. Later, however, I saw that he had a bandage on his wrist-bone. Well, I have to say that I have never claimed to get all those decisions right. With gloves now reaching four inches above the wrist it is more difficult than ever.

Finally, a word about some of the great catches and catchers. Graham Roope (a soccer goalkeeper, as I had been) was superb. Brian Close and Philip Sharpe were in the later stages of their careers when I saw them. Ian Botham is a catcher of astounding skill and the video of 100 Great Wickets shows much of his genius with many great catches taken by him. Two catches which stick in mind – and, I am sure, will do for many years – were both taken in the outfield: Steve Goldsmith's at Lord's in a one-day final and one by Roger Harper in a Sunday League match I umpired at Neath to dismiss Hugh Morris. On both occasions the catch was taken a great distance away from where the fielder had been positioned; both were completed after a tremendous sprint and dive. On both occasions the crowd rose to applaud an outstanding piece of fielding as the player resumed his position in the field. With these, and other efforts, is it any wonder that 50 per cent of the wickets that fall are under Law 32 (Caught)?

One last thought. It is well known that a striker will not benefit from any ball which is illegally deflected by his person, but there is one interesting point which may make some of my colleagues think a bit. Take a situation where a ball is bowled and the striker quite clearly thrusts a pad at the ball. There is no question of an lbw decision being sustained and no appeal is made. The striker makes no effort to play the ball and, indeed, his bat is raised above his head. BUT – suppose that after the ball has hit the pad it jumps up and makes a firm contact with the bat from which it is caught by a fielder. That is obviously *out* under this Law. Now let us take a similar situation where the ball is not caught but flies over the heads of the slip fielders and one run is taken. The ball is then collected and returned to the wicket-keeper by the fielder at third man. To establish a degree of fairness, one might expect a run to be credited to the striker. But no! The Law states: "No runs will be credited from an illegal deflection." Yet the striker can be dismissed from such a deflection, not just under Law 36 (Leg Before Wicket) but also under Law 32 (Caught). It may not appear to be just and I have, on one occasion, taken exactly the action which is required by Law – call and signal "Dead ball", return batsmen to their original ends and ensure no runs are credited – and a few eyebrows were raised.

There are two "out" decisions under Law 32 which will always stick in my memory; both in my opinion were brilliant. In the never forgotten Fourth Test at Edgbaston in 1981, England v. Australia, during the fourth innings Graham Yallop hit a ball hard down on to his boot from where it flew up to Ian Botham (who else?). Upon the completion of the catch all of the England side appealed and Harold Bird signified that he was "out". Some may think that it was not a difficult decision, and from my position at square-leg I could see it quite clearly; but that decision when you are at the bowling end is never that easy. All you see is the ball going straight down from the bat and the umpire has to be certain of many things, especially that it was the boot upon which the ball landed – but no problem for H.D.B.

The other decision was not so much an individual decision but more the way in which the two umpires worked together and the fact that Nigel Plews in only his second match as an umpire on the "Reserve Panel" was not afraid of seeking confirmation of one simple point, having been unsighted by the catcher of the ball. It was an early season match at Cambridge, University v. Hampshire and what happened was as follows. Tim Tremlett was batting and he edged a ball hard to first slip about waist-high, slip failed to gather it first time and from his hands it went down and bounced on top of his boot from where it bounced up behind him. Turning quickly he grasped it and appealed, Nigel by this time could only see the back of the catcher and as the appeal rang out he immediately turned and looked across to me. I had followed the flight of the ball, from bat to hand, hand to boot and boot to hand, and all I did was to raise my finger towards Nigel and he raised his towards the batsman. It all happened so quickly and quietly that not even all the players knew what had taken place; but from Nigel, that was brilliant umpiring – no wonder he gained his rightful place on the "Test" Panel.

A question has recently arisen which may be an interesting discussion point: I put it forward for readers' consideration . A ball is delivered by the bowler, and it first makes contact with the striker's pad, from where it goes straight down on to the ground. From contact with the ground it bounces up and makes a firm contact with the striker's bat and the ball is then held by a fielder without it again touching the floor and an appeal is made. As bowling-end umpire, what would be your decision? I think if you read again the paragraph in regard to the striker being out "Hit Ball Twice", Law 34, although he never makes contact with the ball with the bat at all, you will deduce the correct answer, "Not out".

The reason is, the ball encountering the striker's pad is equivalent to the initial stroke and the second is when the ball makes contact with the striker's bat, but the ball between the two contacts has hit the ground and this will invalidate any catch, as if it had been bat, ground and then bat again.

33

HANDLED THE BALL

I. OUT HANDLED THE BALL

Either batsman, on appeal, shall be out *Handled the Ball* if he wilfully touches the ball while in play with the hand not holding the bat, unless he does so with the consent of the opposite side.

NOTE

(a) Entry in Scorebook

The correct entry in the scorebook when a batsman is given out under this Law is "handled the ball" and the bowler does not get credit for the wicket.

T here have been few recorded dismissals under this Law, and in the period 1872–95 three which *were* recorded involved players who were given *out* while removing the ball from their clothing. It was not until 1899 that a ball so lodged was considered to be "dead". In 1878, the renowned (and wily) W. G. Grace, while taking runs, found that a return from the outfield had lodged inside his shirt ... but he kept on running! When, eventually, he was stopped he refused to remove the ball himself in case an appeal was made for his dismissal under this Law.

It is nearly always with the best of intentions that the striker puts a hand on the ball while it is in play and in first-class cricket (except in one isolated case), nobody would dream of making an appeal if either batsman picked up the ball. It is usually the non-striker who picks up a ball and hands it to the bowler, to save him bending, yet he is also subject to this Law.

I have seen both batsmen handle the ball in self-protection while running and I have seen the striker knock away with his hand a ball which was lifting sharply towards his head. I have also seen the non-striker defend himself by deflecting with a hand a very hard drive. In every one of these cases it was reflex action. They raise an interesting point. What would the umpire do if, from one such reflex action, the ball crossed the boundary line? It is clear that the ball is not "dead". No unfair action has taken place and the batsman would not be given *out* if an appeal had been made. While any umpire would

169

do so reluctantly, and a batsman might be reluctant to accept such a reward, a boundary would have to be signalled.

The action of handling the ball is quite legal if any member of the fielding side has given consent for either batsman to do so. Consent may be by word, action or perhaps even a glance, but it is enough. My advice to all batsmen is: if you have not received such consent, leave well alone. The umpire might find himself faced with an appeal from an enthusiastic player who knows a bit about the word of the Law but little about the spirit of the game. Before answering, I would ask loudly, "Do you wish that appeal to stand, captain?" I bet that in almost every case the appeal would be withdrawn. If it were not, the umpire would be put in the difficult situation of having to indicate that the batsman was *out*, with all the unpleasantness which might follow.

If the ball should be dropping on to the striker's wicket he may knock the ball away with his bat or some part of his person as long as he is not in breach of Law 37 (Obstructing the Field) such as preventing the wicket-keeper from making a catch, but if he knocks the ball away with a hand free from the bat an appeal under this Law would be justified and upheld by the umpire.

An injured batsman is covered by this Law, as is his runner, no matter in which position the runner may be standing at the striking or non-striking end. Should an injured batsman, when not the striker, pick up the ball in a position which is "out of the game" he will not be *out* under this Law but he might be under Law 37 (Obstructing the Field).

Law 33 is one under which I have never had to take any action and I hope that I shall never have to.

LAW
34

Hit the Ball Twice

1. OUT HIT THE BALL TWICE

The striker, on appeal, shall be out, *Hit the Ball Twice*, if, after the ball is struck or is stopped by any part of his person, he wilfully strikes it again with his bat or person except for the sole purpose of guarding his wicket; this he may do with his bat or any part of his person other than his hands – but see Law 37.2 (Obstructing a Ball from being Caught).

For the purpose of this Law a hand holding the bat shall be regarded as part of the bat.

2. RETURNING THE BALL TO A FIELDSMAN

The striker, on appeal, shall be out under this Law if, without the consent of the opposite side, he uses his bat or his person to return the ball to any of the fielding side.

3. RUNS FROM A BALL LAWFULLY STRUCK TWICE

No runs except those which result from an overthrow or penalty – see Law 41 (The Fieldsman) – shall be scored from a ball lawfully struck twice.

NOTES

(a) Entry in Scorebook
The correct entry in the scorebook when a striker is given out under this Law is "Hit the ball twice", and the bowler does not get credit for the wicket.
(b) Runs Credited to the Batsman
Any runs awarded under (3) above as a result of an overthrow or penalty shall be credited to the striker, provided the ball in the first instance has touched his bat or, if otherwise, as extras.

T o uphold an appeal under this Law the umpire to whom the appeal is addressed must be certain that when the ball was hit a second time it was a deliberate act by the striker and not accidental. There are times when one sees a bat make contact with a delivery more than once. For instance, we have all seen a striker play forward to a spin bowler with a steeply angled bat, the bat plays the ball, the ball goes to ground and the ball then bounces back on to the bat. Quite obviously this is not a deliberate act by the striker to hit the ball twice. Now here I must make the point that if, from that second contact of bat on ball, the ball then flies into the air and is caught by one of the fielding side, the decision would have to be *not out* (see Law 32).

There are other ways to make two contacts of the ball with the bat. I am sure that many of us have seen a stroke like a hook-shot played so lustily that the ball is hit a second time as it goes on its way. I have seen this happen more than once and during my playing days I have actually made a catch at second slip from such a stroke. The dismissal of Chris Cowdrey at Dartford (story in Law 2), whilst using a runner, took place in this manner. Remember also that if runs are made from such an occurrence they will count, as both situations mentioned do not involve deliberate acts. If an appeal is made the decision must be *not out*. There are times when the hitting of a ball legally will not allow runs to be scored; but more of that later.

A ball may, of course, be legally hit twice but only in defence of the striker's wicket and it may be undertaken only by the striker. Should the second hit, in the opinion of the umpire, not be for the sole purpose of defending the striker's wicket, he should, on appeal, be given *out*. I have seen it written that the striker should be given *out* from this second stroke if it is illegal but only if he attempts to run. That is not correct. The taking of a run has nothing to do with any consideration the umpire may give to his decision. He should base that decision only on (1) was it a deliberate act or not? and (2) was it made to defend his wicket? The undertaking of this second stroke in defence of the striker's wicket may be made with his bat or any part of his person except his hands. But he may even use his hands as long as they are holding the bat. There is just one restriction on this action by the striker: it may not be taken if the action prevents a catch which a member of the fielding side is trying to effect. This usually refers to the wicket-keeper. Yet such a dismissal would be given *out* under Law 37 (Obstructing the Field) and not Law 34 (Hit the Ball Twice).

Runs may accrue from a ball legally hit twice but only in two situations: (1) if the fielding side concede overthrows and (2) if there is illegal fielding.

To provide a talking-point at gatherings of umpires and cricket-lovers I sometimes ask, "How can a striker be given *out*, 'Hit the ball twice', when he has not even hit it once?" It sounds improbable, so let me explain. The ball need not be struck by the bat to count as a hit. It has only to make contact with the striker's person. So let us say a ball delivered by the bowler hits the striker on the thigh-pad, bouncing upwards and forwards. The striker then kicks it with his other leg out into the field. The first stroke would be upon contact by ball on thigh-pad, the second as he kicks it. As the ball had come forward from the first stroke, the second was obviously not in defence of the striker's wicket. If this is obvious to the umpire he would, on appeal, be justified in giving the striker *out*. But, as we have seen, at no time had the bat made contact with the ball.

At several points in this book I have said there is much that I have never seen in a cricket match and certain actions I have never had to undertake. However, in the summer of 1992 I was involved in an incident which has possibly never occurred previously. I wonder how many umpires would get this one right. It was a Rapid Cricketline match at Horsham between Sussex and Middlesex. The striker, on his back foot, played a ball down to his feet and the ball looked as though it was rolling back towards the wicket. The striker knocked it away with his bat towards the position where short-fine-leg would stand. There was no short-fine-leg fieldsman. As the striker looked round to see where the ball had gone, the non-striker, from the end at which I was standing, hared down the pitch shouting, "Run, run". The wicket-keeper retrieved the ball, threw down the striker's wicket and an appeal rang out. "*Not out*", replied my colleague as the non-striker had made his ground at that end. The wicket-keeper, seeing that the striker had been late in setting off, threw the ball down to the other end of the pitch, hit the stumps and another appeal rang out. "*Not out*" was my reply as the other batsman had made *his* ground. I then instantly called and signalled "Dead ball" and instructed the batsmen to return to their original ends. Everyone looked a bit bemused as I repeated the signal to the scorers and verbally informed them, "No run to count." Later I explained my decision to a fairly large gathering.

As the run was gained from neither an overthrow nor an act of illegal fielding, it could not count. If either of the batsmen had been out of his ground when the wicket was put down, he would have been *out* under Law 38. If the throw at either wicket had missed and then runs had been taken, they would have been legitimately scored. But not the one they had completed. That did not result from an overthrow. I must say it was unusual to see both sets of bails on the ground and both sets of stumps disturbed, both batsmen walking to their original ends and one umpire making various signals and calls to the scorers.

I do not intend to dwell on the situation which would arise if a striker played the ball a second time to either wicket-keeper or a fielder and an appeal was made. Elsewhere in the book I have suggested what might happen to the fielder who put an umpire in the position of having to give a decision on that point. It just doesn't happen, I am very glad to say.

An umpire may go through the whole of a long career without ever encountering an appeal for "Hit the ball twice". There are a number of other points which have to be considered under this Law if there is an appeal. The umpire should base his decision on two points: was the act deliberate, and was it carried out, or not, in defence of the striker's wicket?

35

HIT WICKET

I. OUT HIT WICKET

The striker shall be out, *Hit Wicket*, if, while the ball is in play:

(a) His wicket is broken with any part of his person, dress or equipment as a result of any action taken by him in preparing to receive or in receiving a delivery, or in setting off for his first run immediately after playing, or playing at the ball.

(b) He hits down his wicket whilst lawfully making a second strike for the purpose of guarding his wicket within the provisions of Law 34.1 (Out Hit the Ball Twice).

NOTES

(a) Not Out Hit Wicket

A batsman is not out under this Law should his wicket be broken in any of the ways referred to in (1(a)) above if:

(i) It occurs while he is in the act of running, other than setting off for his first run immediately after playing at the ball, or while he is avoiding being run out or stumped.

(ii) The bowler after starting his run-up or bowling action does not deliver the ball; in which case the umpire shall immediately call and signal "dead ball".

(iii) It occurs whilst he is avoiding a throw-in at any time.

I am amazed there are not more recorded cases of dismissal under this Law when one considers the number of things which can break the wicket to bring about a dismissal – the striker himself, the clothing he is wearing, clothing which has become detached, his bat, parts of his bat and his protective helmet. He can also be out "Hit wicket" if he breaks it during a second effort to protect it and he can also go if he kicks or hits down his wicket as he begins to run.

I am not sure how many strikers I have given *out* under Law 35 in my time but I doubt if I would need the fingers of both hands to count them up. The last batsman I gave *out* on this count was Neil Fairbrother, of Lancashire, in a

Sunday League game at Cheltenham in August, 1989 and I just can't remember the one before that.

Let us take in order the factors which can lead to an *out* decision under this Law. First, the ball must be in play. That means that at any time from the moment the bowler begins his approach – no matter how far away – to deliver the ball, if the striker allows the bat to slip from his grasp during that approach and it knocks a bail from the top of the stumps, that, on appeal, will constitute hit wicket. What the bowler must not do if he sees this happen is stop. For an appeal to succeed the bowler must continue and deliver the ball. If he stops, the ball will be considered "dead". Another thing he must not do is bowl a "no ball" which will invalidate an appeal for "Hit wicket". A lot of cricket-lovers feel it is unfair that the batsman can commit an act leading to his dismissal when the ball has not been released and is, in fact, still in the possession of the fielding side. They may well have a point and it might be better if the Law read "from the moment of the delivery of the ball" rather than "from the moment the ball comes into play".

Next in the possible order of events, the striker may be forced on to the back foot where his heel, or possibly the calf of his leg, might dislodge a bail through contact with the stumps. It may be some part of his protective equipment which removes a bail, such as the flap of a pad, or his batting gloves. Possibly while trying to hit, or hitting a delivery, he knocks down his wicket with the bat; or it may be that the bat slips from his grasp to knock down the stumps or simply remove a bail.

I have twice actually seen pieces of the striker's bat broken off by the ball. Once, during a club game, a small piece of bat actually rested against a stump without removing a bail. The other occasion was in my last match of the 1992 season, at Leicester, and the piece which was broken was about 4 inches by 2 inches. It flew over the wicket to land about 4 yards behind it. It happened off the last ball of an over and as the striker retrieved the piece of willow and handed it to my colleague, the three of us met briefly. I remarked, "That could have been interesting." This was heard by the non-striker, apparently, and he asked my colleague what I had meant, to be told, "He would have given your mate out if it had broken the wicket." When that batsman eventually came down to my end he asked if I had been serious. When I told him. "Yes", his eyes fairly popped. He had never thought that it would constitute "Hit wicket" in such circumstances.

And then we come to the most unfortunate example of a "Hit wicket" situation. This is when a striker is injured (most probably by the ball) and either falls on to his wicket or drops his bat on to it, removing a bail. In such cases you will often find the fielding side refuse to appeal, showing the spirit in which the game can still be played.

Next we come to items of the striker's equipment which fall and remove a bail. Caps have, in the past, been known to fall, though now that heavy helmets are worn by so many batsmen it's more likely that a stump could be removed, let alone a bail. Some years ago in a match between Northants and Worcestershire I gave what I thought to be one of the best decisions of my career, not because it was right but because I arrived at it so quickly. Wayne Larkins played forward to a ball which rapped him very hard on the bottom hand. With an excusable oath he shook his hand so hard that a glove flew off and hit the wicket, removing a bail. There was a shout of "How's that?" and as I ran in to remake the wicket I replied, "Not out". As I restored the wicket Norman Gifford, at gulley, said something to Ted Hemsley who was at slip, and as I ran back to square-leg I saw them both smiling. Over a drink at the end of the day Norman asked if I would like to know what had been said. It was, in fact, what I regard as a massive compliment. Norman had said, "It would be our luck to have Don Oslear standing at square-leg."

When a striker sees the ball is about to hit his wicket after he has played it or if it has rebounded from some part of his person he may try to knock it away with his bat or even kick it. If, in doing so, he breaks his wicket, that will again bring an affirmative response to an appeal for "Hit wicket".

Finally, if the striker sets off for a run immediately after playing, or trying to play the ball, and then slips, his foot (or perhaps the bat) contacting the stumps and removing a bail, again it will constitute "Hit wicket". The operative word here is "immediately", and if there is any delay in running, as after a call of "Wait", then it should bring a *not out* decision because the setting off for a run will not have been immediate.

In the 1947 Code of Law, many of the dismissals I have mentioned would have had to be whilst the striker was "playing at the ball". Under the present Code this term is not used except in Notes to the Law.

This Law has moved a long way since the early Codes. All it said in 1845 was: "The striker is *out* if, in striking at the ball, he hits down his wicket." How much more straightforward than it is now!

LAW
36

LEG BEFORE WICKET

I. OUT LBW

The striker shall be out *lbw* in the circumstances set out below:

(a) Striker Attempting to Play the Ball
The striker shall be out lbw if he first intercepts with any part of his person, dress or equipment, a fair ball which would have hit the wicket and which has not previously touched his bat or hand holding the bat, provided that:
  (i) the ball pitched in a straight line between wicket and wicket or on the off side of the striker's wicket, or was intercepted full pitch; and
  (ii) the point of impact is in a straight line between wicket and wicket even if above the level of the bails.

(b) Striker making no Attempt to Play the Ball
The striker shall be out lbw even if the ball is intercepted outside the line of the off stump if, in the opinion of the umpire, he has made no genuine attempt to play the ball with his bat but has intercepted the ball with some part of his person and if the circumstances set out in (a) above apply.

O f all the ten Laws (30 to 39 inclusive) which relate to the dismissal of a batsman, this is the one which has caused more disagreement, debate and doubt (hopefully not dissent) than all the other nine put together. At top level, there is a very good understanding of the basic elements of the Law, together with superb judgement. In fact within that group of top umpires it is felt that the Law is not difficult to interpret. On the other hand, I know that at other levels it is found to be difficult, and indeed some individuals actually fear being confronted with a decision under Law 36.

The spectator is nearly always unable to reach a reasonable conclusion himself, or to understand some lbw decisions, simply because he or she is so far away from the action. Remember, if perhaps you are tempted to comment on a decision, that the important part of what happens is confined to an area of the pitch about 9 to 12 inches in width and no more than 5 or 6 feet in length. These figures will be recognised as the width from the outside edge of the leg stump to that of the off stump, then a further 3 inches outside the off stump. I imagine that 90 per cent of lbw appeals are made when deliveries have pitched in that area and 5 to 6 feet in front of the striker's person.

There are five basic principles of Law which unfold before the eye and in the mind of the bowling-end umpire. If he can answer "Yes" to all five questions which are posed, then there is no reason for him not to give the striker *out*. If he can say "Yes" to each in chronological order he need have little fear of making a mistake but *all* his questions will really hinge on the fourth one: "But for the interception, would the ball have hit the wicket?" There is a great deal to be considered when arriving at the answer to this part of Law 36. Of the five points, four are simply matters of fact but the fourth is based entirely upon opinion – one person's opinion. It's not a matter for the bowler, or the non-striker, or the fieldsman, or the striker and certainly not the view of the spectator. It is purely and simply the opinion of the umpire at the bowler's end.

Once an umpire reaches a "No" in going through his chronological order of five questions, the rest can be forgotten. The striker must never be given *out* after a "No" because the rest is irrelevant. Even if, in the umpire's mind, the ball would have knocked the middle stump out of the ground, one simple "No" to any of the five questions cancels out all other considerations. Right – let us take the five points in order.

(1) "Is the delivery a fair one?" If, for any reason, either umpire has called "No ball" everything else can be disregarded. On a number of occasions in my career I have called "No ball" for a breach of Law 24 and then seen the ball hit the striker on the pad. The answer to Questions 2 to 5 (which follow) might certainly have been "Yes", but they no longer matter. The delivery was not a fair one and so they do not apply.

But now let us say that the delivery *was* fair. We have our first "Yes" and we pass on to (2) "Did the ball pitch in line between wicket and wicket or to the off side of the wicket?" The umpire standing directly behind the wicket at the bowling end is in the very best position to observe this. I have already referred to a width of 9 inches of wicket plus 3 inches outside the stump but here let me say that I do not insist dogmatically on that matter of 3 inches. Some strikers have been given *out* and correctly, I'm sure, to balls pitching more than 3 inches outside the off stump, especially when no stroke has been played at the ball, and we'll come to that point later. So let's take it that the umpire has answered "Yes" to Question 2 and we now move on to (3). "Was it part of the striker's person which was first hit by the ball, irrespective of the height at which the impact occurred, and was that part of his person in line between wicket and wicket, or to the off side of the wicket?"

This is the most complex part of the Law in my opinion. When the interception is outside the line of the off stump in the umpire's judgement, he has to make the further decision on whether a stroke has been made at the ball. If it has, then no umpire worth his salt will give the striker *out*. It can be said "the ball hit him in the wrong place", but this judgement changes dramatically when the umpire decides the striker has made no stroke at the ball. The interception can be in exactly the same spot as the one the umpire has decided is "the wrong place" but if the striker has made no effort to hit the ball with his bat "the wrong place" now becomes "the right place". Of course, as I emphasise again, the final decision will still depend upon Question 4, which is what I call the 64 thousand dollar question: "But for the interception of the ball by the striker's person, would the ball have hit the stumps?"

Now forget for a moment the matter of the striker being hit in any position other than in front of the stumps. Let us take it that Question 3 has been answered "Yes" and we are dealing purely with Question 4. First I must make it clear that there is one part of the striker's person which will not be considered, and that is a hand or hands which are holding the bat. There are now many points for the umpire to think about and the first of these is the mode of delivery of the bowler.

If the bowler is operating right arm-round-the-wicket, then the line of the flight of the ball, from release from the bowler's hand to its impact on either the pitch or the striker's person, must be accurately observed. If the bowler is a right-arm-over-the-wicket practitioner, then the line of flight will be considerably different. Did the umpire observe any deviation from a straight line in the flight of the ball (i.e. was the bowler able to swing the ball in the air)? If so, by how much and which way? In my opinion, an umpire is not able to watch much of the first third of the ball's progress – he has to have his eye on other things – but he must observe as much as possible. After the ball has hit the pitch, now comes the most vital moment; the umpire who can pick up any deviation from that moment to the ball making contact with the striker's person will be the man who has concentrated hardest and the one who makes least mistakes.

I have mentioned a distance of 5 or 6 feet as being one of the vital areas. By this I mean the distance a good-length ball will travel after being delivered by a medium-pace bowler and hitting the pitch to the moment when it strikes the pads when the batsman is playing forward. I ask this question when I am lecturing: "How far do you require the ball to travel after pitching to observe any deviation?" Answers vary from "Six feet" to as little as "Eighteen inches". The better the standard of umpire, the less distance he will need. Only those umpires in the top half of the members of the first-class panel can, in my view, get it down to as short as 18 inches. That is why they are the best umpires in the world. If, of course, the striker plays the ball off the back foot the distance is proportionately greater and it is easier for the umpire to judge any deviation.

Around the world, but in England in particular, we have many very good seam bowlers who are looking to produce some deviation of the ball, enough to have an lbw appeal sustained by beating the placement of the bat to the ball and encountering the pad. If the movement of the ball, after pitching, is too

179

much, then the umpire may decide it would have missed the wicket. A term often used is "the ball was going down".

Another thing to be taken into consideration, especially on the harder type of pitch, is how high is the ball bouncing after contact with the pitch? You can watch a whole game and see that any ball pitched beyond half-way scarcely bounces above the boot-tops. But the umpire should never assume that all deliveries will be the same. One might possibly hit a piece of loose turf, strike a harder piece of ground or land on a recent abrasion to the surface and "take off". It's disconcerting for the umpire but more so for the batsman. Conversely, a delivery may "shoot" or "skid" along the ground for no apparent reason. So total concentration is necessary; the only delivery which matters is the one currently leaving the bowler's hand.

Obviously, other factors come into the reckoning – the bowler who gets close to the stumps when delivering and the bowler who goes wide, near to the return crease; the man who bowls from many different places along the batting crease to put doubts into the mind of the striker and provide parallel concerns for the umpire.

Spin bowlers probably cause more problems than seam or swing bowlers. The spinner bowls further "up" the pitch and therefore there is less distance (between pitching and making contact with the striker) for the umpire to observe deviation. For a delivery which hits the striker full toss on the boot it should never be said, "I didn't give him out because he has been turning the ball all day so it is logical to assume that one would have turned and missed the stumps." Never *assume* anything. Once you do, you are lost. It may not be generally known that there have been, and still are, bowlers good enough to deliver balls with exactly the same action but one spins and the other doesn't – by design. Ray Illingworth and Abdul Qadir are two of whom it was said that on a pitch taking spin they could judge very closely how much they wanted the ball to turn and they would spin it accordingly.

It was Abdul Qadir who was bowling to Ian Botham at Lord's in 1982 and struck the batsman, full toss, with a ball which hit the pad. Qadir was certainly turning the ball regularly, but this had struck the striker's pad on the full and there was a discussion involving Christopher Martin-Jenkins and Trevor Bailey in which the former insisted that the relevant factor was that the ball was turning and the latter claimed that, in the circumstances, *that* didn't matter. Trevor, of course, was quite right – as you would expect from someone of his experience.

There is a term in current use which is applied to a delivery known as the "arm ball". (It used to be described as "the one that goes on with the arm".) This is usually pushed through a bit more quickly than other deliveries and will not hold, or turn, as it pitches and if all the questions are answered in the affirmative it is one which can result in an lbw decision and will often do so.

At this point, let us insert No. 5 of the umpire's questionnaire which is: "Was an appeal made?" I have had, on one or two occasions, a "Yes" in my mind to all the first four points only to find no appeal coming from the fielding side. In such circumstances we are unable to give the striker *out* – not because we have arrived at a "No" but because the question has not been asked. The umpire can only signify that a batsman is *out* under any Law of the ten governing a dismissal when he is asked, "How's that?" by a member or members of the fielding side.

I am often asked, "How do you know if the striker is really playing a shot at the ball?" How, indeed! An umpire can only base a decision like that on what he sees and by calling on every bit of experience he has gathered during his career. What he must never do is give an *out* decision if he is not sure on this point. Often I have known the most strident appeals from every fielder and have taken what might seem an age, two or three seconds, to make up my mind. All that I am doing there is satisfying myself in my own mind that some sort of shot has been played at the ball, no matter how sketchy it might have been. I have gone through my points in order: Yes. It was a fair delivery. Yes. It pitched 3 inches outside the off stump and the interception which occurred was 1 inch outside the off stump. Yes. It would have hit the stumps but for the interception. Yes. An appeal has been made. *But*, now I am reflecting that in my opinion a stroke was played by the striker and that ensures that my decision is *not out*.

If, of course, the ball had pitched in line, wicket-to-wicket, it wouldn't matter whether a shot had been played or not. It is only when the ball pitches ouside the off stump and the interception is made outside the off stump that the question of a shot being played arises. The really good umpire will spot when the striker thrusts his pad at the ball and then brings his bat down behind the leg. That is not playing at the ball; it is playing at the calf muscle. He will also see when the bat is withdrawn from the line of the ball at the very last minute. It is not the easiest matter to judge, but it has to be done.

One part of the Law in which errors can occur is when everything else in the umpire's mind is clear, all five questions have received an affirmative answer, but he has failed to notice the slightest, feather-fine touch of bat on ball before it hits the pad. It can be so slight there is no deviation of the ball and no sound is heard. There is much more of this type of incident at first-class level where bat and pad are presented so close together. Batsmen have then been known to return to the dressing-room swearing they have "knocked the cover off the ball".

There was an experimental Law between 1929 and 1933 allowing the umpire to give a striker *out* lbw even though he made a slight contact with bat on ball before it struck the pad. This freed the umpire from responsibility for error when some such slight contact occurred but I am sure that would not be good for the game in the modern era. This is always a difficult area; mistakes have been made in the past and will continue to be made. Umpires are normal, fallible human beings. We have to strive constantly to make ourselves better and at the same time be big enough to admit that sometimes we have not got quite right the answer to Question 3.

This raises another interesting point in relation to the double impact but this time, rather than bat, pad, in that order, it is pad, bat; this is the decision which will find us the really great umpires. Not only do they have to be observant enough to discern that there have been two impacts but they have to know which impact was the initial one; if the first was ball against pad, the fact that the ball then encountered bat is of no consequence to an umpire's judgement upon Law 36 (Leg Before Wicket). More than that, they have to make the usual observations to sustain any lbw appeal: but the really great umpires are, then, those who are brave enough to give the striker "Out". It is so easy to "crib out" and give a "Not out" decision in the hope that players will think you were not sure because the impacts were so close together. Obviously if you are not able to split the impacts, then there must be some doubt and the decision must be "not out".

I expect that I give one, sometimes two a season upon a pad, bat contact, and a couple of years ago I was discussing one such dismissal with a colleague. His final summing up not only astounded me but damned him in my eyes forever, when he turned to me and said "No, I never give lbw on that sort of thing, it is not an accepted decision by a batsman." What about the bowler? I bet he is not of the same opinion.

To make up his mind and give a decision, an umpire usually has perhaps two to three seconds, from the moment the bowler's front foot hits the ground to the moment when he has to answer an appeal. That is the time he has to put five questions to himself and get the answers. If 100 per cent concentration is applied, three seconds can be quite a long and adequate time to work it out. I liken it to a camera-shutter operating in the brain, working from what has been seen by the lens which in this case is the umpire's eye and the whole apparatus working from his knowledge of Law 36, his art and technique and, above all, his experience. It is sometimes said that the best umpires are those who do not hurry their decisions and, in general, I agree. Some lbw decisions, however, are so clear-cut that the umpire would know he was going to say "*Out*" even before the beginnings of the appeal were heard.

When I arrived in New Zealand to lecture and umpire, in 1980-81, I was told that an experimental Law was to be operated under which a ball pitching outside the *leg* stump could, in certain circumstances, result in an lbw appeal being sustained. Now this sounded interesting, and so it proved. The special provisos were that the Law would follow the same principles as those applied to a ball pitching outside the *off* stump except that the ball must be delivered from the opposite side of the bowling wicket to the side where the striker's legs were positioned outside *his* wicket. In short, it applied to a right-hand batsman facing a right-arm-over-the-wicket or a left-arm-round-the-wicket bowler. Conversely, a left-hand bat would have to be facing a right-arm-round-the-wicket or a left-arm-over-the-wicket bowler.

I have to say I didn't find it too difficult to operate. When the bowler informed the umpire of his mode of delivery and the umpire in turn informed the batsman, it was for the umpire, then, to note whether the batsman was a left- or right-hander and apply the experimental Law where necessary. It was one more thing to think about, I suppose, but it was quite easy to fix its implications in the mind. Unfortunately, when efforts were made to introduce the experimental Law to cricket in England it was felt by umpires that it was difficult to interpret. That left us with the Law as it is at present, allowing a striker to step back in front of the wicket with both pads to stop a ball which has pitched outside the leg stump. He has complete immunity from being given *out* lbw and it can result in much negative cricket as we have seen recently at Test level. It is surely not good for the game from either a batting or bowling point of view and perhaps we might consider giving the batsman *out* for obstruction as in the Laws of 1774? Surely the New Zealand experiment is worth giving an airing here, for perhaps two or three seasons? It might help bring spinners back into prominence. It would certainly encourage the leg-break bowler and the left-arm, round-the-wicket spinner.

It is worth noting that in four full months of umpiring under this experimental Law in New Zealand I gave only one *out* decision. It was in favour of a left-arm-round bowler against a right-hand batsman.

One way and another, Law 36 can be pretty heavy going, so let me end these thoughts on it on a lighter note. An umpire will judge hundreds of lbw situations in his career – certainly I have – but one in particular stands out and will remain in my mind long after retirement. In a very cold April at the start of the 1981 season I was due to "stand" for the Cambridge University v. Essex match with Nigel Plews, for whom it was his first match as a reserve first-class umpire. It was a pretty miserable month for weather and as the Oxford University match at The Parks was called off because the ground was unfit, ours was the only day's play of first-class cricket taking place in England.

Before the start, I suggested to Nigel that I should take the first over but he would have none of it. He replied, "We'll just walk out and take pot luck on where the bowling starts." I thought about the position and, with Essex in the field, decided that it would almost certainly mean John Lever (left-arm-over) bowling downhill, with a left-to-right breeze blowing, and positioned myself accordingly. I had guessed right, took a couple of sweaters from John, glanced across and smiled at Nigel, who responded with a wink. Lever ran in to bowl to John Peter Crispin Mills, a ball of (very) full length, just drifting in slightly on the breeze. Mills did not come forward but played from the crease, missed the ball and it struck him on the pad in front of middle and off stumps. Any appeal was a formality and I simply signalled *out*. The young man departed and *Wisden* solemnly recorded: "There could hardly have been a more eventful start to the season than this, the lone game to start on the official opening day. Mills was lbw to the first ball of the season – a gentle full toss from Lever." But the story doesn't end there . . .

During the luncheon interval, one of the scorers asked, "Don, did you start by the time on the pavilion clock?" and I replied, "Yes. Why?" The scorer smiled, "Oh. It's just that we noticed it was a couple of minutes fast." So I had not only given young Mills *out* off the first ball of the innings, but also the first ball of the match, indeed the first ball of the season, and the first decision of the season – and I had done it two minutes before the season had officially started. But if Nigel Plews had been standing at the bowler's end it would have had the extra significance of being the first ball of his first-class career.

37

OBSTRUCTING THE FIELD

1. WILFUL OBSTRUCTION

Either batsman, on appeal, shall be given out *Obstructing the Field*, if he wilfully obstructs the opposite side by word or action.

2. OBSTRUCTING A BALL FROM BEING CAUGHT

The striker, on appeal, shall be out should wilful obstruction by either batsman prevent a catch being made.

This shall apply even though the striker causes the obstruction in lawfully guarding his wicket under the provisions of Law 34. See Law 34.1 (Out Hit the Ball Twice).

NOTES

(a) Accidental Obstruction

The umpires must decide whether the obstruction was wilful or not. The accidental interception of a throw-in by a batsman while running does not break this Law.

(b) Entry in Scorebook

The correct entry in the scorebook when a batsman is given out under this Law is "obstructing the field", and the bowler does not get credit for the wicket.

A gain, this is a Law on which I have never had to adjudicate and on which I have never had an appeal of a serious nature. Many cases of obstruction do not really come under this Law because quite often it is the batsman who is obstructed by a fieldsman, but it has to be a *wilful* act for the umpire to take any further action (see Alec Stewart's dismissal – Law 23).

When a decision under this Law is considered by an umpire it should be remembered that the obstruction has to be of a wilful and deliberate nature by the batsman but it need not necessarily be a physical obstruction. A verbal one will suffice.

Things were a little different under the earliest Code of Law. Then, a striker could obstruct to prevent a catch being taken whilst standing in his crease or within the striker's "running-ground" (which I take to mean as he moved over the 22 yards to the other end) as long as he did not use his hand or his bat.

A few years later this concession was limited to the area of the crease and the Law said a striker "could not run from his ground to prevent a catch being taken". The mind boggles at some of the body-checking that must have taken place – more like my old ice-hockey days than a cricket match. It was not until the 1884 Code that it was laid down quite clearly: either batsman could be given out, on appeal, for any act of obstruction. But the act had to be wilful.

In a worthy book on Cricket Law it is said that any involuntary interception of a ball by a running batsman will render the ball "dead" and no run will be credited. That is not so. Note (a) to Law 37 almost covers the point. The fact is that if an involuntary interception occurs the batsmen are quite entitled to run any number of further runs. There is, however, an unwritten law which batsmen invariably follow: they decline to take any further runs.

A couple of times I have known a ball to be deflected by a running batsman and it has gone on to cross the boundary line. There is nothing that can be done in such a situation but to signal a boundary allowance of four runs (and to note the position of the batsmen when the throw was made and to acquaint the scorers with how many runs are to be credited as in Law 19.5 and in what way they are to be credited). The only factor which will make the ball "dead" in such a situation is its crossing of the boundary line, not impact of ball on batsman. It might be interesting to note the reactions if a sort of reverse situation occurred. Suppose, for instance, a batsman was taking a quick single when the ball was thrown at the wicket towards which he was running. An ill-directed throw instead hit his bat and from there ricocheted on to the stumps with him still out of his ground. Would the fielding side then spurn the umpire's decision of *out* if an appeal was made?

Law 37.1 makes it clear which batsman will be out in a normal case of obstruction, and it may be interesting to turn back to Law 18 (Scoring) and recall the incident at Hull. Any runs to be scored in such a case will be found under Law 18.5 (not under this Law), and I stand by the point that I would allow a credit of only one run because the second would not have been completed if the obstruction had not taken place.

Law 37.2 has always been what I considered an unfair piece of legislation until recently when, after a discussion with John Jameson at Lord's, I changed my opinion. I used to think that if the striker had hit the ball back to the bowler who was prevented from making a catch by obstruction from the non-striker, why on earth should it be the striker who was given *out*? He had had no part in any illegal act. John then suggested we take a hypothetical situation where a batting side had just two wickets left to fall. One of the pair at the wicket was a good batsman who seemed capable of winning the match;

the other a not-so-good one. When the good batsman made the mistake of playing a false stroke back to the bowler, the not-so-good batsman could decide to sacrifice his own wicket by obstructing the catch, thereby preserving that of the more accomplished batsman. There was still one wicket to fall. With the No. 11 as a partner, a win might still be pulled off. I take the point. The non-striker in that particular case did not know the Law.

LAW
38

RUN OUT

1. OUT RUN OUT

Either batsman shall be *Run Out* if in running or at any time while the ball is in play – except in the circumstances described in Law 39 (Stumped) – he is out of his ground and his wicket is put down by the opposite side. If, however, a batsman in running makes good his ground he shall not be out run out if he subsequently leaves his ground in order to avoid injury and the wicket is put down.

2. "NO BALL" CALLED

If a no ball has been called the striker shall not be given run out unless he attempts to run.

3. WHICH BATSMAN IS OUT

If the batsmen have crossed in running, he who runs for the wicket which is put down shall be out; if they have not crossed, he who has left the wicket which is put down shall be out. If a batsman remains in his ground or returns to his ground and the other batsman joins him there, the latter shall be out if his wicket is put down.

4. SCORING OF RUNS

If a batsman is run out, only that run which is being attempted shall not be scored. If, however, an injured striker is himself run out, no runs shall be scored. See Law 2.7 (Transgression of the Laws by an Injured Batsman or Runner).

NOTES

(a) Ball Played on to Opposite Wicket

If the ball is played on to the opposite wicket, neither batsman is liable to be run out unless the ball has been touched by a fieldsman before the wicket is broken.

(b) Entry in Scorebook

The correct entry in the scorebook when a batsman is given out under this Law is "run out" and the bowler does not get credit for the wicket.

(c) Run Out off a Fieldsman's Helmet

If, having been played by a batsman, or having come off his person, the ball rebounds directly from a fieldsman's helmet on to the stumps, with either batsman out of his ground, the batsman shall be "not out".

S ince the very earliest days of cricket, parts of this Law have remained unaltered. A batsman has always had to cover the same distance – 22 yds, or thereabouts, depending on where he had to place his bat to complete the run.

Today, this is behind the line of the batting crease (i.e. some 4 feet less than 22 yards) though in earlier days the batting crease was inches closer to the stumps (see Law 9). Even earlier than this, it was into a small hole that the bat had to be placed before the ball was popped into it by a member of the fielding side. If the batsman failed, he was deemed to have been dismissed "run out". It is believed that the action of popping the ball into the hole gave rise to the term "popping crease" or, as I prefer to call it, the batting crease. Today, the batsman will be *out* if he fails to ground either his bat (held in hand) or some part of his person behind the line of the batting crease before the wicket is down.

That is the way it has always been; but over the years there have been many incidents which required clarification, and before the 1947 Code I feel pretty sure that some of the recorded dismissals under this Law must have been incorrect. For instance, if the striker was out of his ground after making contact with the ball and the wicket was then put down by the wicket-keeper, it was recorded as "run out" and not "stumped". All because the striker had made contact with the ball, even though he was not attempting a run at all. This was clarified in the 1947 Code as "stumped" under Law 42 (now Law 39).

I have seen some bizarre incidents in my time, some where the wrong batsman has tried to leave the field. "Run out" sometimes calls for exceptional fielding and in this connection I think particularly of three brilliant practitioners – Graham Barlow, of Middlesex; Peter Squires, of Yorkshire; and Derek Randall, of Notts. All three have "thrown out" batsmen by direct hits on the stumps when it looked as though the run was "on" and they must all have had a fair proportion of hits-per-throws made.

"Run out" requires fine judgement from the umpire, and I am asked frequently: "What do you watch for?" There is only one thing to watch, and that is the batting crease. In your field of vision is the wicket, and you see the bat approaching that line. If the ball registers a direct hit on the stumps there is something of an explosion, and bails and stumps are flying everywhere. And at that moment your decision is based upon: Has the bat made it, or not?

If, on the other hand, the ball is returned from the field to the wicket-keeper for him to remove the bails, it is not so much an explosion as a clatter. Again, you are watching the line, but your field of vision has to take it all in – line, wicket and the action of the wicket-keeper. With a direct hit in a tight situation, I have heard people say, cynically: "He was only given out because it was a direct hit." Of course he was! It is a truism, not a matter for cynicism. What the cynics don't appreciate is that a batsman going flat out for the line can cover quite a distance in the time it takes for the further movements of the wicket-keeper's hands holding the ball to break the wicket – as against the brilliant throw when a direct hit is accomplished. I would suggest the difference is *at least* 12 inches and that's a long way to a first-class umpire.

Of course, if you are the umpire at the non-striker's end a different technique is required. Firstly, you have to be a world-class sprinter over 10 to 15 yards. Then you have to be in line with the batting crease, and standing still. At times you have to be something of a gymnast. My personal *modus operandi* in this situation is not to take my eyes off the ball until it has left the fielder's hands; then (if necessary) I spin round, sometimes while airborne, and focus my eyes on the line. When I am in position, those who know me will recall that I then go down on one knee. There are two reasons for this: (1) if the throw is from behind me it will be able to pass safely over me and, more importantly, (2) I can better observe if the bat is in contact with the ground behind the batting crease when the wicket is broken. I feel that this technique has helped when I am asked for a decision under this Law.

One factor to keep in mind when sprinting into position. It is important to avoid, as far as possible, getting into a spot which is between the fielder and either wicket. You don't want to obstruct the fielder and you don't want to be hit by the ball!

Television replays can be contentious matters. I do not criticise them – perhaps because only once have they shown me to be in error! It was during a NatWest semi-final in 1983 between Middlesex and Somerset at Lord's, and it was one of a number of semi-finals in which I have "stood" which have been tied. Thank goodness my decision did not cost Somerset the match!

During the closing stages I gave Joel Garner "run out" in a very tight situation and the TV replay showed it to have been an incorrect decision. There has, of course, been the other side of the coin when, in my first Test, at Trent Bridge in 1980, I gave both Graham Gooch and Desmond Haynes "run out" in situations where it took the TV replay to establish that the decisions were correct. During the Edgbaston Test against Australia in 1981 I gave Graeme Wood out at the non-striker's end from a direct hit by Chris Old and again it was very tight indeed. In his book, *Phoenix from the Ashes*, Mike Brearley, who was the England captain in that game, wrote afterwards: "Umpire Oslear, in exactly the right position, gave Wood *out*. I confess that at the time I thought Wood was *in* but the action replay showed that the umpire had made a brilliant decision." Thank you, Mr Brearley.

There is much with which I am not able to agree in "Definitions" to Law 38 which, in the main, are the opinions of one person. I certainly don't claim that my views are of all-transcending importance but I can say that what I recommend has worked well for me. Let us take a case in point. "Definitions" takes a case where a ball is hit very hard by the striker straight back down the pitch and the bowler makes contact with the ball which then hits the non-striker's wicket. It says the umpire should do everything possible to get into position to see the crease clearly. *Move* is exactly what I do not do in such a situation. I stand very still behind the wicket and watch, first, the bowler's efforts to make contact with the ball. If he does so, my eyes immediately move to the non-striker's batting crease. Assuming the non-striker has left his ground, the question once more is: Has the bat crossed the line or hit the ground beyond the line before the ball is deflected on to the wicket? To move, anywhere, gives you less chance of seeing a slight deflection by the bowler and no one on earth can cover the distance from an umpire's behind-the-wicket position to get in line to judge, in time.

I well remember an incident at Edgbaston in a Warwickshire v. Sussex Sunday League match. The bowler was Geoff Humpage, believe it or not. (He is best remembered as a wicket-keeper-batsman, of course, but he did bowl a few overs in his time.) His delivery was hit hard back down the pitch and all Geoff had time to do was stick out a leg as he moved away in his follow-through. The ball did not hit any part of his anatomy whatsoever. However, I not only *saw* but *heard* the ball make contact with his flannels, just above the ankle, before it crashed into the stumps with one of the Wells brothers well out of his ground. The ball had made contact with part of the bowler/fieldsman's "clothing or equipment as normally worn" and the non-striker was, therefore, *out*. But what a way to go!

As stated in this Law, the batsman who is out is the one *nearer* to the wicket which is put down, if they have crossed. As far as I am concerned, it doesn't matter whether they have crossed or not, or how many times they have crossed and recrossed. I say this because there are those who look only at the literal words of the Law and think they have found a flaw. Let me assure them: there is none. The crossing, of course, must be between the two batting creases. I have seen batsmen involved in a run-out trying to leave the field because they feel they have been responsible, whereas it is actually the other batsman who is run *out*. Suppose they are simply level? you may ask. Well, if they are level they haven't crossed so the one who is out is the one coming from the wicket which has been put down.

I liken the ground between the batting crease and the wicket, four feet of it, to a castle. The batsman who is there before the other can claim to be "king of the castle" and his castle cannot be captured until he leaves it. Having reached his castle (probably we should now return to saying "made good his ground") that batsman may not leave it until the ball is "dead" except in one instance – to avoid injury. But, remember, he must first have made good his ground.

Whilst I have covered under Law 2 (Substitutes) many matters involving the use of a runner for an injured batsman, it has to be remembered that the runner is there for just one purpose: to run. If he is out of his ground at the non-striker's end or at the injured striker's end and the wicket is put down, the player for whom he is running will be *out* whether it is a fair ball or not. He has no need to be in the physical act of running.

Again, we find something in "Definitions" with which I am unable to agree. It says that from a "no ball" neither the striker nor the non-striker can be run out unless they are attempting to run. This is not the case. Forget the recent clarification with regard to the striker (I will come to that shortly). The non-striker is only involved in the game for one thing at that specific time and that is to run. It must be that he can be run out.

While Law 38.2 states that in the case of a "no ball" the striker can only be run out if he is in the physical act of running, there has been a recent clarification to cover a most unusual circumstance – one which I never expect to see. It will change this part of the Law.

Let us take the case of a striker who takes guard 18 inches outside his batting crease when a "no ball" is delivered to him. He plays it into the outfield and doesn't move a step. The non-striker, however, runs down the pitch, passes the striker and, in effect, "captures his castle". The ball is then returned to the bowler's end – the wicket the non-striker has left – and that wicket is broken in the correct manner. On appeal, it will be the striker who is run out and I agree with that decision. Because the striker had taken guard 18 inches outside his crease and remained there, he has acquiesced in runnings and he and the non-striker have, in fact, now crossed between the two batting creases. And it is the striker who is now nearer to the wicket which has been put down. You are not able to give the non-striker run out as he has fulfilled all his obligations, and you can't deny the fielding side the decision, because everything they have done has been performed correctly. To my mind it is an excellent clarification.

If a batsman is run out only the run which was being undertaken at the moment of dismissal will not be credited. Those taken previously will be allowed unless, of course, either batsman has transgressed the provisions of Law 18 (Scoring) by running short.

The running out of either batsman before the delivery of the ball is, I think, fully covered under Law 24 (No Ball) and the running out of any party when an injured batsman has been granted the concession of a runner is dealt with under Law 2 (Substitutes).

LAW

39

STUMPED

1. OUT STUMPED

The striker shall be out *Stumped* if, in receiving the ball, not being a no ball, he is out of his ground otherwise than in attempting a run and the wicket is put down by the wicket-keeper without the intervention of another fieldsman.

2. ACTION OF THE WICKET-KEEPER

The wicket-keeper may take the ball in front of the wicket in an attempt to stump the striker only if the ball has touched the bat or the person of the striker.

NOTE

(a) Ball Rebounding from the Wicket-keeper's Person
The striker may be out stumped if, in the circumstances stated in (1) above, the wicket is broken by a ball rebounding from the wicket-keeper's person or equipment other than a protective helmet or is kicked or thrown by the wicket-keeper on to the wicket.

T his is the last of the Laws referring to a dismissal and I feel it should be read in conjunction with Law 40 (The Wicket-keeper). To my mind, Law 39 sets out what a wicket-keeper *can* do while Law 40 says what he *must not* do.

The wicket-keeper is the only member of a fielding side who can effect a "stumping". He can do it so long as the striker is not attempting a run and the delivery is not a no ball. But bear in mind that if the bowler delivers the other type of unfair delivery, a wide ball, the striker can be stumped off such a delivery. The striker must be out of his ground when the wicket is put down, generally by the wicket-keeper's hands holding the ball. But this is not always the case. Sometimes the ball rebounds from the wicket-keeper's hands, body or legs and breaks the wicket. I have also seen a wicket-keeper *throw* the ball from a position 16 yards behind the wicket to stump the striker!

I may say that I was personally responsible for the addition of a Note to the second edition (1992) of Law 39 in the 1980 Code. The Note said, "A striker will not be *out* stumped if a ball rebounds from a wicket-keeper's protective helmet and breaks the wicket." I raised the point at a meeting of MCC's Laws Committee because I had noticed one or two wicket-keepers wearing protective helmets and realised that at that time the Law stated that: "the striker would be *out* if the ball rebounded from the person or equipment of the wicket-keeper". I was really making an addition to a point I had raised some years earlier when I had seen the ball on two occasions rebound from the protective helmet of a short-leg fielder and break the wicket, once with the striker out of his ground. The first time I saw this was in 1979 and the next in 1983. I raised the matter at the Laws meeting after that season and it was introduced into first-class cricket. Now it has been extended to include a stumping situation if the ball rebounds from a wicket-keeper's protective helmet.

Law 39.2 is, I believe, fully covered by what I have said on Law 40. It is worth noting that before 1947, if the ball had made contact with the striker's bat, person or clothing and the striker was out of his ground when the ball was retrieved by the wicket-keeper from in front of the stumps and the wicket put down in the correct manner, the decision would have been recorded as "run out", even though no run was being attempted. Since the 1947 Code of Law, this is now recorded as "stumped" unless, of course, the striker is attempting to take a run.

In recent seasons a number of questions have been raised about the wicket-keeper moving closer to the wicket as the bowler is running up to deliver the ball. This is viewed as an unfair action and if it causes any distraction to the striker "dead ball" will be called. We might, in fact, be well advised to go back to the original Code of Law, set out nearly 240 years ago: "The wicket-keeper shall stand at a reasonable distance behind the wicket and shall not move till the ball is out of the bowler's hand." Perhaps they had it right all that time ago – or more right than we have it today?

If we find ourselves in a situation of playing without any bails on top of the stumps because of high winds, all the wicket-keeper has to do to effect a stumping is to take the ball in his hands and merely touch the stumps with his gloves. Elsewhere in this book I mention having umpired without bails on the stumps but I have never had to answer a stumping appeal in those circumstances.

Stumpings have always been recorded, but they were not credited to the bowler until around 1835 and thus many of the old-time bowlers may have had more dismissals than they were credited with. One of the most thrilling sights in cricket is the wicket-keeper standing "up" to a fast-medium bowler and bringing off a stumping . . . just flicking off a bail as the striker merely lets his toes slide across the batting crease. That sort of stumping is much rarer these days and most stumpings have occured off the slower bowlers, and I think that without exception they were all spin bowlers: Freeman bowling to his custodian Ames of Kent and Jenkins bowling to Yarnold of

Worcestershire. In more recent times I have seen Underwood to Knott of Kent. Some of us, too, can recall joyfully the Test combination of Godfrey Evans and Alec Bedser.

There has only been one "hat-trick" of stumpings in this country and that happened exactly 100 years ago, in 1893. Les Ames, of Kent, holds the record for stumping dismissals – 418 between 1926 and 1951 and it must be borne in mind that five of those years were lost to the Second World War. I wouldn't mind betting that Ames' record lives for ever.

Bob Taylor, of Derbyshire, has the highest aggregate of wicket-keeping dismissals in first-class cricket and while only 176 were stumpings (Derbyshire has rarely been a happy hunting ground for spin bowlers) it was one of his phenomenal number of 1,473 catches which provides a final memory for this chapter. My very first match as a first-class umpire was at Derby on 26 April 1975 – a Benson & Hedges Cup tie between Derbyshire and Minor Counties (North). A delivery from my end just flicked the inside edge of the striker's bat and my next view of Bob, standing about 15 yards back, was when he was lying full length on the leg side with left arm outstretched, holding the ball inches from the grass. One of the nicest men ever to play the game, Bob rightly deserves that total aggregate of 1,649 dismissals – again, a record that may never be broken.

LAW
40

THE WICKET-KEEPER

1. POSITION OF WICKET-KEEPER

The wicket-keeper shall remain wholly behind the wicket until a ball delivered by the bowler touches the bat or person of the striker, or passes the wicket, or until the striker attempts a run.

In the event of a wicket-keeper contravening this Law, the umpire at the striker's end shall call and signal "No ball" at the instant of delivery or as soon as possible thereafter.

2. RESTRICTION ON ACTIONS OF THE WICKET-KEEPER

If the wicket-keeper interferes with the striker's right to play the ball and to guard his wicket the striker shall not be out except under Laws 33 (Handled the Ball), 34 (Hit the Ball Twice), 37 (Obstructing the Field), 38 (Run Out).

3. INTERFERENCE WITH THE WICKET-KEEPER BY THE STRIKER

If, in the legitimate defence of his wicket, the striker interferes with the wicket-keeper, he shall not be out except as provided for in Law 37.2 (Obstructing a Ball from Being Caught).

I n the early days of the game the wicket-keeper (or "stumper" as he was sometimes called, simply because he is the only person who can effect a dismissal under Law 39) wore no protective clothing at all. One can see this from old prints and paintings of cricket matches played as early as 1785 – the wicket-keeper has no protective covering of the hands or legs. I surmise that wicket-keeping pads and gloves evolved when bowlers' actions changed from round-arm to over-arm and the ball reached the other end rather more quickly.

It has always surprised me that there is not, and never has been, any reference in Law to what may be worn by the wicket-keeper. Indeed, there is nothing in Law as to what may be worn by a batsman. Only in the case of a runner for an injured striker does apparel which must be worn get a mention under Law 2 and, again under "Definitions" in "Umpiring" and "Scoring", we learn what fielders may not wear on their hands.

The position of wicket-keeper is mentioned under Law 40.1 along with the penalty for any transgression. I am not sure that Law 43.2 in the 1947 Laws was not better as a means of dealing with encroachment by the wicket-keeper. It was then said that "encroachment would be disregarded" as long as it gained no advantage for the fielding side in the wicket-keeper effecting a dismissal or as long as it did not interfere with the striker's efforts to play the ball.

Let us consider a hypothetical case. A ball played back down the pitch by the striker is in the air and the wicket-keeper is able to dive forward and catch the ball. If there had been any encroachment by the wicket-keeper, after consultation by the umpires the decision would be *not out*. Suppose, however, that the ball, after contact with the bat, flies backwards so that the wicket-keeper (with no intervention from the umpire at the striker's end) has to dive *back* to take the catch. In that case a decision of *out* would be correct, whether the wicket-keeper had encroached or not. In the one case the wicket-keeper is penalised because his encroachment gave him an advantage; in the other, the encroachment was actually to his disadvantage, therefore an *out* decision would have been correct.

For an explanation of "encroachment", all one has to do is look at Law 40.1, and what bothers me is this: suppose a wicket-keeper wearing a cap with a prominent peak takes up position very close to the stumps so that the tip of the peak of his cap is level with the front of the stumps. The umpire at the striker's end (i.e. square-leg in normal circumstances) is empowered by Law to call and signal "No ball". This sort of action would, I am sure, be taken only by the most officious umpire but I suppose we've all known one or two in our time. Under the old Law, as we have seen, there was less danger of an interruption to the free flow of the game. There will be those who disagree, but I really can see no unfair advantage to be gained from the wicket-keeper having the front of the peak of his cap in front of the striker's wicket. If it were to happen, the position of the umpire would be far better if he were dealing with Law 43.2 of the 1947 Code. Of course, that is not now the case.

When the ball has made contact with the striker's bat, clothing or person after being delivered by the bowler, the wicket-keeper, from that moment, may come in front of the striker's wicket to retrieve the ball or to effect a dismissal under Law 32 (Caught), Law 41 (Stumped) or, of course, to try to run out either batsman (Law 38). Studying the Law closely, I am puzzled why it makes no mention of the latter point.

During my umpiring career I have seen dismissals effected by the wicket-keeper under all three of these Laws when the ball has been played by the striker a short distance in front of him (perhaps I should say when the ball has made a slight contact with his person). In the case of a run-out, it has usually been the non-striker who is dismissed because he has backed up too far and been unable to make good his ground again. I have seen both a catch and a stumping effected by a wicket-keeper, not of course from the same delivery. In the case of a catch it has usually been at club level and the stumping has usually been in professional cricket.

There is, presumably, an explanation for this. I deduce that first-class batsmen are more proficient in playing a ball down with an angled bat so as to prevent the wicket-keeper having time to come forward and complete the catch. As far as stumpings are concerned, most first-class wicket-keepers are quick and expert as well as such magnificent "readers" of length that they have an advantage over club wicket-keepers. One of the greatest stumpings I have seen, when the wicket-keeper has had to quickly come in front of the stumps to effect a dismissal, was by Bob Taylor, at Queen's Park, Chesterfield, to dismiss Nick Pocock, at that time captain of Hampshire, and I certainly recall a similar one by David Bairstow, at Bradford.

The wicket-keeper must at no time interfere with the striker in playing a shot or attempting to guard his wicket. If he should do so, the striker would only be out under one of four Laws: 33 (Handled the Ball), 34 (Hit the Ball Twice), 37 (Obstructing the Field) and 39 (Run Out). I have never seen any examples involving Laws 33, 34 and 37. In the case of Law 39, I have had to adjudicate many times but never when the wicket-keeper has interfered with the striker.

If the striker in legitimate defence of his wicket interferes with the wicket-keeper's efforts to make a catch he will be given out under Law 37 – but only in the case of a catch. Should he interfere with the wicket-keeper in any other circumstances and he is held to be legitimately defending his wicket, the decision (if there is an appeal) will be *not out*. It could, of course, be a close fieldsman and not the wicket-keeper who is attempting to hold a catch. In that case it is no use the striker thinking he may defend his wicket in such a situation. Not so – if he prevents a catch which is being attempted by anyone, "out".

LAW
41

THE FIELDSMAN

1. FIELDING THE BALL
The fieldsman may stop the ball with any part of his person but if he wilfully stops it otherwise five runs shall be added to the run or runs already scored; if no run has been scored, five penalty runs shall be awarded. The run in progress shall count provided that the batsmen have crossed at the instant of the act. If the ball has been struck, the penalty shall be added to the score of the striker but otherwise to the score of byes, leg-byes, no balls and wides as the case may be.

2. LIMITATION OF ON-SIDE FIELDSMEN
The number of on-side fieldsmen behind the popping crease at the instant of a bowler's delivery shall not exceed two. In the event of infringement by the fielding side the umpire at the striker's end shall call and signal "no ball" at the instant of delivery or as soon as possible thereafter.

3. POSITION OF FIELDSMEN
Whilst the ball is in play and until the ball has made contact with the bat or the striker's person or has passed his bat, no fieldsman other than the bowler may stand on or have any part of his person extended over the pitch (measuring 22 yds/20.12 m × 10 ft/3.05 m). In the event of a fieldsman contravening this Law the umpire at the bowler's end shall call and signal "No ball" at the instant of delivery or as soon as possible thereafter. See Law 40.1 (position of wicket-keeper).

4. FIELDSMEN'S PROTECTIVE HELMETS
Protective helmets, when not in use by members of the fielding side, shall be placed, if above the surface, only on the ground behind the wicket-keeper. In the event of the ball, when in play, striking a helmet whilst in this position, five penalty runs shall be awarded as laid down in Law 41.1 and Note (a).

NOTE
(a) Batsmen Changing Ends
The five runs referred to in (1) above are a penalty and the batsmen do not change ends solely by reason of this penalty.

T his Law applies to all members of the fielding side and any fielding substitute who may be required, and whilst one of them is known as the wicket-keeper who is allowed by convention, not by Law, to wear pads and gloves, he is still subject to this Law and any penalties which may apply.

The wearing of protective equipment by fielders has become much more prevalent in the past 10 or 15 years. Take, for instance, shin pads – and I don't mean the type of protection used in my football-playing days, or when I was even younger and stuffed a month's supply of comics down my stockings! The shin pads worn by fielders at "Boot Hill" (short-leg), and sometimes at silly point, are custom-built, starting below the ankle-bone, encasing the lower leg and with a cup which protects the knee. We also have arm guards and elbow pads (bringing back memories of my ice-hockey playing days); thigh muscles enclosed in a pair of shorts which incorporate padding and a strong "box" to guard the vital parts; and all this is topped off with a helmet which has a strengthened grille.

While all this provides a fair degree of protection, fielders should never be allowed to wear gloves. Having said that, I have to admit I have condoned the use of gloves (Cambridge University v. Essex, 1980). While in fairness to the Essex players I have to say they did try to whip off the glove from the hand with which they fielded the ball, I am not sure they always succeeded!

The bowler should not be allowed to wear bandage or plasters, certainly not on the bowling hand, but here again it is difficult to say "*never*" because a bandage or plaster might be necessary to cover an injury. What umpires must be very careful to observe is that any such covering should not be a help in propelling the ball.

It is often said that so much protection for the fieldsman allows him to stand much closer to the striker than he might ordinarily do, and that is certainly open to debate. What is *not* open to debate is that wearing that sort of protection in no way breaks cricket Law.

To clear up a misapprehension which sometimes arises with regard to Law 41.3 about when the ball is in play – it is in play from the moment the bowler takes his first step in his approach to the wicket. A fieldsman, at that moment, might have a foot on the "forbidden" area of the pitch but remove it before the bowler actually delivers the ball. It would not be right, therefore, for the umpire to call "No ball" because the fielder has a foot in the wrong place while the bowler is still approaching the bowling crease, provided the fielder gets it right before the ball is delivered. A point which requires careful watching, of course.

I well remember, early in my career, calling "No ball" with Chris Waller bowling for Sussex and Tony Greig fielding at silly mid-off. Chris frowned, was clearly puzzled, and I felt he deserved some explanation. I indicated (by signs, actually) that while his captain was standing with his feet placed about 18 inches from the pitch, with those long arms he reached at least 18 inches *over* it. Graham Roope, of Surrey, was another superb fielder in that position (as well as at slip) and Pat Pocock swears I am the only umpire to "call" him.

It was in a match at Worcester and it was due to Graham's eagerness to get in really close for a catch.

The one other incident which springs to mind is one in which a genuine catch was in fact taken, but I called "No ball" when encroachment took place after the delivery of the ball but prior to the striker making contact with it. It was at Lord's; the bowler was Fred Titmus and the catcher was Norman Featherstone.

These occasions were before the adoption of so much body armour. But moving just a little closer to the present, Brian Hardie, of Essex, wore just about everything and I don't blame him one little bit. He stood very close and took some fearful blows from the ball. But he also took some brilliant catches in his days at "Boot Hill".

Two words in Law 41.1 should be carefully noted: "wilfully" and "shall". "Wilfully" means deliberately, something which is done on purpose. If, for instance, a fielder should lose his cap in a chase after the ball and then see his return throw hit the cap as it lies on the ground it can scarcely be construed as a wilful act. One has to accept that the cap fell, or was blown off, accidentally. If, however, the cap has been deliberately placed on or thrown to, the ground this constitutes a wilful act, which is illegal. The penalty of five runs *shall* be applied. The word "shall" is mandatory; the umpire has no discretion.

In discussing Law 20 I mentioned having known nine runs scored from one delivery and it is appropriate to describe this incident at this stage because I was the umpire who awarded five penalty runs in addition to four which had already been run. It followed a chase by the wicket-keeper who, in running to fine leg, had first of all thrown off one glove – to enable him to return his throw, of course. It was in fact a cracking return – right over the top of the stumps where it was caught by one of the fieldsmen. *Most* unfortunately for him he had picked up the discarded wicket-keeping glove, put it on his hand and caught the throw in that! The batsmen having already run four, my penalty of five for a wilful act gave a total of nine runs. There would have been no penalty if the fieldsman had caught the ball in his gloveless hand.

While umpires in TCCB-controlled matches have, for many years, applied this ruling, it was only in 1985 that an experimental Law 41.4 was introduced into *all* cricket. The fielding side were then allowed to place a helmet (worn by one of their players as opposed to one worn by a batsman) in a position behind the wicket-keeper when it was not actually in use. If the helmet was struck by a ball in play, then the penalty had to be applied. (The mandatory word "shall" is the one in the Law; the umpires have no discretion in the matter.) In recent years I have made the award twice and on both occasions, at the same venue, I have been severely abused and taken criticism from people who should know better. So let me repeat: the penalty is mandatory and the umpire has no option but to apply it.

The penalty of five runs will be in addition to any other runs which have been completed, or when the batsmen have crossed, at the time the illegal fielding takes place. It might appear strange that if no runs are scored (or an even number of runs have been credited) when the penalty is imposed, the batsmen will be at their original ends when the next ball is bowled (i.e. the ends they occupied before the act of illegal fielding took place). This is because the five additional runs on the total are a penalty and the even number of runs (or no runs) taken by the batsmen is what determines their remaining at the original ends.

In "Definitions" it states that the ball becomes "dead" at the instant of call and signal of "Dead ball". I say it becomes "dead" before that – immediately the act of illegal fielding takes place. This is, perhaps, a small point; but there could be some delay in the act occurring and the award being notified to the scorers. With careful attention to Law 23.1(f) it will be seen that my contention is correct.

How is the penalty (and any other runs) credited? If the ball has been hit by the striker they will be credited to him – all of them, penalty included. If not, all the runs (penalty included) will be credited as byes, leg-byes, wides or no balls as the case may be.

The ball striking a helmet which has been placed on the ground behind the wicket-keeper is not particularly unusual these days, but an incident in Sri Lanka when I was umpiring there in March 1991 certainly was. A ball "bounced" a bit and eluded the wicket-keeper down the leg side. It looked pretty certain to reach the boundary and neither batsman showed any inclination to take a run. However, as a fieldsman closed in from long-leg the ball stopped, just short of the boundary. Seeing this, the non-striker called his partner for a run, taken at a leisurely stroll, whereas if they had set off as the ball passed the wicket-keeper they might have had a comfortable three. Then came the return throw – which landed directly on the helmet (behind the wicket-keeper) and ricocheted away to square-leg, inspiring the batsmen to try another run. By this time I was not interested in the ball, the batsmen or the run. The ball was dead. After sending the batsmen back to the ends they occupied after taking the first single I turned towards the scorers and raised my arm above the head to signal byes. I called to the scorebox, "And it is six of them."

One of the most unusual cases of a penalty awarded for illegal fielding again has Essex connections. They were in the field in a match where a ball was hit into the outfield and as the batsmen turned for a second run, one of them dropped his bat. Naturally, he left it where it was and continued running. But when the throw came back from the deep, another Essex fieldsman had picked up the discarded bat – and stopped the ball with it. It was almost certainly a light-hearted gesture, but one made without thinking of the possible consequences. The umpire, quite correctly, imposed a penalty of five runs. It was illegal fielding, light-hearted or not.

Law 41.2 makes a restriction upon the number of fielders behind the line of the batting crease on the leg side – no more than two – and it states that this is from the moment the bowler delivers the ball. This wording is strange in my opinion, because there is a conflict of sorts with Law 41.3. In Law 41.2 a fielder can be fielding at deep square-leg and, as the bowler is running up to bowl, the fielder can also start running round the boundary, making sure that he is not behind the line of the batting crease when the bowler delivers the ball. He can be 10-15 yards behind the crease when the ball is hit by the striker, which may have a great bearing on his efforts to make a catch. In Law 41.3 the fielder has to stay in a certain position until the ball has been struck, and I would like to see both parts, i.e. Law 41.2 and 3, read the same.

LAW
42

UNFAIR PLAY

1. RESPONSIBILITY OF CAPTAINS
The captains are responsible at all times for ensuring that play is conducted within the spirit of the game as well as within the Laws.

2. RESPONSIBILITY OF UMPIRES
The umpires are the sole judges of fair and unfair play.

3. INTERVENTION BY THE UMPIRE
The umpires shall intervene without appeal by calling and signalling "Dead ball" in the case of unfair play, but should not otherwise interfere with the progress of the game except as required to do so by the Laws.

4. LIFTING THE SEAM
A player shall not lift the seam of the ball for any reason. Should this be done, the umpires shall change the ball for one of similar condition to that in use prior to the contravention. See Note (a).

5. CHANGING THE CONDITION OF THE BALL
Any member of the fielding side may polish the ball, provided that such polishing wastes no time and that no artificial substance is used. No one shall rub the ball on the ground or use any artificial substance or take any other action to alter the condition of the ball.

In the event of a contravention of this Law the umpires, after consultation, shall change the ball for one of similar condition to that in use prior to the contravention.

This Law does not prevent a member of the fielding side from drying a wet ball or removing mud from the ball. See Note (b).

6. INCOMMODING THE STRIKER
An umpire is justified in intervening under this Law and shall call and signal "Dead ball" if, in his opinion, any player of the fielding side incommodes the striker by any noise or action while he is receiving the ball.

7. OBSTRUCTION OF A BATSMAN IN RUNNING

It shall be considered unfair if any fieldsman wilfully obstructs a batsman in running. In these circumstances the umpire shall call and signal "Dead ball" and allow any completed runs and the run in progress or alternatively any boundary scored.

8. THE BOWLING OF FAST SHORT-PITCHED BALLS

The bowling of fast, short-pitched balls is unfair if, in the opinion of the umpire at the bowler's end, it constitutes an attempt to intimidate the striker. See Note (d). Umpires shall consider intimidation to be the deliberate bowling of fast, short-pitched balls which by their length, height and direction are intended or likely to inflict physical injury on the striker. The relative skill of the striker shall also be taken into consideration.

In the event of such unfair bowling the umpire at the bowler's end shall adopt the following procedure:

(a) In the first instance the umpire shall call and signal "No ball", caution the bowler and inform the other umpire, the captain of the fielding side and the batsman of what has occurred.

(b) If this caution is ineffective he shall repeat the above procedure and indicate to the bowler that this is a final warning.

(c) Both the above caution and the final warning shall continue to apply even though the bowler may later change ends.

(d) Should the above warnings prove ineffective the umpire at the bowler's end shall:

(i) At the first repetition, call and signal "No ball", and when the ball is dead direct the captain to take the bowler off forthwith and to complete the over with another bowler, provided that bowler does not bowl two overs, or part thereof, consecutively. See Law 22.7 (Bowler Incapacitated or Suspended during an Over).

(ii) Not allow the bowler, thus taken off, to bowl again in the same innings.

(iii) Report the occurrence to the captain of the batting side as soon as the players leave the field for an interval.

(iv) Report the occurrence to the executive of the fielding side and to any governing body responsible for the match who shall take any further action which is considered to be appropriate against the bowler concerned.

9. THE BOWLING OF FAST, HIGH FULL PITCHES

The bowling of fast, high full pitches is unfair. See Note (e).

In the event of such unfair bowling the umpire at the bowler's end shall adopt the procedures of caution, final warning, action against the bowler and reporting as set out in (8) above.

10. TIME-WASTING

Any form of time-wasting is unfair:

(a) In the event of the captain of the fielding side wasting time or allowing any member of his side to waste time, the umpire at the bowler's end shall adopt the following procedure:

(i) In the first instance he shall caution the caption of the fielding side and inform the other umpire of what has occurred.

(ii) If this caution is ineffective he shall repeat the above procedure and indicate to the captain that this is a final warning.

(iii) The umpire shall report the occurrence to the captain of the batting side as soon as the players leave the field for an interval.

(iv) Should the above procedure prove ineffective the umpire shall report the occurrence to the executive of the fielding side and to any governing body responsible for the match, who shall take appropriate action against the captain and the players concerned.

(b) In the event of a bowler taking unnecessarily long to bowl an over, the umpire at the bowler's end shall adopt the procedures, other than the calling of "No ball", of caution, final warning, action against the bowler and reporting as set out in (8) above.

(c) In the event of a batsman wasting time (see Note (f)) other than in the manner described in Law 31 (Timed Out), the umpire at the bowler's end shall adopt the following procedure:

(i) In the first instance he shall caution the batsman and inform the other umpire at once, and the captain of the batting side as soon as the players leave the field for an interval, of what has occurred.

(ii) If this proves ineffective he shall repeat the caution, indicate to the batsman that this is the final warning and inform the other umpire.

(iii) The umpire shall report the occurrence to both captains as soon as the players leave the field for an interval.

(iv) Should the above procedure prove ineffective, the umpire shall report the occurrence to the executive of the batting side and to any governing body responsible for that match, who shall take appropriate action against the player concerned.

11. PLAYERS DAMAGING THE PITCH

The umpires shall intervene and prevent players from causing damage to the pitch which may assist the bowlers of either side. See Note (c).

(a) In the event of any member of the fielding side damaging the pitch the umpire shall follow the procedure of caution, final warning and reporting as set out in (10 (a)) above.

(b) In the event of a bowler contravening this Law by running down the pitch after delivering the ball the umpire at the bowler's end shall first caution the bowler. If this caution is ineffective the umpire shall adopt the

206

procedures other than the calling of "No ball", of final warning, action against the bowler and reporting as set out in (8) above.

(c) In the event of the batsman damaging the pitch the umpire at the bowler's end shall follow the procedures of caution, final warning and reporting as set out in (10 (c)) above.

12. BATSMAN UNFAIRLY STEALING A RUN

Any attempt by the batsman to steal a run during the bowler's run-up is unfair. Unless the bowler attempts to run out either batsman – see Law 24.4 (Bowler Throwing at Striker's Wicket before Delivery) and Law 24.5 (Bowler Attempting to Run Out Non-Striker before Delivery) – the umpire shall call and signal "Dead ball" as soon as the batsmen cross in any such attempt to run. The batsmen shall then return to their original wickets.

13. PLAYER'S CONDUCT

In the event of a player failing to comply with the instructions of an umpire, criticising his decision by word or action, or showing dissent, or generally behaving in a manner which might bring the game into disrepute, the umpire concerned shall, in the first place, report the matter to the other umpire and to the player's captain, requesting the latter to take action. If this proves ineffective the umpire shall report the incident as soon as possible to the executive of the player's team and to any governing body responsible for the match, who shall take any further action which is considered appropriate against the player or players concerned.

NOTES

(a) The Condition of the Ball

Umpires shall make frequent and irregular inspections of the condition of the ball.

(b) Drying of a Wet Ball

A wet ball may be dried on a towel or with sawdust.

(c) Danger Area

The danger area on the pitch, which must be protected from damage by a bowler, shall be regarded by the umpires as the area contained by an imaginary line 4 ft/1.22 m from the popping crease and parallel to it and within two imaginary and parallel lines drawn down the pitch from points on that line 1 ft/30.48 cm on either side of the middle stump.

(d) Fast, Short-pitched Balls

As a guide, a fast, short-pitched ball is one which pitches short and passes, or would have passed, above the shoulder-height of the striker standing in a normal batting stance at the crease.

(e) The Bowling of Fast, Full Pitches

The bowling of one fast, high full pitch shall be considered unfair if, in the opinion of the umpire, it is deliberate, bowled at the striker and if it passes, or would have passed, above the shoulder-height of the striker when standing in a normal batting stance at the crease.

(f) Time-Wasting by Batsmen

Other than in exceptional circumstances, the batsman should always be ready to take strike when the bowler is ready to start his run-up.

L aw 42 is one which, I feel, should not be necessary in the game and what has to be written regarding certain aspects of the Law is something which I find obnoxious.

Law 42 has always been a contentious one and I therefore have no wish to break any contract which I have signed. It is within these constraints that I offer my thoughts on Law 42 (Unfair play).

Law 42.1 places the responsibility on the captain of a team not only to conduct himself in a manner in keeping with the game of cricket but to be responsible for the conduct of all other members of his side. At this juncture, I must say that the one or two "bad apples" in county cricket will not spoil the remainder in the barrel: they possess far too much sense and professionalism. I have known, in my time as an umpire, a number of captains who have had the complete respect of every player within their clubs. There may have been players who felt they were beyond reproach but they never "tried it on" with men like Ray Illingworth or Keith Fletcher. Both of them led sides who not only knew that strict discipline was expected of them; both led by example both on and off the field. Yet the two sides were quite different. Leicestershire played to a strict code in every way. Essex were more a happy-go-lucky collection of disciplined players and perhaps if they had been just a little more like Leicestershire they might have won honours earlier than they did. What I can say is that while Essex played many pranks on each other – and on me – they always conducted themselves in an impeccable manner. Leicestershire, perhaps a little more intense in the way they achieved results, were a tremendous side in my early days of umpiring and I seemed to "stand" with them a great deal in those days. But it was at his personal peril that any individual player put a foot wrong or made a single comment which was out of place. Their captain would have nailed the culprit to the dressing-room door.

Mike Denness and Mike Brearley were two others who commanded the respect of all their players, but all four I have mentioned played some years ago. There is one of more recent vintage who is well worthy of mention and news of his appointment came to me in a far-off land.

In January 1987, after umpiring a match at Harare Sports Club in Zimbabwe, I was in conversation with a Surrey committeeman who was there on holiday. He asked me to guess the name of the Surrey captain for that year and although he gave me more than one clue I failed to come up with the name. I am not sure why I was surprised when he named Ian Greig, because the five years that Ian occupied the position were the best thing that had happened to the club for some decades. Ian was no mean cricketer and he was a great disciplinarian. Now he no longer holds the position of captain. I do hope that the standards which he set will be maintained by those who follow in his footsteps.

Law 42.4 and 5: while there were reports of ball-tampering as early as 1920, much that I could write on these two sections might lead me into conflict with the authorities because what I shall write is not only the truth, it is also fact and, whilst all books and articles have to be submitted to the TCCB for their approval prior to publication, this will not sway me in any way. I do know the restrictions which are placed upon me as an employee of the TCCB and I have never been one for breaking either my word or the terms of any contract which I have signed. With this in mind, I say that there is much that is unable to be written until my contract ends in September 1994.

I have mentioned in Law 3 certain strong umpires, of which I am one, and throughout the last two seasons I have submitted to the TCCB five reports on ball tampering, the contents of which are a confidential matter between myself and the TCCB. Looking back at my copies of these reports, I notice that three of them involve the same side during a period of 35 days. I am also aware that the TCCB took some action after receiving them but it appears to no avail, as the abuse of cricket balls continued. I feel that this aspect of the game is one to which the authorities and umpires must pay a great deal of attention, and certainly be prepared to give each other full support. I am sorry to say that I have recently had brought to my attention the fact that whilst I have not entirely been the only person to have reported this abuse of Law 42, any other report has been an exception.

It would be absurd to say that no player has ever interfered with the ball, so what I shall do is cite instances of what I, personally, have known to happen.

In my first season, a ball in one game was hit to the boundary and then returned to the bowler, who missed it. As the ball ran towards me I bent and picked it up – and felt as though a sharp piece of metal had rubbed against the palm of my hand. I must have been a bit naive in those days. In the following game I mentioned this experience to my colleague, an ex-player, and he showed me how a thumb can be run round the stitching of the cross seam. The next instance I recall was in 1983 and at the close of an innings I found I could pick up the match-ball by a piece which had been picked out at the join of the cross-seam and quarter-seam.

The application of lip-salve is reasonably easy to spot. (Someone secretes the stuff in the bottom of a pocket and rubs it into the ball with the fingers.) After a while the ball gives off a distinctive odour – but try to establish who has the substance in his pocket! No umpire is going to go around levelling accusations like that. Much more difficult to detect is the wax spray which is applied to trousers in the dressing-room and the ball rubbed on the waxed area.

During 1990 I stopped play and asked for the ball, which my colleague and I inspected. We then called together the captain and the senior professional of the fielding side together with the two batsmen, one of whom, fortunately, was the captain of that side. We showed them the ball, which had virtually been "skinned" on one side – and this after only nine overs! I certainly did not mince my words and interference with the ball stopped. But during those nine overs the ball had swung around to claim three wickets, all leg before wicket. During the next 33 overs not one wicket fell and the match was drawn. The ball in this situation was not changed as instructed in Law 42.5, as it would have been impossible to have found one of similar wear. What I did was to rub the ball between my hands to smooth the side which felt like a suede shoe and, whilst there was no way in which I could return it to pristine condition, it did make it into a matt finish rather than a very rough one.

The 1991 season was full of problems, and there were a number of reported cases of the quarter-seam being opened up. The ball swung around to great effect. What happened in the summer of 1992 gained a lot of publicity and I don't intend to prompt further speculation on the matter here. What I can say is that what happened in 1992 was more in the nature of what had happened in 1990 than in 1991. I certainly made reports on all the matters with which I was concerned (except the first one) and while I and other umpires are reluctant to take action when we cannot identify individuals who abuse Law 42.4 and 5, there are practices which everyone must make an effort to eradicate from the game.

I have avoided mentioning names and venues but in one case I don't mind doing so because what happened was done with a great deal of innocence. At the start of an innings at Swansea, the ball was thrown to Rodney Ontong and while the captain, Alan Jones, was setting the field, Rodney – right in front of me – bent down and began scrubbing the ball in a bowler's footmarks. Politely, I asked him just what he thought he was doing and Rodney replied that he thought his action was legal. I told him it certainly was not and went to the pavilion for another new ball. Rodney was profuse in his apologies. No report was ever made on the matter to the TCCB because the action was not undertaken in any sort of underhand way. This practice, by the way, was outlawed in the mid-fifties.

When the condition of the ball has been altered illegally the remedy in Law is to replace it with a ball of similar condition; but if such action is taken in TCCB-organised matches, a ball of much inferior condition is used as the replacement.

As stated under Law 5 (The Ball), there are many ways in which the condition of the ball may be changed. I can't vouch for the bottle-top or one-inch metal nail treatment but by the speed at which the condition of the ball deteriorates at times, it is not simply normal wear and tear. Sometimes it makes finding a ball of inferior condition rather difficult.

For the 1993 season the TCCB at a meeting of the Cricket Committee decided that, if a ball was to be changed because in the opinion of the umpires it had been tampered with, in the first instance a box of balls (six) would be produced and the batsman would be able to choose the replacement. The balls in the box would range from a new one, right through to one which had been used for years in the nets for practice. Should this action not suffice and it was again seen by the umpires that the ball was still being abused, then the bowler who was bowling at the time of the inspection would be barred from bowling again during that innings. I expect and hope that very severe action would then be considered by the Disciplinary Committee of the TCCB against the culprits, both individual, team and club.

The obstruction of a batsman by a member of the fielding side (Law 42.7), if deliberate, is an unfair act. Should it take place, the umpire (either of them) must call "Dead ball" to ensure that the batsman is not dismissed and any runs being attempted at the time will be credited. The batsmen will change ends even if they have not crossed when the call is made. In all other instances the batsmen have to cross on the run being attempted for it to count. But not in this one. If, for example, the bowler grabs hold of the non-striker as he is about to set off on a run, he may not even have left his ground at the bowling end but the run will count, and the batsmen will change ends. If the ball is on its way to the boundary when the obstruction occurs, the umpire will not call "Dead ball", as the batting side will be credited with the most runs possible. The only time "Dead ball" will be called is to ensure no dismissal follows if illegal obstruction has occurred.

Law 42.8 deals with the bowler who delivers an excessive number of fast, short-pitched balls and three principles are laid down for deciding whether the delivery is unfair: (a) the delivery must be fast; (b) it must be short-pitched; (c) it must rise above the shoulder-height of the striker whilst he is in the normal batting stance. All three criteria must apply to the same delivery, or no warning can be issued. In 1990 Test Matches, (a) and (b) applied but in (c) the height to which the ball could rise before a warning was issued was increased. Again, it was above shoulder-height but *whilst he was standing upright*. The bowler was allowed one such delivery to each batsman in the over, but a further one would automatically draw a warning from the umpire at the bowler's end. This provision was brought into all cricket for the 1992 season, and I see it as a step towards its being brought into Law in the near future. I am totally against this new regulation and am making efforts to get it rescinded in favour of a return to the height as in Law. It has been said in many quarters, and it is certainly desirable, that this type of bowling, if not eliminated completely, should be severely restricted. As I see it, the "standing upright" regulation means that a delivery may be pitched shorter and allowed to rise even higher.

During 1982 I was involved in a most unusual incident at Southend when I ruled, in effect, that Stuart Turner, of Essex, had three innings. For that season the TCCB had introduced a regulation that only one short-pitched ball an over would be allowed at a batsman. Essex were playing Middlesex, always a spirited encounter, and Stuart was frustrating the Middlesex bowlers. Wayne Daniel bowled one such ball and I told him that was his "allowance". So when he bowled another later in the over and Stuart gave a catch to Phil Edmonds, in the gulley, I called and signalled "No ball". A few overs later the bowling was changed and Simon Hughes did exactly the same thing to Turner, who was again caught by Edmonds in the gulley while I called and signalled "No ball". Who said lightning doesn't strike twice?

Law 42.9 deals with the fast, high, full-pitched delivery – often referred to as the "beamer". A proposed change to this part of the Law was due to be put before MCC in May, 1993. Up to that point the criteria for an unfair delivery were that it has to be (a) fast; (b) full-pitched and (c) high. The height once again was given as above the shoulder while the striker was in his batting stance. If the proposed change goes through (and I see no reason why it shouldn't), the height would be much lower – "above the waist while he is standing upright". Along with Barry Dudleston I was involved in an unsavoury situation a few years ago at Northampton when this Law was abused. When this type of ball is bowled it can be very dangerous. I am in favour of the proposed change, but I am not sure I approve of the height being raised again, which is the effect of applying the words "standing upright".

I must confess that it was Law 42.9 which caused me to shout at a player on the field for the one and only time in my career. It was during the Roses match at Headingley in 1982, and I am not proud to tell the story. It was, however, a nasty incident and I am afraid I almost lost my temper.

Lancashire set a target in the last innings and Yorkshire were going fairly well when Kevin Sharp decided to chance his arm against Colin Croft. He went down the wicket and tried one or two rather ambitious shots. Croft told him, "You won't do that again." To me, he said, "Round the wicket, umpire." As I informed the batsman of the change in the mode of delivery I sensed what the bowler was going to do, but there was no way I could stop him. Sure enough, the next ball was going full pitch straight for Sharp's head and how he managed to deflect it with his glove is something I suppose neither of us will ever know. I was furious and I shouted, "That was deliberate and this is a warning." I mentioned the incident in my report but I am not aware that anything came of it.

Law 42.11 sets out a good and clearly stated course of action when bowlers cause damage to the pitch while they are bowling and moving into what is referred to as "the danger area" of the pitch. Bowlers can be and have been suspended from bowling for the remainder of an innings: but what about batsmen who run up and down the central area of the pitch? We are not able to suspend them. To try to cope with such a situation I have formulated my own course of action. If a batsman, generally the striker, "trespasses" in this area, I give him, first, a "friendly" warning, then two official warnings. If he transgresses again after that I call and signal "Dead ball" and instruct the scorers to discount any runs attempted or completed. Some people say I am not allowed to take this action. I say I am, under Law 42.3 and also 42.2, which holds that "The umpires are the sole judges of fair and unfair play." If neither the batsman nor his team is going to be allowed the runs the practice of running down the middle of the pitch will soon cease.

Certain batsmen when spoken to regarding an infringement under this part of Law 42 will state: "But umpire, I am only wearing crepe soles." I am not sure what that has to do with the matter; those who have seen a crepe sole slide down the pitch will know that it can cause as much damage to the turf as a studded boot, if not more. There was one individual I saw, and it was not an isolated instance, take a kick at the pitch as he was completing a run and remove the top surface with his studs, always on the length around where the ball would be pitching and when his bowlers would soon be operating. When he took this action in a match in which I was "standing" he received more than a flea in the ear. Fortunately he is no longer playing on our circuit because that type of cheat I am unable to accept.

On Law 42.13, I have to say that I consider myself "strong" when it comes to discipline and I don't think I allow players to get away with transgressions of the Law. Whilst I have only submitted an official report on a couple of occasions, I have several times asked a captain and an offender to come to the umpires' room at the end of a day's play, and made my feelings abundantly clear. No one, I am glad to say, has ever made such a visit twice.

And so we come back to Law 42.1, which requires strong captaincy. It is good to be able to say that bad behaviour is not common in our game. What is unfortunate is the fact that it is the few who spoil a wonderful band of sportsmen who play the game with a great degree of skill and, more than that, conduct themselves in an impeccable manner. We, the umpires, are in a favoured position and should be those who uphold not only our own dignity and skills but try to ensure that others do likewise.